MIND
SHAPES

MIND
SHAPES

UNDERSTANDING THE DIFFERENCES
IN THINKING AND COMMUNICATION

Alan R. Kahn, M.D.

Kris Austen Radcliffe

PARAGON HOUSE
St. Paul, Minnesota

First Edition
Published in the United States by

Paragon House
2285 University Avenue West
St. Paul, Minnesota 55114

Cover image by Robert Tinney, printed with permission.

Library of Congress Catalog-in-Publication Data

Kahn, Alan R., 1932-
Mind shapes : understanding the differences in thinking and communication
/ Alan R. Kahn, Kris Austen Radcliffe.--1st ed.
    p. cm.
    ISBN 1-55778-849-9 (pbk. : alk. paper) 1. Cognitive styles. 2. Thought and
thinking. 3. Human information processing. 4. Individual differences.
    I. Radcliffe, Kris Austen, 1968- II. Title.

BF311.K23 2005
153--dc22

                        2004026980

Manufactured in the United States of America

The paper used in this publication meets the minimum requirements of American
National Standard for Information Sciences—Permanence of Paper for Printed
Library Materials, ANSIZ39.48-1984.

10 9 8 7 6 5 4 3 2 1

For current information about all releases from Paragon House,
visit the web site at www.paragonhouse.com

Dedication and Acknowledgements

From Alan

To Dr. Walter Lowen, who provided the basis for the material presented here in his book *Dichotomies of the Mind,* and whose generous ongoing collaboration has guided its development.

To Barbara Pratt, who for the past 20 years has participated in every aspect of the building and application of the cognitive model and is responsible for many of its insights.

To the many others who have participated in the testing and applications of the material described in *Mind Shapes,* especially to Dr. David Shupe, Dr. Mojgan Samardar, Alexandra Rambusch, Dr. Norma Wagoner, and Peter Seidel.

From Kris

To Peter, Evvie, Fiona, and Betty for their loving support.

CONTENTS

11

12

13

LIST OF FIGURES

LIST OF TABLES

FOREWORD

Two take-home points present themselves in both this book and its companion volume, *Who Are We Now? The Evolution of the Sociocognitive System:* One, you are part of something bigger than yourself. In fact, as a contemporary human, you are part of several somethings bigger than yourself. And two, your brain evolved steeped in the structures of those somethings.

Those "somethings" are the human groups people form when they come together to share labor or resources. Some groups are small, like individual nuclear families, and some are large, like multinational corporations. These groupings are filled with like-minded individuals who operate using the same language and the same rules of living. They protect and feed, but are also subtly structured creatures made of living, breathing, conscious humans who think and process information.

There are many special things about the human brain—several of which we will touch on in this book—but chief among them is the human knack for specialization. This ability goes beyond picking a vocation; the human brain actually differentiates in how it processes in order to support the human group.

Have you ever wondered why you chose the profession that you did? Or, on the other hand, why is it that you don't like your job and instead dream of designing airplanes or finding the beauty of the cosmos? Why is it that you are good with numbers but are bad at fixing pipes? Why is it that you always see the complexity of a situation and are perplexed when others don't?

If these questions hit home, then your brain is set up to produce quality output in a specific, abstract arena. Your abilities include the conscious manipulation and refinement of the data flowing between members of a group. Your role is to strengthen the group by strengthening the data structures that tie it together.

Of course, you may be shaking your head or curling your lip at the suggestion that your calling is to strengthen data structures. You may think that helping others is the core of what you do—helping them come together, helping them talk to each other, and helping them be coherent as a group. Or maybe your calling is to build the infrastructure in which the group lives, either physical in the form or tools or homes, or as data in the form of computer programming. Or maybe your calling is to move—move your body, move goods and services, or move the soil and make things grow. You know that you have nothing whatsoever to do with strengthening data and everything to do with keeping the individuals of the group fed and protected.

In order for the group to survive, everyone must play their roles. Differentiation refines the abilities of the individuals in those roles. Instead of doing a little bit of everything tolerably, we can focus on a specific area and do it very well, knowing that the rest of the group will fill in the gaps in our talents.

Differentiation is the ultimate focus of *Mind Shapes*. In this book we get down and dirty in the brains of the like-minded individuals that operate within a group. For that reason, this book is more personal in nature, and it will lay out for you why it is that you process information the way you do as well as what that processing entails.

—Kris Austen Radcliffe and Dr. Alan Kahn

PREFACE

Deep in the hominid past, one of our ancestors experienced a genetic change that altered how their brains processed information, and that change became the foundation for all of the human adaptations that followed. *Mind Shapes* looks at the blueprint that change established and how it configures modern cognition and communication. It is the most "personal" part of the Human Dimensions Model (HDM)—the theory that encompasses the *how* and *why* of human cognition and group interaction. It describes *how* and *why* an individual brain thinks and communicates. Here, the focus is on understanding yourself and the people you interact with on a daily basis.

Where it all started

The development of the Human Dimensions Model (HDM) began in late 1982 when Dr. Kahn acquired a copy of Dr. Walter Lowen's book *Dichotomies of the Mind*. Dr. Lowen's work is a highly theoretical model of the infrastructure of human cognition that describes in detail the different cognitive processes used by different kinds of people. Dr. Kahn was struck by the synchronicity of Dr. Lowen's model with his own experience in neuroscience and physiology. The two soon began to collaborate and develop a close friendship.

Dr. Lowen, now a retired professor emeritus and founder and chair of the Systems Science Department at SUNY Binghamton, developed *Dichotomies of the Mind* as a way to look at the differences in people as an integrated system extending beyond the different cognitive types. He built on the acute observations of Carl Gustav

Jung's *Psychological Types* published in 1921, and the Myers-Briggs Type Indicator (MBTI), through which the Jungian description of differences among people is familiar to most of the public.

In 1943, Isabel Briggs Myers integrated Jung's ideas into an understandable and workable model, creating the MBTI. The Human Dimensions Model (HDM) builds upon the Myers-Briggs model and restructures the Jungian nomenclature to match how the brain processes information. The HDM also provides Lowen's model and the MBTI with evolutionary evidence to explain *why* humans are the way they are.

Also, in the time since Walter Lowen described the model in 1982, Dr. Kahn began to find the work of other scholars that mirrored the Human Dimensions Model (HDM), often in unexpected places. Anthropological and archaeological evidence appeared that supported Dr. Kahn's theories of the neurobiology that provides the infrastructure for the model. Patterns emerged of how our human evolutionary past supports the current complex system. These observations and others led Dr. Kahn to expand Dr. Lowen's model to include the physiological, evolutionary, and historical information presented in this book.

Also, preliminary experimentation revealed that the Human Dimensions Model (HDM) had the potential to provide useful tools for improving the understanding between people and the management of human interactions in a variety of situations. Dr. Kahn subsequently formed Human Dimensions, Inc. to further develop the model and its potential applications.

For twenty years, Human Dimensions Inc. has developed the practical applications of the HDM, including work in human communications, education, organizational management, and team-building. During this time, Human Dimensions Inc. has conducted more than one thousand in-depth studies on human subjects; analyzed student classes at two medical schools; worked with the marketing departments of large firms; and for the past ten years, provided graduate courses at two major universities concerning the material in this book.

Mind Shapes: Understanding the Differences in Thinking and Communication has been in process for approximately ten years. It has taken this long because the information and insights have been in a continual state of development, making it difficult to establish a fixed point at which to stop and report. Fortunately, one of Dr. Kahn's students, Kris Radcliffe, became interested in assisting in the preparation of this book. The collaboration started with her as a writer, but from the beginning she offered improved perspectives and new insights of her own, including some key concepts on narrative and consciousness as well as a few "bridge" areas to complete the model. Our collaboration developed into a partnership in which we are coauthors of this book.

The purpose of this book

Our goal in writing this book was to enrich understanding of the current differences in how people process information and how those differences fit into the modern world.

To reach this goal, we took an integrated approach that enhanced traditional scientific understanding with a multidisciplinary view. Archaeology and evolutionary theory supplied the view of the past; neurobiology, anthropology, psychology, child development, and other sciences provided the view of the present.

All of these fields provide evidence of an alignment between how our ancestors processed information and how we process today. From this insight grew the theories and hypotheses of the HDM, including a description of the relationship between different cognitive behaviors depicted in the patterns of our ancestors' artifacts and those demonstrated by modern humans.

Indeed, the four stages of hominid evolution are directly recapitulated by the four stages of growth and development of a contemporary human child. Further, a detailed mapping of the different cognitive processes used by different individuals in the world today reveals four major groupings with behaviors that are clearly derived from the four stages of child development. When viewed together, this shows a convincing similarity between the four cognitive groupings in today's population and the four stages of hominid evolution.

Previously, studies in the three areas of human evolution, child development, and sociology have been isolated from one another. By bringing them together into a single perspective, the close alignment of our cognitive evolution, our growth and development during childhood, and the different ways people think today, we find that each area supports the others. This provides a much deeper understanding of the development of our cognition and who humans are today.

Enriching the understanding of *how* people are different with an understanding of *why* they are different helps to build more accurate models. It also provides additional tools to further understanding of the differences between people in daily life, including family, education, work, and communication.

Another advantage relates to an individual's understanding of him- or herself. Humans are a product of our evolution, and we must function on a day-to-day basis within the societal system in which we evolved. The broader context that brought about the insights of evolution and society also brought about insights into the mechanisms for *how* humans deal with our world. Processes that had been thought metaphysical are now made physical through the application of the theories and hypotheses of the HDM.

Features and benefits of the work

The Human Dimensions project offers a multidisciplinary, holistic view of the cognition of humans and societies in which we live. Through our work to draw together this information, we have found that previously unrelated disciplines support each other to enhance and enrich understanding of how humans process information.

From these features, the reader can expect to gain a heightened awareness and understanding of him- or herself; an appreciation and enjoyment from implementing his or her new understanding of the differences among people; and a new set of tools to bridge these differences. Among the areas to which these gains can be applied are in education, organizational management, family life, and team-building. Another area of application that the reader will take away from this book is a new comprehension of *how* we live in our societies and *what* those societies actually are.

A word about sources

This book stands on the mountains of information developed over many years by countless scholars. Chief amongst those works are: Walter Lowen's *Dichotomies of the Mind,* which lays out in detail the cognitive processing profiles used by the Human Dimensions Model, and Merlin Donald's *Origins of the Modern Mind,* which describes the same four modes discussed by Lowen from an evolutionary standpoint. Written at different times and completely separate from each other, these two books form a complementary pairing.

Also important was Richard Dawkins' *The Selfish Gene* for his in-depth discussion of deterministic replicators and for providing us with the concept of the "meme." Herbert A. Simon's discussions of reasoning and bounded rationality also informed our work. We would also like to point to the many works of Joseph Campbell and his brilliant discussions of myth and narrative as well as the books of Thomas Cahill for his excellent portraits of life during the turning points in human history.

Other sources of great importance include William Calvin's works, and in particular *The Throwing Madonna* and *A Brain for All Seasons.* Gerald Edelman's work on the brain in *The Remembered Present* was fundamental in understanding how the brain functions during consciousness. Also extremely important in that area was the work of Antonio Damasio, and in particular his book *Descartes' Error.* Another book of great importance was *Nature's Thumbprint* by Peter and Alexander Neubauer for its discussion of nature versus nurture.

How to use this book

Each chapter starts with an overview and ends with a summary. We have provided these additions to help the reader gain the clearest understanding of the information as possible. Also, we have learned from experience that different individuals will process this information differently. This phenomenon is a manifestation of what this book is about, and the overviews, summaries, and included diagrams help bridge these differences.

Important terms are italicized throughout the book and are listed in a quick reference glossary in the back.

That said, we invite you to step into the Human Dimensions Model. You will learn new ideas, new terms, and new tools for dealing with the world.

1

INTRODUCTION

Overview

The *Human Dimensions Model (HDM)* is a model of cognition based on the processes used by the human brain. The HDM describes how humans process *memes*, the scripts that code a sequence of actions people use to respond to a situation. Within the HDM are the *cognitive processing modes,* which act as "databases" for processing. The modes correlate with Piaget's four stages of child development. Also within the HDM are the *cognitive processing steps,* which allow a person to create a meme within a mode. In combination, the modes and the steps produce a *cognitive processing profile.*

Two changes allowed humans to develop the modern cognitive processing profiles: The first was the development of the *Left Procedural Cortex*, the area of the left hemisphere where humans create, practice, and store memes. The second was the creation of *memetic organisms,* which allowed humans to live in large groups and specialize in different skills.

Note: The material covered in chapters 1–6 is also covered in greater depth in the companion volume to this book, *Who Are We Now? The Evolution of the Sociocognitive System.* If you have read *Who Are We Now,* you may wish to skip directly to chapter 7.

INTRODUCTION

Most people will come to this book looking to solve a communication problem. People process information in different ways, leading to different ways of understanding and different viewpoints. Often these differences lead to misunderstandings. They also can lead to self-esteem issues that arise from "not fitting in" or "not living up to expectations." Understanding the processes behind how people differ will give the reader tools to deal with the problems that arise from the interaction of different viewpoints.

Descriptions of the *how* are only part of the picture. Examining how people differ will achieve nothing more than a picture of observations—a picture that can be viewed from many angles and be developed in many ways. Many such "pictures" exist already, including the Myers-Briggs Type Indicator and its offspring.

Also, studies of learning styles have produced several other systems describing how cognition shapes how people take in and produce information. But "learning styles" are descriptive too. They are state models—models that look at the current *state* of a data set and organize it by grouping similar items.

A state model is essentially correlational—that is, we see x and predict we will see y because we know that we usually see x and y together. What we don't know is whether x leads to y, y leads to x, z leads to x and y, or x and y just have a coincidental connection. In the learning styles models as well as in the MBTI, correlations are made by looking at past groupings of similar responses from data sets in similar states. Visual learners may tend to organize data in a particular manner, or people who have certain traits tend to answer questions in a certain manner, but we do not know *why* these items correlate with each other or *how* that correlation occurs, only that

3

they travel together. State models are a good way to collect information and form hypotheses, but they don't look at *how* and *why* those items are in the data set to begin with. And both the *how* and the *why* are very important.

Theories help determine which alternatives are true, and we can judge the quality of a theory by its ability to make testable predictions. A model that describes process helps a great deal in judging causal direction and identifying useful tests. If *x* leads to *y*, which then leads to *z*, you should be able to observe each element separately, presuming that you can find a way to observe the process in action. Most good theories contain elements of *how* a process works, because they are directed at answering *why* the data is the way it is.

The model that this book is based on is a process model. It is the *Human Dimensions Model (HDM)* and it is based on the *how*—the methods that the human brain uses to process information. These processes produce the data that are used in all state models that deal with cognition. From understanding the how, the HDM gives the reason why the data is in the set, and allows them to be organized in a manner that is predictive of how they will interact.

The HDM isolates the elements of cognition and describes how they interact with each other. It includes both cause and effect as shown by modern brain imaging and brain studies. From this work developed a highly predictive model with causal movement—if element x and y come together, then this is the result. It describes human cognitive processing, which is the way a person processes information, both from the senses and from the intuitive world of words.

What this book offers is an understanding of the process. It is a different way of viewing how we think than to say "everyone who answered x to question one is one type of learner and everyone who answered y is another." By understanding the process, the reader can delve under the "wannabe" factor of answering questions the way a person believes they should be answered, and look at what happens during the actual cognition.

The HDM and society

Other *whys* have come from the Human Dimensions Model (HDM), the most important to this book being *why* humans do what we do. It is not simply that we are all different and that's "just the way we are." Evolution produces responses to an animal's context; it does this for squirrels, dolphins, monkeys, and also humans. We are the way we are because our ancestors needed to be this way to survive. They needed the differences in how we think; and they also needed to use those differences in the most advantageous manner. So no matter how frustrating or anxiety-producing those differences may be for the modern individual in a modern situation, they aren't just the "way we are," they are *necessary*.

Those differences stem from two very important changes to the human animal: The first took place several million years ago with the appearance of *Homo habilis,* the first human ancestor to leave evidence of tools. These tools, along with evidence from fossil brain imprints showing differentiation on the left side of the brain (Wilkins and Wakefield 1995), indicate a change that provided the first step toward human cognitive processing.

The change produced the *Left Procedural Cortex,* the part of the human brain that creates, perfects, and remembers sequences of specific, context-free actions. These sequences are *memes,* and they are unique to humans.[1] Our ability to process memes gives us our hallmark adaptability and our ability to "learn on the fly." As the *Homo* genus evolved, new and increasingly more powerful ways of dealing with memes were layered on top of earlier structures. Modern, big-brained humans are the current manifestation of that evolution.

The second change occurred not long ago, in one of the worst climatic periods of the last ice age. Humans were few and far

---

1. Some birds may be using a rudimentary precursor form of the processing we will be discussing in this book (Grant and Grant 1999). More studies and future evaluation of evidence should shed some light on this question.

between, and we were in danger of extinction from the onslaught of the ice sheets. Humans were living in hunter-gatherer groups of no more than about thirty-five individuals. Everyone in the group did a bit of everything, making everyone jacks-of-all-trades.

Some groups began to take advantage of the different types of cognitive processing that manifest in humans. They began to live in larger communities and to specialize, allowing those that, for example, were good at making arrows to spend all of their time producing and perfecting arrow technology, and those that were good at hunting to spend their time hunting and perfecting their techniques. Those that were good at communicating and organizing became the tribal leaders.

On the frozen plains of Southern Europe where the Ice Age humans congregated, the *memetic organism* arose, a way of grouping humans to take full advantage of the different ways people process information. The memetic organism survives on the human ability to create, process, and transfer memes. It is a very powerful way of group living that allows the *group* to outcompete everything and everyone else in the environment.

Humans still live in memetic organisms. Our groups have allowed us to go from near extinction to completely dominating the planet in a time frame that, geologically speaking, is a mere blink of an eye. All because, as a species, we have brains that differentiate between individuals and specialize into specific types of cognitive processing.

As situational context varies, sometimes one particular set of problem solving skills enhances survival better than another. Some problems are immediate and present a danger to the physical well-being of those involved, like fighting a fire or hunting prey. Some involve how to manufacture tools to best support immediate survival, such as fire fighting gear or bows and hunting weapons. Communicating how and when to use the tools produces another set of challenges that involves skills that go beyond the immediate *now*. Finally, there are the problems that arise from organizing and designing production, both of which require strategy and logic to resolve.

These four sets of problem-solving skills—*body-oriented* and physical; hand-oriented and tool-using; *communication-oriented* and word-using; and *logic-oriented* and abstract—form four separate "databases" of knowledge within the human mind. We all have these databases; but each of us specializes in using one of them, filing and formatting how we think with knowledge specialized toward one kind of problem. Body-oriented people specialize in physical responses to the immediate situation, such as athletics, fire fighting, nursing, and sales. Hand-oriented people build and refine tools and specialize in the building trades and accounting. Communication-oriented people organize others and create with words and metaphor, and specialize in the arts and in teaching. Logic-oriented people specialize in finding the underlying structure of phenomenon and events, and are the abstract intellectuals who do research and development as well as strategic planning.

The how and why of the HDM

People who use different databases think very differently from each other. They often do not even think about the same problems. When they do, solutions are very different. A firefighter considers the physicality of a building while fighting a fire—where the stairwells are, how many rooms, the best way to get to the people quickly and safely. An engineer, on the other hand, thinks in terms of construction and materials, whereas an architect thinks in the abstract terms of flow and space. Together, these experts produce the best, safest building for the citizens of their group, but their viewpoints and ways of thinking are very different.

These differences in how people process information provide the foundation of the Human Dimensions Model (HDM), the theoretical basis for the information within this book and its companion volume, *Who Are We Now? The Evolution of the Sociocognitive System*. The HDM covers both the inner workings of *how* the human brain processes information as well as the social motivations of *why*. Together, *how* and *why* form the *sociocognitive system*—the interweaving of human thinking and the social and cultural structures it supports.

This volume focuses on one slice of the *how* and *why* of the HDM—the differences between how individuals cognitively process information. The *how* involves the different ways of thinking. The *why* deals with the different roles that we all must play in assuring that our memetic organisms grow and prosper. Under the *how* and *why* are the everyday interactions in which we all engage. Some of those interactions happen smoothly and with little effort; others are difficult or sometimes impossible.

Everyone has faced a time when he or she has had a hard time communicating with someone else. Examples abound: Team members who just can't seem to explain their thoughts to each other in a clear manner; children who don't seem to fit into the family; or bright students who don't "apply" themselves to a lesson. Other people may not seem to register what is being said to them at all, or perhaps appear to minimize parts of the project, family, or lesson that are the most important to others involved.

Most people do not minimize the efforts of others in order to personally attack them. They do not willfully ignore, either. They simply process information differently. *Output,* which is cognitively produced information that is transferred to others via communication, is *shaped* by the way of thinking of its producer. Each way has a specific "shape," and sometimes that shape is very difficult for a listener to comprehend. Thus, misunderstandings and problems occur.

The four "databases"—body, hands, communication, and logic—correspond to the four layers of human development and are the *cognitive processing modes.* These layers are reflected in both the evolutionary history of the *Homo* genus and in the cognitive development of modern children. They developed with humans and build upon one another. Each layer has its function within a memetic organism, and together they allow modern human civilization.

Also, there are four ways of using each of the databases while cognitively processing information. These four *cognitive processing steps* reflect different functions of the human brain as it manages novel solutions. Humans also specialize in one of the steps, refining problem-solving skills one more level beyond the modes. Together, the cognitive processing modes and the steps create sixteen distinct *cognitive processing profiles*.

Every profile has a communication style in which *input* and *output* are shaped by how the profile processes information. The input looks for information that fits the database—information that is produced by other people who think in the same database with a similar viewpoint on the problems a mode is best equipped to tackle. If the input does not fit, it is not immediately comprehensible to the individual and requires some sort of translation.

This applies to all types of information, including schoolwork, verbal communication from coworkers or family members, the news in the newspapers or on television, how products are advertised, how documents are designed, how web sites are navigated, and so on. Understanding how the profiles work together and how best to maximize communication will help any group avoid problems and increase productivity and efficiency.

This volume is designed to help the reader investigate and understand those differences. It is only one aspect of the Human Dimensions Model, but the most immediate to a person's life.

Archaeological evidence left by our *Homo* genus ancestors includes signs that point to the development of each of the modes. *Homo habilis*, the oldest ancestor to be considered human, left simple tools that indicate an ability to create gross-motor, or body-oriented, solutions. They also left impressions in their skull fossils that showed differentiation in the left cortex, the side of the brain that allows humans to learn on the fly. *Homo erectus*,[2] the next ancestors to show major changes, left complex tools and were the first to spread themselves beyond Africa, indicating more complex behavior and the ability to coordinate hand movements for fine motor control. After the intermediate *Homo heidelbergensis*, *Homo sapiens* appeared with our ability to talk and create tools used to make other tools. More recently the Greeks formalized the process with logic.

Also, the four modes are directly reflected in Piaget's description of the developmental stages of modern children:

Table 1: Childhood Development

Age	Piaget's stage	Skill
0–2 years	Sensorimotor	Gross motor / Body
2–7 years	Preoperational	Fine motor / Hands
7–12 years	Concrete Operational	Verbal-Social / Communication
12–15 years	Formal Operational	Abstract Intellectual / Logic

Piaget did not connect his findings to the differences in cognition among adults. Carl Jung, though not the first to notice the modes in adults, was the first to fully describe the modes in a workable model. Jung did not live in a time when he had access to brain science, so he was unable to understand *how* the modes did what they did.

While assembling the HDM, we had access to modern understanding of how the brain works as well as the work of Piaget, Jung, and a multitude of archaeologists. We also had the work of Walter Lowen, which supplies the vast majority of the diagrams and the understanding of how the cognitive processing profiles interact with each other that are used throughout the book.

Dr. Walter Lowen developed the basic structure of the cognitive processing profile part of the HDM. In this book, we will look at how the model fits together and how it describes the cognitive

2. There is some controversy as to whether the *H. erectus* fossils in Africa are from another species, *Homo ergaster*. One phylogeny organizes the African *H. ergaster* as the origin species of *H. erectus,* which spread out through Eurasia, and for *H. heidelbergensis,* the species considered to be the precursor to humans.

processing of individuals. Dr. Lowen's book, *The Dichotomies of the Mind,* includes a deeper technical discussion about how he arrived at the basis of the model we use today. His work includes perspectives on Jung and child development as well as insights from the dynamic processing of systems. We will not go into the details of the development of the model here, but will instead point the reader to Dr. Lowen's work.[3]

Gene and meme: deterministic replicators

This book will give the reader an understanding of what the cognitive processing profiles are as well as how they use different capabilities within the human brain. Before we can discuss the profiles, we must have an understanding of what those capabilities are.

As we have stated, the hallmark of humanity is our adaptability. Human adaptability is special—it is unlike any other behavior malleability in the animal kingdom. Humans, as we know, create and implement novel solutions, and we do it on the fly. We can do this because the human brain can process memes, which are scripted responses to a particular context.

Animals live in a pattern of *trigger* and *response*. A trigger is a change in the environment that is noticed by the organism, either as a chemical difference in the environment around a cell, or as a perception for more complex organisms. A response is what a living organism uses to counter the trigger and maximize the organism's benefit at that moment.

Living things always respond to a trigger by expressing a deterministic replicator. *Deterministic replicators* are the repeatable and transferable scripts that encode responses to environmental triggers. When a replicator *expresses*, it releases a controlled expenditure of energy in the unfolding of its response to a trigger.

The deterministic replicator that encodes the scripts for how

---

3. Please see References and Suggested Readings at the back of this book.

to build a biological, genetic organism is the *gene*. Without the gene, there is no body. The deterministic replicator that encodes the scripts for how to think is the *meme*. Without the meme, there is no language and no thought. Genes and memes interact to create a person.

For example, humans learn to think. We learn the language in which we think, and we learn the frameworks we use to guide our thinking. Learning and thinking are actions of the brain, which is part of the human body. The first step to learning and thinking is to produce the biological infrastructure that supports these actions. To do this, a human body must first express the scripts that are the genes encoding the cellular processes, muscle movements, and instinctive responses that reside in our cells. These expressions build the body, its perceptual systems, and the brain that processes the incoming information.

The second step in learning to think involves retaining and remembering sequences of genetic responses. Humans seem to be the only species on earth capable of this feat. The sequences humans remember are best responses to the triggers that we encounter in our environment. By remembering the best responses, we maximize the precision of our response to the trigger and minimize the need for our brains to produce a new response every time the same trigger occurs.

This encoding in memory of sequences of genetic responses is a meme. Richard Dawkins coined the term "meme" in his book *The Selfish Gene,* where he used it to describe culturally transmitted information. The HDM has tightened the definition of a meme to a precise sequence or hierarchy of body actions as learned and remembered by the human brain. Memes are the scripts of culture as Dawkins labeled them, but they are also much more, that is, the muscle movements needed to pitch a baseball, or speak a word, or knit a sock. We also learn and remember the rules of grammar and logic.

Not only are memes repeatable, but they are transferable as well. We can watch and mimic, remember the precise sequence we see, and then practice it. We can talk to each other, exchanging the instructions that shape thoughts. Or we can read books, and understand thoughts with a depth of detail not possible through speech alone.

When we exchange information, we are using our sequencing abilities to encode and then decode the transferring memes. In this case, memes ride on the carrier of language, which we build through combining our sequences into hierarchies. The ability to make hierarchies has produced everything in modern life that expands exponentially—technology, knowledge, society, and culture.

Summary

- The model this book is based upon is the *Human Dimensions Model (HDM),* a process model of how the human brain processes cognitively.
- State models are a collection of observations that identify like items that "travel together." A good theory will add *process* to the model, allowing causal connections between those items. Process models are also highly predictive.
- The *Left Procedural Cortex* is the part of the human brain that creates, perfects, and remembers sequences of specific, context-free actions, called *memes.*
- The *sociocognitive system* is the interweaving of human thinking and the social structures it supports.
- There are four sets of problem-solving skills that form four separate "databases" of knowledge within the human mind:
  - Physical, gross-motor, and *body-oriented*
  - Procedural, fine-motor, and *hand-oriented*
  - Word-using, verbal, and *communication-oriented*
  - Abstract, and *logic-oriented*
- Memes fall into four basic modes of cognition, with each mode being processed differently by the brain. These are

the four "databases." They also correlate to Piaget's four stages of child development.

- Humans also use four *cognitive processing steps* during cognitive processing. These steps allow a person to create a novel solution to a situation.

- The step and mode you use consciously determine your *cognitive processing profile*.

- Every profile has an *input* and an *output* that are shaped by how the profile processes information.

- Animals live in a pattern of *trigger* and *response*. A trigger is a change in the environment that is noticed by the organism, either as a chemical difference in the environment around a cell or as a perception for more complex organisms. A response is what a living organism uses to counter the trigger and maximize the organism's benefit at that moment.

- Deterministic replicators are the repeatable and transferable scripts that encode responses to environmental triggers.

- When a replicator *expresses*, it releases a controlled expenditure of energy in the unfolding of its response to a trigger.

- The deterministic replicator that encodes the scripts for how to build a genetic organism is the *gene*.

- The deterministic replicator that encodes the scripts for how to think and how to build a memetic organism is the *meme*.

2

CONCEPT CHAPTER:
THE COGNITIVE PROCESSING STEPS

Overview

This chapter offers a quick overview of the basics of the HDM. Humans live at the intersection of two *deterministic replicators:* the *gene* and the *meme*. Genes encode how our bodies are built; memes encode what we do with them. In humans, genes and memes have evolved in tandem, producing a brain with a *Left Procedural Cortex* and the capacity for memetic processing. This evolution did not happen overnight. Organisms evolve replicators by using four steps: *explore, try, evaluate,* and *implement*. These steps manifest in humans as the four *cognitive processing steps*.

EVOLUTION AND THE COGNITIVE
PROCESSING STEPS

B ecause the Human Dimensions Model is based on how the brain processes information, much of the language used to describe the cognitive processing profiles is based on how the brain works. In the introduction we introduced some of those terms—deterministic replicator, meme, cognitive processing mode, cognitive processing step—and the concepts behind them. In this chapter we will continue building those concepts. Also, we will establish how the brain evolves memes by using the cognitive processing steps as well as what those steps are and how they work.

The human brain is the hardware on which our replicator scripts run. The brain reads the scripts and produces the neurological signals that tell the body how to express them. The biological mechanisms used by the brain differ from the computer mechanisms with which we are familiar, but as a metaphor, computers work well to explain the process.

All of the higher human cognitive functions depend on the combined efforts of the *Right Perceptual Cortex*—the cortex of the right hemisphere where sensory information is built into a model of the world, and the *Left Procedural Cortex*—the cortex of the left hemisphere where the brain builds, practices, and retains memes, its responses to the model built by the perceptual cortex.

The differentiation within the human brain gives humans what can be described in computer terms as two processors running two very different programs. The program on the right creates a picture of the world, and the program on the left creates and chooses the best action in response to that picture. They work together, but they do very different things.

For higher animals, both the right and left cerebral cortices process *now* information—sensory data comes in and is used to determine the correct reaction for that particular moment. Both perception and reaction are combined to form a snapshot of that *now*. Life is a stream of *nows*, with no past or future, only the current moment and its context. Because both cortices process *nows*, there is no room for, or a mechanism to allow, the recording of memes. This works well for animals, but in terms of hardware, the animal brain can read only genes—the scripts with which it was born. Basically, the animal brain works with read-only memory installed at the factory with very little room for upgrades.

Humans, though, have an added feature in their brains. Unlike other animals, our left posterior parietal cerebral cortices do not process snapshots of *nows*, but instead record and process the body actions that are executed over a series of *nows*, forming *sequences* of actions retained as memes. Our right cortex remains *perceptual*—bringing in and processing sensory information, but our left cortex has become *procedural*—creating, perfecting, storing, and executing the procedures coded in our memes.

The Left Procedural Cortex is a major upgrade in brain hardware and gives humans a disk-drive that not only supports our ability to learn, but also to perfect. Without the Left Procedural Cortex, there would be no complex tools, no language, no culture, no societies, and no human cognition.

First, we must look at the gene—the biological deterministic replicator that builds our bodies and brains, and the meme—the cultural deterministic replicator that moves between people within a memetic organism and allows humans to work together and to "learn on the fly."

The gene: building the "hardware"

Genes encode *action directives* that express as discrete functions in response to a trigger within the cellular environment. These functions either build proteins or control the building of proteins, all of which come together to build the cells that make up the individual bodies of human beings.

The accumulation of different expressions forms genetic traits and instincts. In order for a gene to express and a trait or instinct to develop, there must be a need for the behavior it supports. These behaviors run the gamut from internal cellular functioning to flight from a predator.

A gene can express differently depending on environmental stimuli within the cell. The amount of external pressure will determine the amount of internal response, giving the organism some "wiggle room" to adapt. Not much room is available though, because a gene is hard-coded in deoxyribonucleic acid (DNA), and can increase or decrease response only within the production template of the DNA. This makes a gene like a little die-cast mold—a cell makes proteins and enzymes to function by copying bits of its DNA. It cannot change that mold, only ramp up production or decrease it depending on stimuli.

Instincts are the primitive driving forces behind everything we do to keep ourselves alive—eating, sleeping, mating, avoiding pain, and so on. They manifest as a series of action directives hardwired as pathways in the brain. You are born with these pathways intact; you do not need to learn them. Some instincts can be tempered by learning, but a person without neurological damage will always pull back from a hot object or jump when startled by a snake.

The action directives that are the basis of motor functions such as moving the hands and using the vocal cords are genetic. They are hard-coded and cannot be changed, though there are expressive differences between individuals. Motor functions are the base scripts we use to build everything that we do. Most humans are unaware of these instinctive origins of our world; we see only the trappings of culture.

The meme: the "software"

The remaining scripts are encoded as memes. These are the scripts
produced and executed by the Left Procedural Cortex. At its most
basic level, a meme is the encoding of a sequence of action directives in the Left Procedural Cortex.

Unlike the Right Perceptual Cortex, the Left Procedural Cortex does not process perceptual information. Though the left side
of the brain does process sensory information for the right side of
the body, it does not build that information into perception—that
function is carried out by the Right Perceptual Cortex. Instead,
the Left Procedural Cortex focuses only on the action part of the
now.

This very big switch away from full perceptual processing in
both cortices came from a very small change. In our prehominid
ancestors, the left cortex functioned as it does for all other non-
hominid animals—it processed and built *nows*. When our first
hominid ancestors *Homo habilis* came along, it appears that they
carried a mutation that dropped perceptual modeling of sensory
information out of the processing of the left cortex (Gazzaniga
1998). The *Homo* genus, which includes *H. habilis, H. erectus,* and
modern human *H. sapiens sapiens,*[4] has built successively complex
adaptations on this one small mutation.

The Left Procedural Cortex maintains all of the processing
architecture of the Right Perceptual Cortex, but instead of building
the entirety of a *now* with the vast amount of sensory information
included, it takes only the actions needed to respond to a situation
and use its considerable processing power to build the entirety of a
behavioral sequence derived from a series of *nows*, from beginning

---

4. Modern humans carry the scientific designator *Homo sapiens sapiens,* of
which the second *sapiens* classifies us as a subspecies of *Homo sapiens.* Cro-
Magnon, one of the best-studied groups to be classified as *H. sapiens sapiens,* left
evidence of a culture capable of toolmaking marked by greater diversification and
specialization than earlier *H. sapiens* groups as well as a more developed artistic
tradition.

to end. This behavior is a procedural "snapshot," which is stored as a sequence. A sequence can stand alone as a meme or be linked together with other sequences to form more complex memes.

A memetic sequence is not genetically hard-coded into the brain when an individual is conceived. Instead, it is built by the brain as the individual gains experience throughout life. The resulting neurological pathway becomes a template for future responses in much the same way as a gene is a template for cellular functioning. Just as a cell can make many copies of a gene so it can build enzymes, a human can repeatedly express a meme so that he or she can speak the same word in the same way over and over again; produce multiple perfect baseball pitches over several games; or build the different components of a clock.

Since memes are not chemically hard-coded like genes, they are much easier to modify. A meme coding an interaction with peers can change rapidly and radically over just minutes, whereas genes coding mating behaviors can take thousands of years to differentiate. The speed at which memetic scripts can be built, modified, and refined gives humans a major advantage in adapting to rapidly changing environments.

As scripts, genes replicate from cell to cell; memes replicate from person to person. Where genes function as the instruction packets for the cells of our bodies, memes function as the instruction packets for us, the "cells" of our cultures. They bind us together, bring us into alignment, give us consistent language and thought structures so that we can communicate, and bring the dynamic flow of life to our societies.

The rapid mutation of memes and the speed at which they respond to environmental triggers—both long-term and transient triggers—gives them much more wiggle room than genes. A bad meme is more likely to be replaced with a good one than to stick around and become cancerous in a culture. Together, genes and memes form the scripts of human life. They are both deterministic replicators—carrying coherent information from one part of the system to the next.

Context

Replicators do not work alone; they need to respond to environmental *context*, which is everything that can be perceived either chemically for the cell or with the senses for an organism. The configuration of triggers within the context of a situation determines the responding replicator, which will play out from the beginning of its script until the end, regardless of the context changes during the expression.

The interplay of replicator and context has built an intricate, diverse multitude of life with different levels of internal complexity. Top-line predators such as big cats and wolves have evolved highly tuned perceptual systems that allow them to match fine distinctions in context with finely defined, genetically coded responses. This is what allows a cat to jump and catch a mouse as it streaks by—the cat's perceptual system is so intricate and finely tuned that the cat matches each nuance of the mouse's movements with its own appropriate muscle responses.

The muscle responses of the cat are the result of *action directives*. Each action directive that occurs in the expression of a genetic instinctual behavior such as catching a mouse, that is, the neurons firing and causing the context for each cell in the cat's muscle to change, change the perceived context around the cat. This produces the next contextual *now* for the cat to process.

The next *now* triggers the next response, and so on. The cat "loops" through the instinctive behavior, processing and reprocessing

Figure 1: The "looping" processing of instinctive behaviors

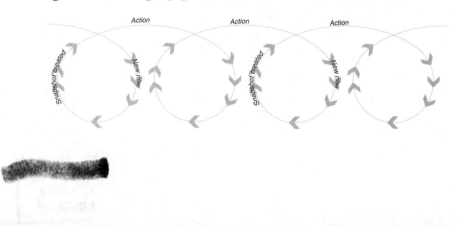

every *now* as it goes. This type of processing relies more on frequent feedback from the context than on the use of deterministic replicators to produce the large-scale action—in this case the instinctive behavior. It is essentially environmentally oriented, and we will refer to it as *contextual*.

Like the cat, humans pick up the small-scale triggers with our very refined perceptual systems. For example, when facing a cougar, each *now* produced by perception is variable and contextual. The cougar may be moving—forward, backward, through the trees, or perpendicular to the path. It may or may not be growling, and it may be audible before it is visible. The shadows from the trees may disguise its location or its direction of movement. An obstacle may block the person's retreat. The person may also be tired and hungry, which will affect muscle response, or be totally distracted in conversation with a friend and miss the cougar altogether. Every single one of these variations—and countless more—has the potential to combine to make a unique situation best processed from *now* to *now* with small-scale triggers. Not all situations, though, are best suited to genetic, instinctive responses.

The memetic replicator

The memetic replicator steps beyond instincts. The Left Procedural Cortex stores and executes specific sequential steps of body action directives, learned from previous behavioral activities, and

Figure 2: The initial *now* activates a sequence. Context is not reprocessed as the sequence is executed

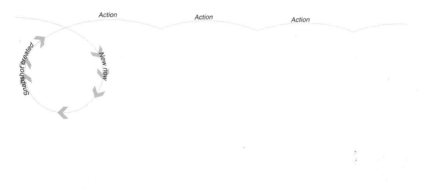

distills them from the context in which they may have originated. The new meme is executed as an entire sequence of action directives that is triggered by the initial *now*. Sequential processing relies on the brain's aggregation of sensory data just as instincts do, but a sequence, unlike a genetic, instinctive response, will *always* ignore the changes in context as the meme is expressed. For this reason, this type of processing relies more on the replicator than the context, and will be referred to as *deterministic*.

For example, humans can throw. We perceive the context of a target and that context becomes the trigger for a throwing meme. Once triggered, a throwing meme will express rapidly from beginning to end and ignore all changes in the environment as the meme is being expressed, including such possibilities as the target moving or the wind changing. Once the expression is completed, then a snapshot of a new *now* is formed.

To create and retain the meme, the Left Procedural Cortex remembers the best sequence of action directives used in the past to hit the target. When the target appears again, the brain responds by expressing the meme, and the entire sequence of the best throw is executed again, greatly increasing the likelihood that the thrower will hit the target.

Memes are not tangible and therefore hard to pin down. But they are deterministic replicators, and they do have all of the features of a replicator, just like genes. For memes, the environment is also the *context* and the source of triggers, but instead of starting with triggers on the cellular level, memetic triggers start with sensory perceptions.

More fully developed memetic structures allow for adaptation to more triggers in the environment. Humans can process information about details like when the salmon spawn, where along the banks of the river to fish, and how to make the nets to catch the fish. Humans have also learned how to prepare the fish for eating and how to preserve it to be eaten later. Memes allowed people to model the future and predict triggers.

The four steps of natural selection

Organisms must often respond to new situations for which they do not have replicators. When this happens, the organism must evolve new replicators for the new context, may those replicators be genes or memes. Evolution is how life changes over time in response to changes in the environment. It is essentially the creation of new replicators in response to new triggers. Traditionally, natural selection and the choosing of the fittest genes for survival have been seen as the core of evolution. Natural selection, though, can be broken down into four steps: *explore, try, evaluate,* and *implement:*

Figure 3: The Four Steps of Natural Selection

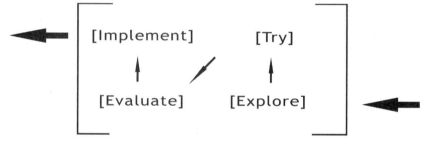

Replicators do not adapt by themselves—the system adapts its replicators to its needs. This may seem like a trivial distinction, but it is not—the "motivation" for change does not come from the replicator, but from the organism built from the replicator. It is only as an organism that a group of cells can build systems capable of perceiving subtle contextual triggers. It is these systems that perceive the environment.

Higher mammals like cats, dogs, and humans have highly efficient perceptual systems and they use them to register the current conditions. For an animal on the open plain, what triggered the storm brewing overhead doesn't matter. There are only the conditions of the *now.* This "here and now" is the world to the animal and is everything the animal knows.

The animal's knowledge of the world is incomplete—it is a

model that allows the animal to distinguish the features of the current set of contextual triggers and to respond to those triggers with the appropriate instinctive behavior. Knowing what started the storm isn't going to make one bit of difference in how the animal responds to it, but recognizing it as a storm and matching that recognition to a behavior will.

A *sensing model*—either one run by a big cat with a highly developed perceptual system or one run by a worm that is limited to sensing moisture variations in the soil—is still only the *now*. The repertoire of behaviors the animal uses in response to its model is limited to those coded in its genetics. Finely tuned genes will increase the chances that the animal will survive the storm. But no matter how intricate the genetics of an animal is, if a significant new trigger comes along that isn't encoded, its species will need to adapt.

The first step to adapting to a new set of triggers is to *explore the environment*. Adaptation to a new environment cannot happen unless knowledge of the change is brought into the animal. The sensing model that an animal uses to determine the context of the situation is built in this step. Here, the organism takes it all in, gains a maximum array of contextual perceptions, scopes the territory, and so on, and the animal's perceptual system brings in information about the new triggers.

Animals of the same species will view the world similarly because of genetic coherence, that is, their perceptual systems are built from the same genetic blueprint, and the same set of new triggers will stress all of the individuals of a species in a similar manner. Contextual triggers will be internalized throughout the genome, and new triggers will stress several individuals.

If the animals detect an unmanageable set of circumstances, their first response is to try the behaviors they already have. In the face of new triggers, their genome will execute the replicators that are normally triggered by contexts with similar features and that come closest to maximizing benefit and survival. The fittest traits will continue to be passed to offspring.

For example, geological changes tend to cause climate shifts.

What was once warm and wet becomes cool and dry, and a rain forest thins to groves of trees and open savanna. An animal adapted to rain forest life may have fur that is thick to shed rain. On the dry savanna, that fur does not go away, but continues to serve its protective purpose. Instead of blocking rain, though, it blocks the harmful rays of the sun.

If the current configuration of traits does not stand up to the new context, the species will continue to be stressed. Poorly performing replicators cause the system to rearrange their application or to add a new replicator. This is made possible by the mutable structure of the replicator carriers. As the new conditions hold and the species starts to die out because it cannot cope, new combinations of genes appear in the offspring of the individuals that remain. This way, the system *tries the new combinations.*

In the example, on the open savanna, the thick fur adapted to the rain forest may be too thick and cause the animal to overheat. If too many of the species are overheating and dying before they can reproduce, they will die out. Those that do manage to reproduce are so stressed that their offspring carry mutations. With enough different trials of possible mutations, somewhere within the species individuals with thinner fur will appear.

Once the new combinations of responses are out in the environment, natural selection e*valuates the performance of the new replicators.* Replicators that perform well are triggered more often and quickly come to dominate within the evolving species. The new genome adapts to the new environment, carrying the fittest genes forward.

In the example, the animals with the fur better adapted to savanna life flourish. Those with the thicker fur die out.

Now finely tuned to the new environment, the newly evolved species *implements its new genome and fills its niche in the system.* The more robust replicators spread out through the entire genome, sometimes carrying an entirely new species with them.

In the example, the new animals spread out across the savanna with their newly adapted fur that lets them hunt in the grass without overheating.

Figure 4: Evolution of Genes

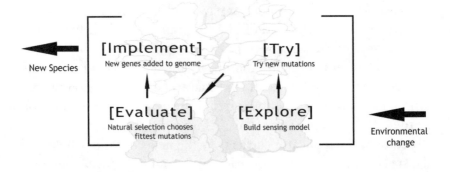

Evolution and the meme

The four-step process—explore, try, evaluate, and implement—is universal to generation and evolution of deterministic replicators and appears in memetic evolution as well. Memes are created in response to a new situation, tested in context, edited, and given to the world. Innovation, creation, even a conversation can evolve a meme by moving it back and forth between two people who refine it as they discuss it.

Memetic evolution requires both the Right Perceptual Cortex and the Left Procedural Cortex in the human brain. As one individual creates and evolves a meme, it is passed to another person, who then adds personal touches to it. Every human specializes in one of the four steps. Using consciousness, each of us either prefers to explore, try, evaluate, or implement the memes that come to us. We are the parts of the engine of evolution that propels our societies forward, creating, evaluating, perfecting, and implementing the tools, technology, knowledge, and systems that support modern day humans.

Memetic evolution starts with exploring the environment. To build a world model, a person *internalizes* each *now* by forming it into a snapshot in the perceptual processing areas of both cor-

Figure 5: Evolution of Memes

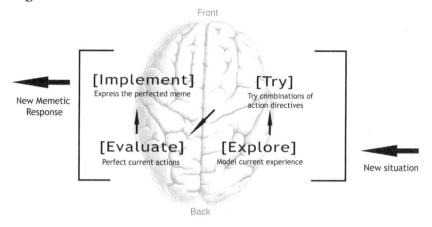

tices. When a snapshot is matched to an appropriate action, the whole *now* is stored as an *episode*. This process of exploration of the enviroment via the senses is the *explore step* we use today when we observe new situations. It is Contextual and Internalizing, and occurs in the world-modeling areas of the Right Perceptual Cortex, which are located in the rear of the right side of the brain. We will refer to it as the *CI explore cognitive processing step*.

The current snapshot is explored by comparing it to other episodes stored in memory. If it matches a stored episode that contains an *action plan* of action directives for muscle movements that respond accordingly to the trigger, the person's motor control areas in the front of the brain *externalize* the action. In this way, a previously stored response is tried in the current *now*. This *try step* process allows the person to respond to the environment with already learned memes. We use it today when we try one of many possible solutions to a problem. It is Contextual and Externalizing, and occurs in the action-taking areas on the right side of the brain. We will refer to it as the *CE try cognitive processing step*.

The CI/CE cycle is trial and error, and is used in all kinds of higher mammals. These processes are old, stable, and prolific within the animal kingdom. We see them in the other primates.

We see them in dolphins, too, with their huge perceptual cortices, and in birds, when they compare one episode moment with another and mimic back the correct response for that situation. Without it, we—and they—would be cut off from the world.

Even though the left side of the brain processes sequences, its basic structures have not changed. Internalization still takes place in the rear of both cortices. In the Left Procedural Cortex, though, the sequence of action directives tried by the individual is brought in as part of that person's sensing model.

While internalizing, instead of enhancing the richness of the perceived model of the world, the Left Procedural Cortex enhances a sequence of actions derived from a series of *now* snapshots. As people practice and perfect, they make use of an attribute of the posterior parietal associative cortex that allows the brain to learn from single events. This quick learning capability is unique to this area of the brain and is the basis of short-term, working memory. In the right cortex, it takes a sensory snapshot for an episode, and in the left cortex, it makes a sequence.

This *evaluate step* process allows the person to practice a sequential behavior, perfect it, and store it in the Left Procedural Cortex[5] as a sequence for future use. It is Deterministic and Internalizing, and occurs in the modeling areas on the left side of the brain. We will refer to it as the *DI evaluate cognitive processing step*.

The CI explore and CE try steps produce sample behaviors. With each practice attempt, the Left Procedural Cortex senses a sequence of action directives and continues to evaluate and alter that sequence until the DI processing step stores the final, perfected procedural sequence.

When a perceptual match identifies a situation as needing a specific meme, a person executes the procedure using the action-taking areas on the left side of the brain. We will refer to this *implement step* as the *DE implement cognitive processing step*. The function of the DE process is to perform predetermined action sequences

---

5. Broca's area is part of this storage area.

based upon perfected procedural sequences. If the implementing DE step does not produce a satisfactory response, practice continues until the DI step perfects the procedure. This type of deterministic sequencing is quite different from the trial and error mode of the CE, which is designed to deal with contextual uncertainty and does not save a perfected procedure.

DE implementation starts with an accurate initial perception in the form of an accurately sensed trigger in the environment. This is followed by the execution of a predetermined sequence that ignores any contextual changes during its performance. The DE process assumes a stable internal and external context in which to operate. For example, while throwing a baseball pitch, the DE implement step executes the procedure while assuming certain behaviors from the hitter and the catcher, like not running while swinging the bat and not running away. Once the throw starts, it is followed through until the end, no matter what happens around the pitcher.

The CI explore, CE try, DI evaluate, and DE implement cognitive processing steps allow a person to use consciousness to evolve a meme. This evolution needs a "database" in which to operate—a database provided by the cognitive processing modes. In the next four chapters we will take a closer look at how each mode operates.

Summary

- *Deterministic replicators* are the scripts that encode responses to environmental triggers.
- There are two types of replicators: the *gene* and the *meme*.
- The gene is hard-coded in *deoxyribonucleic acid (DNA)* and provides scripts for operating cells.
- The meme is created and stored in long-term memory in the Left Procedural Cortex and scripts learned behaviors.
- For animals, both the right and left cerebral cortices process *now* information—sensory data comes in and a snapshot of the current moment is used to determine the correct reaction for that particular *now*.

- The human left posterior parietal cerebral cortex does not process snapshots of *nows* but instead records and processes the sequences of body actions resulting from a series of *nows* that are executed as memes.
- The human right cortex remains *perceptual*—bringing in and processing sensory information that triggers specific actions.
- The left cortex has become *procedural*—creating, storing, processing, and executing the procedures resulting from extended sequences of actions.
- Genes code *action directives* that express as discrete cellular functions.
- *Instincts* are the primitive driving forces behind everything we do to keep ourselves alive—eating, sleeping, mating, and avoiding pain. They are made up of genetically built pathways in the brain.
- *Context* is everything that can be perceived either chemically for the cell or with the senses for an organism.
- Processing that relies on context to determine the next step in a response is *contextual*.
- Processing that plays out through an entire sequence of actions while ignoring changes in context during expression is *deterministic*.
- Evolution operates via natural selection, which can be broken down into four steps: *explore, try, evaluate,* and *implement.*
- The animal's knowledge of the world is incomplete—it is a *sensing model* that allows the animal to distinguish the features of the current set of contextual triggers and to respond to those triggers with the appropriate instinctive behavior.
- Memetic evolution uses both the Right Perceptual Cortex and the Left Procedural Cortex in the human brain.
- When a snapshot is matched to an action, the whole *now* is stored as an *episode.*

- An *action plan* contains the action directives for muscle movements that had previously maximized the animal's survival as stored in a previously experienced episode.
- The *contextual internalized* process of exploration of the environment via the senses is the "CI explore" cognitive processing step we use today when we observe new situations.
- The *contextual externalized* process of responding to the environment is the "CE try" cognitive processing step, which we use today when we try possible solutions to a problem.
- Action directives are pulled together and stored as a *procedural sequence*.
- A procedural sequence is an entire action sequence—a whole throw, or the whole process of chipping a rock.
- In the right cortex, the posterior parietal associative cortex takes a sensory snapshot for an episode, and in the left cortex it creates a model of a sequence.
- With the *deterministic internalized* "DI evaluate" cognitive processing step, humans practice a sequential behavior, perfect it, and store it in the Left Procedural Cortex as a sequence for future use.
- The *deterministic externalized* "DE implement" cognitive processing step performs predetermined action sequences based upon perfected procedural sequences.

COGNITIVE PROCESSING MODES: SENSING FEELING (SF)

Overview

The *Sensing Feeling (SF)* cognitive processing mode developed early in hominid evolution with *Homo habilis*. This mode of processing corresponds to Piaget's "sensorimotor" stage of child development. It is *sensing* in that it deals with the sensed world, and *feeling* in that emotions are part of the *episodes* being processed. Subsequently, *H. habilis* laid the foundation for the *SF cognitive processing mode* used by modern humans, and also the first DI evaluate and DE implement cognitive processing steps.

THE FIRST MODE: SENSING FEELING (SF), THE MODE OF THE BODY

The addition of the DI evaluate and DE implement cognitive processing steps opened the hominid brain to memetic processing. The foundation formed by this change is how humans use our bodies. People move in ways that are not duplicated anywhere else in the animal kingdom. For example, lions do not attack prey with the surgical precision of a ninja. Gorillas do not do yoga. Dolphins, too, even with their amazing acrobatic abilities, do not play water polo.

Skipping, dancing, playing sports, and throwing all take practice and precision, and rely on body memes. We learn these behaviors through imitation and practice, and the memes involved are much more than how to move the body, they also contain how to situate the body in the right position to start the meme correctly.

Body memes are the gross motor memes; they are represented by Piaget's "genetic epistemology" timetable that traces the development of a modern child's thinking.[6] They form the first level of cognitive development. In this level, infants learn to position their bodies to better achieve the effect they desire. This is Piaget's "sensorimotor" stage between the ages of birth and two where infants practice and perfect their gross motor skills; they learn to walk, make sounds, and control their arms and legs.

For adults, throwing is the quintessential example of gross motor memes in action. People play ball—baseball, soccer, American football, rugby, lacrosse, basketball, jai alai, golf, and dozens of

---

6. Please see Appendix A: Child Development.

other variations. We hit the ball; we kick it; we run with it; and we dodge it when it comes our way. Mostly though, we throw it, making it go in the precise direction at the precise speed needed to hit the target at which we are aiming.

Throwing is deep-seated; it's a primitive passion that transcends human cultures. At its roots, it is an essential hominid survival skill, and modern humans still hold it dear. Throwing, along with other gross-motor memes, maximize outcomes by *always* responding to a situation with the best possible body movements.

As anyone who's ever pitched a game knows, anyone can throw, but throwing *well* is an art that happens only through practicing and perfecting. Without the DI evaluate and DE implement cognitive processing steps, the gross motor memes of throwing could not be learned and could not rise to the level of expertise.

The expertise comes from the human ability to *aim*. Aiming is more than seeing something and throwing a rock at it; it involves positioning oneself so that the target can be hit. Pitchers get their bodies ready to throw when they wind up, and their throws are precise and aimed because they follow the same set of action directives for the throw *every time,* including the initial body posture. If a pitcher were checking the context of the situation moment to moment, the windup would never be the same, and neither would the pitches.

The brain structures that support the ability to aim are the core of human memetic processing. They consist of making a sequence from the action directives generated over a series of *nows* as needed to produce a desired result. This process mirrors the instinctual response, except the instinct is replaced by a previously perfected and stored meme.

We know that the differentiation from strict perceptual processing to memetic procedural processing happened sometime in human evolution. The Left Procedural Cortex appeared at some point, just like human bipedalism and our naked skin. *Homo habilis* was the first human ancestor to leave evidence of developing new procedures, strongly suggesting that they were the first hominid species to use the mutations supporting memetic processing.

H. habilis, a bipedal ape that lived between 2.4 and 1.5 million years ago, inhabited the sub-Saharan plains in and around the Great Rift Valley. They were descended from one of the Australopithecus species, most likely *A. afarensis,* and had some small anatomical differences in cranial capacity, molars, and hand construction. The new hominid's main distinction was that it appeared in the fossil record alongside the very primitive Oldowan culture tools.

As a bipedal ape, the *H. habilis* was not well adapted to life on the savanna. For a mammal, two legs are slower and clumsier than four, leaving the animal vulnerable to predation and less able to hunt efficiently. A brain adaptation such as a Left Procedural Cortex could help the animal learn on the fly, giving it a better chance at survival.

For humans, the skills generated by the Left Procedural Cortex can compensate for a great deal of our physical inadequacies. Athletes train to learn and practice how to best position and use their bodies. So do firefighters and police officers. People learning a sport train their bodies to achieve the best execution of physical movements. Humans learn and practice all sorts of gross motor skills, from how to lift without hurting their back to how to fill the lungs for the best breath support while singing.

Body memes allow humans to be good at what we do not because we are physically built to be the best runners or the best hunters, but because we can learn and practice how to always use the best of what our bodies are capable of producing. With body memes, humans—and all of our ancestral species that had access to memetic processing—were capable of learning how to *always* perform a behavior at top capacity no matter how the environment changed around the behavior's trigger.

H. habilis and the Human Dimensions Model

With body memes, whole, perfected procedures were accessed for implementation, giving the *H. habilis* fluid physical actions. Modern humans who use this mode tend to participate in and do well at body-active sports, testifying to the natural environmental advantage of "sense and respond" processing.

The processing associated with this mode grounds its users very much in the "here and now." It is a mode of sense and respond, both in the "trial and error" cyclical, contextual processing, and the sense and implement, deterministic processing. It is "of the body" and its sensations at that moment—may they be happy, hungry, satisfied, or frightened. Because of this, the mode infrastructure that appeared with *H. habilis* was very tangible and based on direct sensory perceptions, and will be labeled *sensing* (S).

Also, the emotional system has evolved to check one episode at a time. This is a much older way of processing than the evolutionarily new Left Procedural Cortex. Based on analysis of the emotional system of modern animals and also of modern humans, we can reasonably assume that the emotional system of *H. habilis* had the same basic functioning (Damasio 1999).

The emotional system also works much faster than the higher cognitive functions and "tags" a perceptual episode or procedural sequence before the brain is done processing cognitively. This gives the animal, hominid, or modern human an emotional "kick" with perception, that is, whether or not what is being perceived is good or bad for survival.

Also, with the emotional system, "one at a time" processing is a crucial element—the emotional system will tag only one perceptual episode or one procedural sequence at a time. Since the Left Procedural Cortex in *H. habilis* was sense and respond, sensing one complete episode then responding with one complete procedural sequence, the emotional system was able to apply an emotional tag to guide each response. With the tag in place, every time *H. habilis* remembered an episode or sequence, he or she recalled the emotion, too. Thus, we will label the mode *feeling* (F). When combined with sensing to make "SF," this mode is sensory and emotionally tagged.

The action memes generated by the SF mode are gross-motor, physical, and based in the body. The SF mode processes internal and external sensations and matches that information to stored perceptual episodes. Today, human infants first use the SF infrastructure in their first stage of development as they learn to control their bodies.

When we diagram the HDM, the SF mode is placed at the left of the model:

Figure 6: The SF Mode and the Human Dimensions Model

Internalizing and Externalizing in the hominid brain

Even though the left side of the early hominid brain processed sequences, its basic structures did not change. Internalization still happened in the rear of both cortices. In the new Left Procedural Cortex, though, the sequence of action directives tried by the individual was brought in as part of his or her sensing model. For hominids and the humans that came after them, this is the fundamental difference in processing between us and the animals—the left cortex of the *Homo* genus brain makes models of responses, actions, and reactions instead of duplicating the models of the context made by the right cortex.

While internalizing instead of enhancing the richness of the perceived model of the world, the Left Procedural Cortex enhances a sequence of actions derived from a series of snapshots. It perfects the sequence until it produces the desired results when the sequence is implemented by the action areas in the front of the brain.

The following diagram illustrates memetic development as it proceeds from the modeling areas in the back of the right cortex to the implementing areas in the front of the left cortex:

Figure 7: Memetic Development from Modeling to Implementing

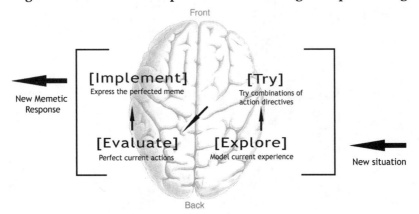

Figure 8: Model-Making Areas of the Brain

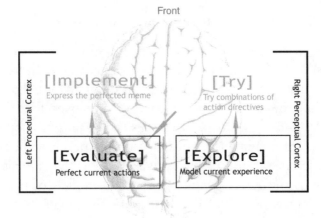

Figure 8 highlights the two internalizing, model-making areas of the brain—the "explore" area in the back of the right cortex where the perceptual model is constructed, and the "evaluate" area in the back of the left cortex, where sequences are built.

Implementation occurs in the action areas in the front of the brain. These areas send the neurological signals to the body telling it how to move. In animals, both the left and right cortices send responses based on genetic instincts to these areas. In hominids, the left cortex sends responses stored as memes.

The following diagram highlights the action areas of the brain—the "try" area in the front of the right cortex where genetic combinations are tried, and the "implement" area in the front of the left cortex where memes are implemented:

Figure 9: Action Areas of the Brain

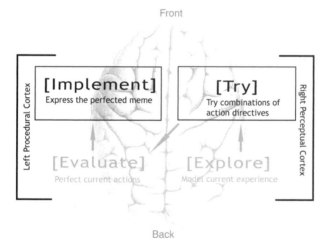

Once one individual perfected a meme, the others of the group could perceive, internalize, evaluate, and implement the same behavior. Even without language, gross motor memes could spread throughout an entire population very quickly, maximizing responses for any individual who learned them and increasing the likelihood of the survival of anyone carrying the Left Procedural Cortex mutation.

Quick, immediate learning makes memes much faster to evolve and implement than genes. Though *H. habilis* gross motor memes were restricted to the number of action directives that could be contained in a single episode or sequence, they still opened an evolutionary floodgate of adaptability that eventually carried the *Homo* genus to its current manifestation as *H. sapiens sapiens*.

Human capacities and the SF infrastructures

The body-oriented, gross-motor memes that first manifested with *H. habilis* were the first step to everything memetic that humans would evolve—the procedures we use for building tools, the sequences we access when we produce vocalized words, and the thoughts we use to organize our world.

As part of today's world that functions with memetic organisms, some humans process consciously within this SF mode.[7] This benefits the society by providing an internal group that is grounded in the physical—people who literally think in the action of the world. They are our firefighters, our athletes, our surgeons, our warriors, and our salespeople. They are the dancers, and they are the people who teach us how to move without hurting ourselves. They take the entirety of human cognitive processing and filter it back through the "here and now"—the physical world that *is*. People today who specialize in the SF cognitive processing mode make sure that one foot of the human race is always planted firmly on terra firma.

Summary

- Action directives are pulled together and stored as a *procedural sequence*.
- The fundamental difference in processing between us and

---

7. The profiling work done to date suggests that the profiles are split fairly evenly within the population, making about one-quarter of humanity SF.

other higher animals is that the left cortex of the *Homo* genus brain makes precise models of responses, actions, and reactions instead of duplicating the rich models of the context made by the right cortex.

- The grounded, sense and respond mode infrastructure that appeared with *H. habilis* was very tangible and based on direct sensory perceptions, and will be labeled *sensing*.

- Since the Left Procedural Cortex in *H. habilis* functioned one complete procedural sequence at a time, the emotional system was able to apply an emotional tag to guide each procedure.

- When combined with sensing to make the *sensing feeling* "SF" mode, the *H. habilis* mode processed single episodes or sequences that were sensory and emotionally tagged.

- The first stage of child development—labeled "sensorimotor" by Piaget—is learning to use the SF infrastructure.

4

COGNITIVE PROCESSING MODES: SENSING THINKING (ST)

Overview

The Sensing Thinking (ST) cognitive processing mode developed with *Homo erectus*. This mode of processing corresponds to Piaget's "preoperational" stage of child development. It is *sensing* in that it deals with the sensed world, and *thinking* in that it processes *procedural strings*, of which emotions are *not* a part. ST mode cognition also introduced *dexterity* and the ability to mime into the Homo genus.

THE SECOND MODE: SENSING THINKING (ST), THE MODE OF THE HANDS

The next infrastructure appeared with *Homo erectus*. *H. erectus* roamed the planet between 1.8 million and 300,000 years ago, leaving fossil evidence in lands as distant from Africa as Java on the Pacific Rim, where they survived until the arrival of *H. sapiens*.

H. erectus was the next hominid ancestor to show evidence of an advancement in memetic processing. *H. erectus* took an already present ability of the primate brain and applied it to the sequences of the Left Procedural Cortex. All primates—including humans and presumably our hominid ancestors also—have a well-developed associative linking capability within their posterior parietal areas of both cortices. Basically, "similar enough" episodes can be linked easily in primate brains.

H. habilis left no evidence that they applied this ability to link together the sequences of the Left Procedural Cortex. *H. erectus*, on the other hand, left archaeological evidence of more complex toolmaking, suggesting that they were the first hominid ancestor to use the linking ability of the posterior parietal area of the Left Procedural Cortex to link together sequences.[8] Linked procedural sequences became *strings*, which are longer, more complex memes.

A modern automobile assembly line works well as a metaphor

---

[8]*Homo ergaster*, an early, African version of *H. erectus*, appeared with the Achulean stone tool industry, which consisted of large cutting tools and "hand axes." These tools were significantly more advanced than the tools of *H. habilis*.

for procedural strings. Each station on a line is a separate procedural sequence—at the first station the chassis is put into position. At the second station the engine is dropped in. At the third the body is attached. Because the sequences are on one line and done consecutively, they produce one thing—a car. In the case of a procedural string in the brain of an *H. erectus* or a modern human, the entire production line would produce one procedural string meme.

Within the SF cognitive processing mode, the entirety of a procedure was a single sequence—it began and ended in one *now*. For the new mode, the initial *now* is at the beginning of a string of procedures. This is fundamentally different from SF matching. With string memes, the sequences that will lead to the full implementation of the meme are not directly part of the procedure built from the initial *now*. Instead, they spread away from the initial *now* like beads on a string—with each sequence as a distinct "bead."

Humans—and presumably our hominid ancestors as well—reconstruct remembered episodes with information stored in the memory data store. Reconstruction effectively highlights what was in the context that triggered the string meme in the first place, attaching more importance to that feature than to the rest of the perceptual data in the episode.

This resulted in a new ability to extract and match component features of an experience rather than requiring a complete match to an entire episode. These features "mark" a string meme. For example, a modern SF, who processes consciously with whole episodes, and an ST, an individual who processes consciously with string memes, will respond to a visit to a new locale differently. When first experienced, the SF will match the entirety of perception of the new place to memories of places visited in the past. The *entire* sensory landscape of colors, smells, textures, sounds, and so on, will be taken as a whole snapshot and matched to memories of other places.

An ST, on the other hand, will look at the new place and examine the features separately. The new place may have trees like one episode, but a stream like another. It may feel cooler, but have different sunlight. Each of these features marks a string meme response, and the ST will be able to implement a meme in response to each of the features, as opposed to implementing based on the entirety of the episode. In effect, feature matching breaks up a big *now* into several little pieces, each of which can be used as a trigger for a meme. For example, a certain type of branch, no matter where it fell, becomes the trigger, as opposed to the entire perception of the branch as it has fallen.

Though more possibilities for implementation existed in every *now*, the memes expressed were still linear. This follows from how memes are executed—beginning to end with no changes for context. String memes are no different; they are executed first step to final step on down the line. The initial trigger elicits a memetic response that plays out sequence-to-sequence, until the meme reaches expression. Steps are not interchanged; that is, Ford engines do not go into GM cars. Modern humans who use this extended, sequential infrastructure as the core of their cognitive mode also process consciously in an extended linear manner.

Emotional tagging

The emotional system checks one episode or sequence at a time and a string meme's procedure covers more than one sequence. This means that the string meme exists outside of what the emotional system can handle, leaving string memes emotionally untagged.

No tags meant no emotional information stored with the string. Individuals who use this cognitive processing mode rely on a non-feeling *thinking*[9] way of observation and process to determine if a behavior represented by a procedural string maximized survival. Today, we call this process "objectivity."

The difference between *feeling* and *thinking* can best be summed

---

9. The original designation of this type of processing as "thinking" comes from Jung. Walter Lowen also uses it in his model, and we will continue to use it here in the HDM.

up in a scene from modern life: Take, for example, a first kiss under an apple tree in the blush of spring. It is an emotionally charged scene, and the memory of the moment is emotionally charged as well. For a feeling "F" individual, the memory of the day recalls all of the day's emotions, and the individual relives them physically in much the same way that in their mind's eye they can see the scene[10]. The feelings are very much a part of the memory, and they color all connected memories. For example, an apple may always bring a blush to the cheek.

A thinking "T" individual, on the other hand, is more "objective." Though the emotions were fully felt that day under the apple tree, they are not vividly relived when the memory is recalled. They may be remembered, but not in the same way as for the feeling F individual. For the thinking T person, the emotions are a feature of the memory, something that is labeled and categorized, and thus sorted. There is no visceral response to the memory, just the objective "well, I felt good that day," allowing the memory to be sorted with other "felt good" memories. In objectivity, emotions can be ignored, and an apple will always be just an apple.

Dropping emotional recall may seem like a great loss, but it also came with a great gain. The thinking T process enables a linking ability not available to F feeling. The T can work with and manipulate more information at a finer level of detail. For the *H. erectus*, this meant more advanced technology and the adaptability to move into and survive in habitats outside of Africa.

The objectivity of the T process also allows an individual to circumvent limiting and inappropriate emotional system responses. For example, humans have an emotional response to protect our territory, but we can circumvent it and keep ourselves from fighting over parking spaces, a "feature" of territory for which the fight emotional response is inappropriate. We do this by using the ST database to access a meme designed to cope with the "parking space" feature.

---

10. Not all people can "see" a scene in their mind's eye. We will discuss this phenomenon in later chapters.

These memes are procedural and deal with the situation "objectively," ignoring emotions and helping society function smoothly.

The new thinking T ability did not change the tangible, sensing component that *H. erectus* inherited from *H. habilis*. *H. erectus* individuals in this mode were still grounded in the here and now, working with what their senses told them and with what they could hold. The difference was that they worked and processed using larger memes to encompass more extensive procedures. This allowed the development of memes for situations that were "features" of general instincts, such as protecting territory and choosing a mate, which set the stage for refining of social interaction.

The new *H. erectus* mode became the *sensing thinking (ST) mode*. On the HDM, ST is placed at the bottom of the model:

Figure 10: The ST Mode and the Human Dimensions Model

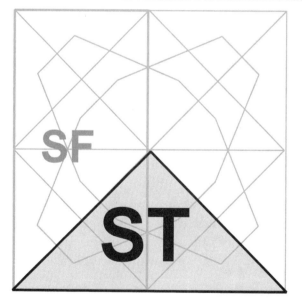

Dexterity

Not only did the change to strings increase the overall size of the memes with which *H. erectus* could work, but it also increased the intricacy of motor control with the hands. Humans have very good control of our fingers and hands, and it's not just because we have an opposable thumb. Chimp hands are very similar to ours,[11] but chimps can't touch-type, use power tools, or embroider because a chimp's brain isn't set up to string together sequences of action directives to do anything as intricate as typing, drilling, or needlework.

The magic of a procedural string is that the meme ceases to be one sequence. Once that happened, the brain was able to link together all of the little moves we make with our hands—the pinching of leaf buds, the grasping of rocks and fruits, the waving of this finger to stirring up a termite nest and the pointing of another to indicate location—and was able to string them together into something more than they were before.

String memes that express as intricate hand movements are one manifestation of the ST mode. They are also an obvious and important manifestation, and one that is still with humans to this day. And while handedness is in no way limited to humans, the fact that we have hands that can write, type, and shuffle a deck of cards is. In the majority of humans, the dominant hand—the hand that does most of the work—is the right hand. The left cerebral hemisphere of the brain controls the motor functions of the right side of the body, and vice versa. The cortices provide direction to the hands, with the Left Procedural Cortex more directly providing the directions for the right hand. This manifests as precise fine motor control and dexterity.

Human children develop the ST infrastructure during their toddler and preschool years. In Piaget's epistemology, he refers to this time between the ages of two and seven as the "preoperational"

---

11. Our thumb is more flexible and our hands are shorter, allowing a pincer grip.

stage. It is marked by the increasing use of the hands and increased exploration of the tangible world around the child.

While the SF mode gives modern humans body precision, the ST mode gives us tool precision. STs work with the physical, tangible, tactile objects of the world and manipulate them with their precise manual, fine motor control. Those that aren't building the world's infrastructure through carpentry and the other trades use their procedural string linking to build our information infrastructure with data entry, bookkeeping, and computer coding. They give us organization and all of the sequential procedures we use to run our daily lives.

Summary

- To make a string meme, a person links together sequences involved in a process and remembers the entire *string* as a procedure.
- The ST infrastructure uses feature matching, as opposed to the whole episode matching of the SF infrastructure.
- Each sequence in a procedural string is stored separately, rendering the entire meme represented by the string inaccessible to the emotional system for checking.
- Without the emotional system checking the meme, no emotional tags were stored with the string.
- This new ability did not change the tangible, sensing component that *H. erectus* inherited from *H. habilis*. *H. erectus* individuals in this mode were still grounded in the here and now, but working and processing using larger memes to encompass more extensive procedures. The new *H. erectus* mode became the *sensing thinking* ST.
- Thinking is "objective," whereas Feeling is "subjective."
- The ST infrastructure manifests in child development between the ages of two and seven and is Piaget's "preoperational" stage.

5

Cognitive Processing Modes: iNtuitive Feeling (NF)

Overview

The modern human brain processes *hierarchically,* utilizing *abstractions* and *generalizations*. Abstractions are sequences of internal brain functions that the brain has learned and stored in the Left Procedural Cortex. Generalizations are abstractions "played" on the sensory cortices and used by the Right Perceptual Cortex as perceptions. Abstractions allow categorization, which enabled hierarchical processing. Abstractions and generalizations also made possible the *intuitive model,* which is the foundation of *consciousness*. The intuitive model made possible a new cognitive processing mode— the *iNtuitive Feeler NF*—the mode that works with and creates intuitive episodes based on abstractions and generalizations. The NF thinks in words and is particularly good with language, metaphor, and interpersonal relationships.

THE THIRD MODE: INTUITIVE FEELING (NF), THE MODE OF COMMUNICATION

Modern *H. sapiens sapiens*—the version of *H. sapiens* walking the earth today—are so named because of our specialized technology and large social groupings. Physically modern *H. sapiens* evolved approximately 130,000 years ago in Africa, but modern *H. sapiens sapiens* appeared in Eastern Africa during the Ice Age. About 55,000 years ago, Cro-Magnon and other Ice Age groups left archaeological evidence of toolmaking specialization and social groups larger than hunter-gatherer bands. These humans were also the first to leave evidence of work of art and religion.

With the evolution of *H. sapiens sapiens*, humans fully developed the *intuitive model,* a new way of modeling the world. The intuitive model runs on language and is not based directly on the perceptions of the body. Instead, the intuitive model is based on the human ability to name distinctive and specific features within the environment. The "names" are the brain's way of holding onto and working with its impressions of the "features." The "names" are *abstractions*, and they are the specific concepts within consciousness that sit behind words.

For example, the abstraction of **yellow** is not a particular perception, but is built from all of the "yellowness" that has ever been perceived by the individual. This new sequence is purely intuitive—it is not of the world per se, but is built by the brain in order to organize all that is yellow. It is an *abstraction* and its purpose is to give all things yellow a descriptive annotation. This annotating abstraction also connects all memories containing yellow.

The abstraction of **yellow** is a "pure" sequence in the Left Procedural Cortex—it is a sequence built from the processes the brain uses to perceive the color yellow. This kind of processing is a new order of magnitude in the brain's memetic abilities. Not only can the human brain create sequences for the body to use by remembering, evaluating, and implementing the action directives it needs to produce the best movement, it can also create sequences based on *its own processing*. This internal labeling, that is, the brain recognizing that a perception is "yellow," builds the intuitive model.

The human brain can also manipulate abstractions by forming them into "perceptions" and responding to them as if they were actual, physical manifestations sensed by the eyes, ears, nose, tongue, or hands. These intuitive "perceptions" are *generalizations* that occur when abstractions are "played" through the sensory cortexes, creating an intuitive episode. To the brain, these intuitive episodes are very similar to the sensory episodes of the sensing model.

Abstractions also allow a new type of interconnection between episodes and sequences. The abstraction of **yellow** can be annotated to a multitude of different perceptions in a multitude of different episodes containing such perceptions or abstractions as the sun, a flower, a bee, or a road sign. All of these very diverse episodes are connected by **yellow**, and allow the human mind to move from one to another following the annotated abstraction links.

This type of linking is very different from the linear string meme, and it requires a new way of organizing the information. In the ST mode, a string meme is a chain of sequences laid out one after another, like an automotive assembly line. There are no "if/then" or "either/or" gates at any of the points where the sequences are linked. There are no alternatives to any of the sequences presented. A string meme cannot be anything other than a straight line.

Modern humans use abstractions as "if/then" gates. A meme can jump between vastly different sequences via an abstraction. To organize the many possible branches, a human uses a *hierarchy* to knit together routes through the maze of possibilities.

Hierarchies are formed around category abstractions such as **yellow**. The intuitive generalization built from the abstraction of the color yellow becomes the episode to which everything—that is, memories and new perceptions—within the **yellow** hierarchy is matched. All perceptions, intuitive or sensory, are subordinate to it. **Yellow** is the label and category to which all yellow perceptions belong, and without the "pure" abstraction, the hierarchy would not exist.

For example, a person may choose **yellow** as the category abstraction they wish to work with at a particular moment. **Yellow** becomes the top of the hierarchy and all matching revolves around it. The person will use consciousness to locate and form understanding around that particular color and will bring all that is yellow together under the label.

Consciousness

One aspect of the intuitive model that is very important to humans is *consciousness*. Thinking—the modeling of what memes should be used in any given circumstance—uses a stream of language to manipulate abstractions and generalizations. What is being thought about is the *subject* and replaces the environmental trigger of the sensing model. What to do in response to the subject is the *verb* and is the intuitive application of a meme.

Consciousness occurs when one is unsure of what verb to apply to a subject. The person must build a new response by evolving a new meme. To do so, consciousness uses CI explore, CE try, DI evaluate, and DE implement to intuitively and internally "talk through" options, try possibilities, practice outcomes, and implement a new solution.

Consciousness allows a virtual modeling of future possibilities without putting the individual through demanding and possibly dangerous physical attempts. Those possibilities are different hierarchical connections running from the main focus of the triggering verb. For example, the question may be what to do with a tree. The tree is green, so the individual may run through all of the connections using **green**. The tree is also **big**, and **made of wood**. All or some of these connections will filter out into a hierarchy that ultimately produces the best response to how to use the tree in that circumstance.

People with different cognitive processing profiles use consciousness in different ways. The cognitive processing steps of CI explore, CE try, DI evaluate, and DE implement shape *how* a person processes. For example, a CI individual will focus more on the first part of developing memes, which is the exploration of the environment. CIs will watch, consider, take in, and gather. They will continue to do this and often have a difficult time finishing a task. On the other hand, a DE will do, act, finish, and release to the world. DEs always finish their tasks, but they do it quickly and without seeming to take in the environment. This can make them appear rash or overconfident.

The cognitive processing modes of SF sensing feeling, ST sensing thinking, NF intuitive feeling (which we will explore more in the next section), and NT intuitive thinking (which we will explore in the next chapter) shape *what* a person processes. The modes are body, hands, words, and logic, and the type of meme a person's consciousness evolves depends on that person's mode. Combined with the cognitive processing step, the cognitive processing mode sets up a profile that specializes in processing a particular part of a meme particularly well.

Consciousness is the brain running the processes of a person's specialized cognitive processing profile. The brain uses a stream of language to manipulate a subject and verb pairing intuitively and then translates the meme it evolves into physical activity. Which part of this cycle a person is aware of depends on the person's cognitive processing profile.

Hierarchical concepts and the modes

For people who process consciously in the S modes, perception of the physical world is what their brains process first. For people in the new intuitive "N" modes, it is reversed, with abstraction processing and matching via the hierarchical routes happening first.

The SF matches their *now*—what their body is telling them—with the memes they need to react to that *now*, giving their cognitive processing mode a body-oriented framework. Body-oriented processing gives SF people better knowledge of their physical body and the action directives that control it. An SF thinks primarily in this body language and will use abstractions and the hierarchies they access to group and organize concepts about physical movements as the second step in processing. The SF then communicates these concepts through language, and can also translate back to physical movements any action memes that have been communicated. A good example of SF body-oriented processing is a basketball player using episode-to-episode matching to move quickly and precisely. He then follows up the game with a verbal description.

The ST links sequence to sequence to perform a procedure. ST processing manifests primarily in terms of the fine motor control of the hands. The ST then intuitively labels the procedures involved, grouping them hierarchically so that they can be communicated via language. For both the SF and the ST, working in the intuitive model is the second half of an integrated process. A good example of ST string processing is typing. Each trigger in each *now* is responded to with a dexterous string meme. Any description of the process comes later.

Instead of processing in terms of the physical, the new intuitive N modes—with the *iNtuitive Feeler NF* as the first to appear—processes in terms of abstractions. The N's primary language of thinking is words, making processing of perceptions second. This sequence is reversed from the S modes.

N processing is the processing of language—it is, at its simplest, the replacing of an action with a verb in a stream of language.

The N works virtually, moving abstractions with the action of language.

The S and N components of the human mind run parallel to each other, forming two systems of modeling and comprehending the world. The S models the sensed world—the physical context in and around that person. The N models the intuitive world—the virtual context of abstractions and language. The two weave in and out of each other, supporting and augmenting understanding; but they are different models, and they model different things.

Where the SF works with the body, the NF works with words. Instead of using perception to frame matching, the NF uses language, building connections between perception and abstraction. Communication-oriented processing allows NFs to construct and transmit memes verbally with great precision—a very valuable ability in a memetic organism. A good example of the NF ability to transmit intuitive memes precisely is actors. A fine actor can transmit multiple layers of memetic information with timing, posture, and tone, getting across exactly what needs to be said in a very efficient manner.

The *feeling* F component of the NF mode operates in the same manner as the feeling component used by the SF. Single sequence or episode processing is accessible to the emotional system in both the sensing and intuitive models, making abstractions emotionally tagged. In the HDM, the NF mode is placed at the top of the model (Figure 11).

NFs, with their sensed-to-intuited processing, are very good at using language to describe the world and the memes used to interact with it. They do this processing consciously, using the mapping tools of the brain to sort and work with intuitive information.

The NF works with intuitive episodes—the episodes created by the brain from the "pure" sequences in the Left Procedural Cortex. The NF manipulates these episodes by replacing the object of attention in the perceived world with the object of a sentence in the intuitive world. They then operate on the object by implementing a verb with language.

Figure 11: The NF Mode and the Human Dimensions Model

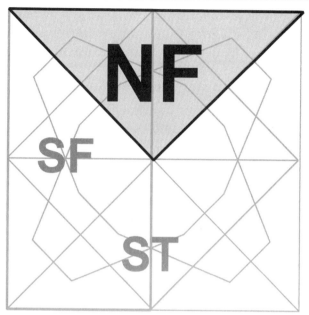

Everything can be described and labeled, and the NF matches a circumstance by building an intuitive episode to best describe it. These intuitive episodes are built from the abstractions annotated to the sensory perceptions of the circumstance. By internally building and rebuilding intuitive episodes, the NF can create many more shades of gray in understanding than the straightforward SF matching of one *now* to one episode in memory.

A good example of this process in action is the classic literary metaphor. All of the cognitive processing modes have a metaphor structure all their own, but the NF metaphor is the one that all children are taught in elementary school. A *metaphor* matches a feature of an object, person, or event to the feature in the sensory world. The simplest form is the simile—"the flower is yellow like the sun." The cross connection between the two is the abstraction **yellow**. The listener uses the abstraction of yellow to cross-link the descriptive hierarchies of the sun and the flower.

NFs grab all internal intuitive abstractions and give them form as a sentence. The sentence, as it flows, produces an ongoing intuitive story, drawing attention from one point to another, building on important features by drawing on one metaphoric connection and then another.

This is also the purpose of Piaget's concrete operational stage of child development. In this stage the child connects concepts and observations. For example, a child will realize that the concept of gravity applies to all perceptions and will form a hierarchy around that concept. Children also do this type of concept-to-perception connection-building with people in this stage. For example, they begin to build a notion of what it means to be them, and what it means to be their friend or their teacher.

The NF mode is the mode of metaphor. NFs talk, write, draw, paint, film, and sculpt metaphor. They excel at creating the "deep" understanding of human existence—it is the NFs of the world who communicate the abstractions so that we all can build common intuitive episodes.

It is the "commonality" of the NF mode that allows humans to connect and build modern memetic organisms. We transfer to each other the memetic rules of conduct within a group via the NF metaphor. These rules are abstractions of behaviors, and in order for them to be transferred with their meaning intact, they need to be communicated in terms of the common ground of the sensing model.

In this way the people who operate within the NF mode act as translators between the memetic organism and the individual. They create the metaphor that fills the stories that are told to the entire population. These stories transmit the rules of the memetic organism via the example of the characters while at the same time also transmitting an acknowledgment of the individual needs and wants that the characters represent.

This transmission is manifested as some of the great stories of humanity: The hero who loses everything and goes on to find something new in a new memetic organism. The hero who is martyred because he refuses to break the rules of his home memetic organism. Finding love and fulfillment with a mate who is a stand-up citizen.

But artists also transmit individual needs back to the memetic organism as well. Themes of loneliness and betrayal, hurt, loss, hunger, and so on, are all designed to spread understanding of pain from one area of the memetic organism to another. They build empathy and help keep the group healthy by encouraging helping behavior.

NFs codify this strengthening of the memetic organism through religion and art, both of which make physical the abstractions of the intuitive model. Religion manifests the memetic organism rules in terms of action and ritual as physical examples of behaviors. For example, praying synchronizes a group, brings them together, and gives them a common set of rules to follow. Art makes physical everything else—the abstractions of what it means to be a **horse**, or to be **joyous**, or to be a **citizen**.

The modern memetic organism is built by the strength of metaphor—those who can transmit their memes the best create the best communication within the population. Memetic transmission is the key—it is how memetic organisms grow and reproduce. Without the NF mode there would be no language, no metaphor, and no transmission.

Summary

- *Abstractions* are the specific concepts within consciousness that sit behind words. They are "pure" sequences built from all of the perceptions a person has experienced of a specific feature.
- *Generalizations* are abstractions "played" through the sensory cortexes, creating an intuitive episode.
- Humans run a model of the world that uses abstractions— the *intuitive model*.

- Abstraction and generalization form *hierarchies* of connections, with the abstraction as the "label" of the hierarchy.
- The *subject* replaces the environmental trigger of the sensing model.
- The *verb* replaces the response and is the intuitive application of a meme.
- *Consciousness* occurs when one is unsure of what verb to apply to a subject. This person must build a new response by evolving a new meme.
- An *iNtuitive Feeler NF* processes information in terms of words and metaphor.
- A *metaphor* matches a feature of an object, person, or event to the feature in the sensory world.

6

Cognitive Processing Modes: iNtuitive Thinking (NT)

Overview

The fourth cognitive processing mode to develop was the *iNtuitive Thinker NT.* NTs use logic—the set of memetic rules used to consciously organize hierarchical thinking—to facilitate their mode. NTs are unconcerned with the sensed world and excel at conceptual and abstract thinking such as science, math, and strategy.

THE FOURTH MODE: iNUITIVE THINKING (NT), THE MODE OF LOGIC

There is an intrinsic difference between the sensing and the intuitive models that goes beyond "real world" vs. "imagination." The information that "fills" the SF and ST databases is immediate and provided by perception. It is what it *is*—the information is produced by the physics of the world in and around the individual.

The intuitive model is different—it is "filled" by abstractions and generalizations, the production of which is controlled by the processes within the brain. Abstractions also are not refreshed immediately by the flow of the next perception coming in; they must be moved along by language. Using, manipulating, and communicating the contents of the intuitive model requires language, a support infrastructure that is not necessary for the sensing model.

Language allows the NF to use metaphor to connect the physical world of the sensing model to the abstract world of the intuitive model. Words are the labels on abstractions—they are the similar utterances by which we transfer to each other an abstraction. The NF must know how to connect words to form sentences so that they can create intuitive episodes. These episodes are then transferred to another person via the common language, where they "play" in the other person's cortexes. Without words, and in particular without *grammar*—the memetic hierarchies of rules used to order those words—the NF literally has nothing to do and cannot

71

function as an NF. The memetic infrastructure of language supports and facilitates the NF mode.

Language is ubiquitous, but not every human uses the same language. Memetic organisms, as collections of people, have their own set of cultural rules, including their own languages. Those rules shape what is noticed and described, and therefore what is available to "fill" the intuitive model of the group's members. This is most obvious in the differing artistic traditions of different cultures. Words and grammar bring order to what would otherwise be the individual chaos of abstractions.

Language also refines abstractions. For example, there is a subtle difference between **yellow** and **yellow-orange**, a difference that would not be easily distinguishable without words. Well-developed languages provide their users with a cornucopia of descriptions; descriptions ripe for linking and manipulating.

In the correct sociological conditions, the fourth cognitive processing mode of the *iNtuitive Thinker* NT develops. The genetic potential for NT most likely appeared at the same time as NF because the ability to produce *thinking* objectivity was already in the population. NT, like ST, orders memes into larger wholes than the one-*now*-to-one-sequence of the feeling modes. NT manipulates abstractions and generalizations into hierarchical memes by using the brain's ability to group multiple sequences. This is the same ability the ST uses to order sequences of body moves into strings.

Like NF, the use of the NT within a group is also shaped by the memetic organism. It depends on a well-developed language to provide material to be ordered into hierarchical memes as well as an ordering infrastructure to support the mode.

Different cultures have different NT traditions. For example, the difference between the "Western" focus on toolmaking and technological advancement coupled with self-reliance is markedly different from the "Eastern" focus on administrating and social coherence. This book uses examples focusing on the codified traditions of Western culture.

The appearance of the Western NT

Humans created technological specialization and the modern memetic organism during the last Ice Age. Both adaptations were memetic responses to a changed environment and allowed our species to continue. We pulled together and divided up the work in a manner that best used the talents available.

When the Ice Age ended, the environment became considerably friendlier. Humans, though, were still memetically adapted to a very harsh life. Memetic organisms and specialization allow a group to respond optimally all of the time—in very much the same way that the original memes allowed a body to respond optimally to environmental triggers all of the time.

Up to this point, contact between memetic organisms had been limited by the sparseness of the human population. Ice Age peoples did trade with each other; archaeological evidence of the spread of technology and the distance inland traveled by goods made with sea materials shows that Ice Age peoples traded a great deal. But trading is a choreographed dance of interactions in which one person interacts with another, exchanges are made, and everyone returns happy to their home memetic organism. Interaction was brief and had a defined end.

Not so with the population explosion that followed the Ice Age. Between 8,000 to 5,000 years ago, humans of different memetic organisms not only traded with each other, but needed to live with each other, too. Natural disasters caused wave after wave of migrations. Specialization advanced technological expertise, and specialized guilds of traders, priests, farmers, and artisans appeared. Memetic organisms fractured, contracted, shifted, and mingled.

The adaptations of the Ice Age quickly forced a new context for humans, and in particular those of the Fertile Crescent. The tightly packed memetic organisms varied too much—there were different gods saying basically the same thing but from different social points of view. Something had to change.

Out of the confusion, the Greeks cultivated a new ordering

system. They took what the human brain does naturally and did it consciously—they rigorously applied the categorizing, hierarchical system of human thought to everything around them, from the nature of the universe to the nature of the individual person.

This is *logic*—the set of memetic rules used by humans to consciously organize hierarchically. Logic manifests as the *scientific method*, which is used to establish and verify connections between abstractions in many different areas. The scientific method is a rigorous, conscious, and socially exchangeable version of what humans do anyway—we connect abstractions intuitively and then verify them by looking for examples in the sensing model.

For example, scientific hypotheses are followed by experiments to verify their validity. Social laws are verified by their effect on a social grouping. Inside an individual, we make sweeping statements, for example, "Boys always ignore me," and we look for examples of these statements in how our lives manifest before us.

Logic and the scientific method can be applied to all of these areas of hierarchical thinking. What the Greeks did was codify their use in the social arenas of science and politics with definite rules. On the individual level, they took all of the competing rules from all of the memetic organisms mashed together in one area and generated a prioritizing system. That system became the *Self*, the logic-based, internal system used to prioritize what rules from which memetic organism an individual will follow in any given circumstance.

The Self is highly individual. It depends on what memetic organisms a person deals with in life and how well those memetic organisms meet the needs of the person. What works for one person may not work for another. Though the rules for prioritizing may be the same from person to person, what they are prioritizing is not, and how a person applies those rules will also vary depending on biological needs as well as the cognitive processing profile. The Self, though designed to facilitate social interaction by allowing a person to switch from the rules of one memetic organism to another, is not in itself a social structure. This makes codifying how it works extremely difficult.

The Greeks essentially harnessed an underused segment of their population and gave them a socially supported and useful method to manifest themselves. For the Greeks and all of the "Western" cultures that descend from them, logic and the scientific method build a hierarchical social infrastructure of memes for laws, tools, and written communication, which manifested as the phonetic Greek alphabet.

The NT mode

NTs are unconcerned with the sensed world. They work totally

Figure 12: The NT Mode and the Human Dimensions Model

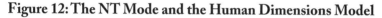

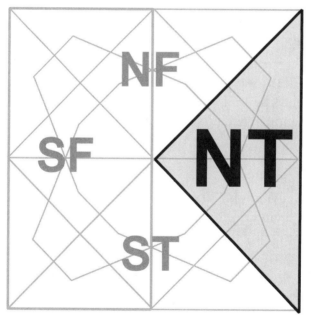

in the realm of the intuitive and are very aware of the work of language in their consciousness. Like the ST, the NT steps away from the episode-to-episode matching of the feeling modes. The ST organizes memes into procedural strings that function like a macro operation in a computer program. Stripped of context, these macros are inaccessible to the emotional system. The NT does something similar, but instead of procedural strings, the NT organizes cognition into hierarchies. In a string meme, the organized procedures are sensing and body-based. In an NT hierarchy, they are abstractions.

In the HDM, the NT mode sits on the right side of the model (Figure 12). The contents of the hierarchy can be anything, including abstractions that lead to other hierarchies that include information in either the sensing or intuitive models. NTs build hierarchies of hierarchies, examples of which are the hierarchies built to sort experiences within multiple memetic organisms, or the hierarchies needed to do advanced mathematics.

The NT mode corresponds to Piaget's formal operational stage of child development. It is in this stage that adolescents gain an understanding of logic and the "bigger picture" of the world by allowing a refined organization beyond what can be immediately sensed. With the support infrastructure of logic, NTs knit together large "wholes" beyond perception, such as societal law, physics, strategic planning, and other such abstract concepts.

Summary

- The *iNtuitive Thinker NT* cognitive processing mode uses the brain's ability to group multiple sequences. This is the same ability the ST uses to order sequences of body moves into strings.

- *Grammar* is the memetic hierarchy of rules used to order words. Without grammar, the NF literally has nothing to do and cannot function as an NF. The memetic infrastructure of language supports and facilitates the NF mode.

- *Logic* is the set of memetic rules used to consciously order abstractions and generalizations into hierarchies. Without logic, the NT literally has nothing to do and cannot function as an NT. The memetic infrastructure of logic supports and facilitates the NT mode.

- The ancient Greeks codified logic into a socially usable support structure for Western NTs.
- The NT mode corresponds to Piaget's formal operational stage of child development. It is in this stage that adolescents gain an understanding of logic and the "bigger picture" of the world by allowing a refined organization beyond what can be immediately sensed.

7

THE PROFILES: CAPACITIES AND TRANSACTIONS

Overview

Within the Human Dimensions Model is a map of *capacities* and *transactions* that describes the structures and movements of human cognitive processing. This map is constructed using the dichotomies we have already learned about: *Internalizing/Externalizing, Contextual/Deterministic, Feeling/Thinking,* and *Sensing/iNtuitive.* The first two dichotomies make the cognitive processing steps, the second two the cognitive processing modes.

Capacities are areas of activity within the human brain. Capacities are not behaviors; instead a capacity "makes" information. Transactions are the movement between capacities as work is performed on the information. It is from this work that behaviors arise.

The beginning capacity of a transaction makes the "subject" of the episode, and the ending capacity acts on that subject as the "verb." Every capacity performs a distinct activity and "makes" a distinctive form of information.

THE HUMAN DIMENSIONS MODEL
COGNITIVE PROCESSING PROFILES

The first six chapters of this book provided a quick tour of some of the theory and evolutionary history behind the Human Dimensions Model (HDM). We learned about replicators, the four cognitive processing steps, the four cognitive processing modes, and how each operates to evolve memes.

The four cognitive processing steps of CI explore, CE try, DI evaluate, and DE implement manifest from two dichotomies within the brain—*Contextual vs. Deterministic* and *Internalized vs. Externalized*. Contextual (C) / Deterministic (D) reflects the human capability to process perceptual and procedural information. Internalized (I) / Externalized (E) reflects the animal capability to perceive and respond—an ability that predates humans.

The four cognitive processing modes of SF sensing feeling, ST sensing thinking, NF intuitive feeling, and NT intuitive thinking manifest from two other dichotomies within the brain—*Sensing vs. iNtuitive* and *Feeling vs. Thinking*. Sensing (S) / iNtuitive (N) reflects the most recent change in the *Homo* genus and the human ability to process information in two models of the world. Feeling (F) / Thinking (T) reflects the human capability to involve or not to involve the emotional system in matching.

The steps are the brain's way of evolving a new memetic replicator in response to a situation. The modes are the "databases" in which these new memes reside.

The remaining chapters will focus on how modern humans cognitively process information in today's world. What follows is a fairly detailed discussion of what happens when each of the cognitive processing profiles "thinks." This information is charted onto the *HDM map*—the diagram that illustrates how information flows within human cognition. On this map the cognitive processing steps manifest out of *transactions* between *capacities* within the brain. The capacities process information in a specific way. The movement of information between two capacities forms a transaction. The cognitive processing steps are descriptive of the type of processing handled by different transactions within the different cognitive processing modes.

Dr. Walter Lowen developed the basic structure of the cognitive processing profile part of the HDM. In this book, we look at how the model fits together and how it describes the cognitive processing of individuals. Dr. Lowen's book, *The Dichotomies of the Mind* (1982), includes a deeper technical discussion about how he arrived at the basis of the model we use today. His work includes perspectives on Jung and child development as well as insights from the dynamic processing of systems. We will not go into the details of the development of the model here, but will instead point the reader to Dr. Lowen's work.

Capacities

There are sixteen *capacities,* with each capacity corresponding to a mechanism used to generate a certain type of memetic processing. The capacities support the brain's ability to evolve memes by using each of the four cognitive processing steps within each of the four modes.

The capacities used in consciousness differ between individuals, depending on how the person uses the dichotomies of the cognitive processing steps and modes. The first pair of dichotomies determines the person's cognitive processing step: The *Contextual/ Deterministic* dichotomy shows whether the individual's consciousness uses Contextual (perceptual) or Deterministic (sequential) processing. The *Internalizing/Externalizing* dichotomy shows whether the individual's consciousness uses capacities located in the action-taking or world-modeling areas of the brain.

The second pair of dichotomies determines the person's cognitive processing mode: The *Sensing/iNtuitive* dichotomy shows whether the person's consciousness sits more in the sensing model or the intuitive model. The *Feeling/Thinking* dichotomy shows whether the emotional system is able to contribute to the primary matching process.

All of the possible combinations of S/N, F/T, C/D, and I/E make up all of the capacities that human cognition can potentially use while processing information. Consciousness uses a subset of these capacities. In this way, consciousness acts as a lens that focuses memetic processing onto a specific set of capacities.

Think of consciousness this way: if you poke a hole in a sheet of paper and hold it up in front of a light source, the hole will focus a point of light onto the surface behind the paper. Depending on where in the sheet of paper the hole is punched, it will focus light onto a different region of the surface. The hole represents the input into consciousness, and the region on the surface where the light is focused is the "subject" capacity consciousness uses. All of the other capacities that fall under the shadow of the paper are unconscious.

The hole and the region on the surface have adapted to each other; the hole best focuses the light that illuminates that particular region most clearly. This adaptation is *attention*, and it filters out information that cannot be processed easily by the capacities used by the individual's consciousness.

Once the "light" gets to the surface, though, it needs to be processed. The capacities of the brain are activities that produce information, *not* behaviors. To produce a behavioral change in the organism, the brain performs a *transaction* between two capacities. This movement is driven by the subject/verb structure of the episode, the *subject* being what has the individual's attention, and the *verb* being the response to the subject. Subject and verb operate in both the sensing and the intuitive models.

The beginning capacity of the transaction serves as the holder of the subject of the episode. This capacity "makes" the information that will be acted upon. As we will see, each capacity does a different activity, so a particular "picture" develops out of the processing of this first capacity. For example, the SF capacities produce different "pictures" from the NT capacities.

The ending capacity of the transaction serves as the actor providing the verb. This is the process worked on the subject. This process provides the response to the environment and motivates the person to move on to the next *now*.

The "purpose of action" of the transaction can be specified as either Internalizing (I) or Externalizing (E) . (E) transactions move to an action-taking capacity and use existing modeled information to take action in the world. In an E transaction the modeled information is the subject, and the action taken is the verb. (I) transactions move to a world-modeling capacity and take action in the world to position the individual to better build a world model. In an I transaction, the action taken is the subject, and the modeling that occurs because of the action is the verb. Another important concept to keep in mind when considering transactions between the world-modeling and action-taking areas of the brain is that this movement is the pinnacle of a brain's work. All sensory information-processing is in place so that the animal or human can know what it faces in the environment and react to that information in the best possible way. Essentially, the I/E dichotomy's "purpose of action" motivates all the manifestations of processing a brain does, no matter which capacities are in use.

Earlier in the book we mapped the cognitive processing steps onto areas of the brain. The cognitive processing steps are the steps of evolution and are a combination of Contextual or Deterministic (C/D) with Externalizing or Internalizing (I/E). They represent the outcome of processing, and where in the brain the "verb" of a transaction will be applied.

The other two dichotomies of Sensing and iNtuitive (S/N) and Feeling and Thinking (F/T) combine to make the cognitive processing modes. The modes are like filing systems that order information. They form memory databases and are akin to a film

Figure 13: Cognitive processing areas of the brain

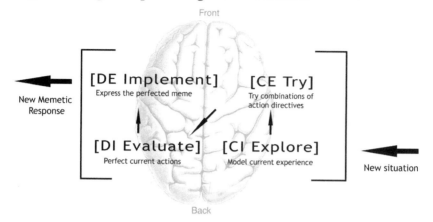

emulsion on the above metaphorical surface, behind the sheet of paper. The emulsion can help or hinder the focus of the picture, depending on the emulsion's components and what kind of light is coming through the hole. The modes can have a similar effect on cognition. For example, NF communication-oriented memes do not "focus" well on ST procedural, hand-oriented emulsion.

Like a film emulsion, the brain's mode processing areas are made of many different bits and pieces. This makes placing the functioning of the modes on a map of the brain nearly impossible, at least with modern imaging technology. This is particularly true, since the sensing and intuitive models run on the same perceptual infrastructure.

The S/N and F/T dichotomies, though, along with C/D and I/E, can be easily mapped onto a diagram. This map lays out the capacities of human cognitive processing and shows how the transactions flow from one capacity to another. The rest of this chapter will focus on how to read the map, and on what each area and line means in terms of what we have already discussed.

A barebones look at the HDM map is shown in Figure 14. The three terms that we have previously introduced are of particular importance when using the HDM map:

Figure 14: Bare bones look at the Human Dimensions map

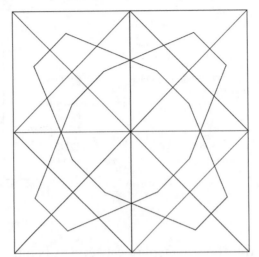

- *Capacity:* Each triangle on the HDM represents a *capacity* of human cognitive processing. There are sixteen capacities, one for each of the cognitive processing steps within each mode.

Figure 15: One of 16 capacities on the HDM model

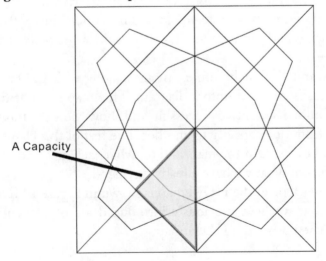

- *Transaction:* Human cognitive processing is not static and relies on the movement of *transactions* from one capacity to another.

Figure 16: A transaction on the HDM model

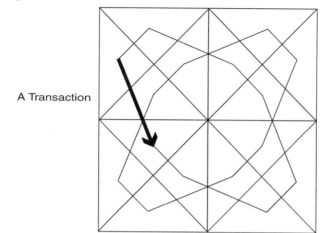

A Transaction

- *Dichotomy:* The steps and modes of the HDM form four dichotomies, which are divided into two groups. First are the *Contextual/Deterministic* and *Internalizing/Externalizing* dichotomies of the cognitive processing steps. Second are the *Sensing/iNtuitive* and *Feeling/Thinking* dichotomies of the cognitive processing modes.

Figure 17: The SN and FT Dichotomies on the HDM model

The dichotomies are an outgrowth of the steps and modes. They are another path to understanding the capacities and transactions. The dichotomies are most relevant when learning the theory of the HDM. They are also particularly relevant when working one-on-one in an interview situation, where they allow the identification of behaviors. For this reason, we have integrated them into our discussion as we move through the model.

Internalizing and Externalizing, giving movement to transactions

For our pre-*Homo* ancestors, life was a continuously looping series of *nows*, with each episode generated by a *now*. Every response consisted of a CI explore and a CE try, followed by another CI explore and another CE try:

Figure 18: The "looping" processing of CI/CE

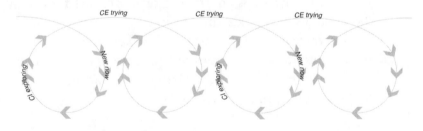

At this point in hominid development, the only dichotomy present was the movement between the world-modeling areas in the back of the brain and the action-taking areas in the front of the brain. Left and Right differentiation had not yet occurred.

In CI explore, the animal created a model of the world. In CE try, it tried an action plan in response. In going from CI to CE and back again, the australopithecine brain generated the first transactions of what would become human cognitive processing:

Figure 19: The side view of the brain

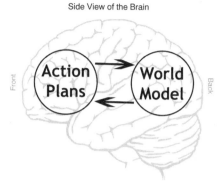

Side View of the Brain

As shown on the diagram, there are two transactions between the action planning and world modeling areas of the brain. The first moves front to back as the animal takes action to position itself for the best possible input. This enables the creation of the best possible model (CI). The second transaction moves back to front, with the animal acting in response to the world it has already modeled (CE). Both sides of the brain do the same type of processing in animals. In humans (and our hominid ancestors) only the Right Perceptual Cortex engages in CI/CE processing:

Figure 20: The right perceptual cortex engages in CI/CE processing

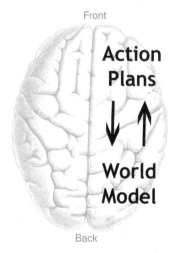

These transactions are named for their result, meaning that the transaction that starts with world-modeling to produce an action in the world is *Externalizing*, and the transaction that starts with an action to better construct the world-model is *Internalizing*.[12]

On the HDM, the Internalizing and Externalizing transactions represent a dichotomy of purpose of action. The Internalizing person takes action to be placed in the best position for receiving input and build a personal conscious model, whereas an Externalizing person uses a personal model in order to determine how to take action.

For the Internalizer (I), taking action facilitates model-building in the modeling areas of the brain. For the Externalizer (E), the model facilitates action in the expression areas of the brain.

On the HDM map, the capacities represent either the ability to model or the ability to take action. The world-modeling capacities are on the inside of the map. The action-taking capacities are on the outside of the map:

Figure 21: Externalizer and Internalizer models

The action-taking capacities   The world-modeling capacities

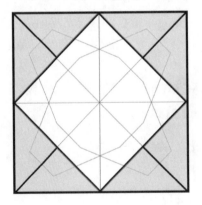 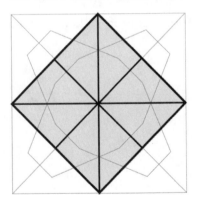

---

12. If you have pets, watch them carefully one day. Dogs and cats exhibit preferences for either the internalizing or externalizing processes.

Some examples of Internalizing processing in people:

- Internalizing (I) people gather information. CIs are conscious of creating a model of the world and DIs are conscious of building procedures to work within the world.

- For an Internalizer, all input is new information for the model, including just-generated output. This gives an Internalizer cyclical conscious processing because every new idea is a new place to start. This can lead to difficulty finishing projects.

- An Internalizer will use phrases such as "I found myself doing," "I let things come to me," "That's the way things happen."

- The Internalizer tends to place herself as the object of the predicate while speaking.

Some examples of Externalizing processing in people:

- E people act on information. CEs try possibilities and DEs implement procedures.

- For an E, input triggers an output and the person moves on. Externalizers do not continually reprocess information about a topic.

- The Externalizer will tend to place himself as the subject of the sentence.

Table 2: "Quick Glance" I/E Differences

Internalizing	Externalizing
Protective	Aggressive
Passive	Proactive
Learn it	Apply it
Let it	Try it
Test it	Do it
Perfection	Good enough
Think about it	Do it now

Contextual and Deterministic

Homo habilis arrived on the scene with hemispheric differentiation. On the left, they had developed a deterministic, procedural cortex, and on the right, they retained their contextual, perceptual cortex. This led to a new type of processing, one executed sequentially:

Figure 22: The sequential processing of DI/DE

Instead of engaging in only the CI and CE transactions, with the addition of deterministic processing the brain also engages in DI and DE transactions.

Figure 23: The new DI/DE transactions in *Homo habilis*

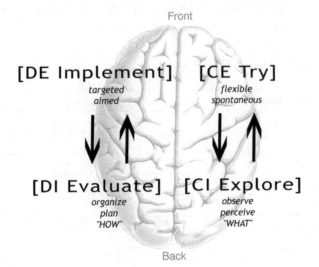

As shown on the diagram, the CI explore/CE try transactions still function as they did in prehominid ancestors. Added to them are the new DI evaluate/DE implement transactions. These new transactions give rise to a new dichotomy: Contextual vs. Deterministic.

Which half of the Contextual/Deterministic (C/D) dichotomy used by a person's consciousness is determined by which cortex's processing that person is aware of. Contextual (C) people are aware of and use the environment-oriented, contextual processing of the Right Perceptual Cortex. Consciousness in the Right Perceptual Cortex also uses generalizations in its processing, as opposed to abstractions.

Deterministic (D) people are aware of and use the start-to-finish, procedural processing of the Left Procedural Cortex. Consciousness in the Left Procedural Cortex is aware of its own process of building and using abstractions, and does not rely upon the generalizations generated by those abstractions in the Right Perceptual Cortex.

Some examples of Contextual processing in people:

- C people use incoming perceptual information even while in the middle of a task. This allows them to change directions quickly and respond to new input without finishing what they have started. This gives the C good multitasking abilities, but it also means they can have more difficulty completing an activity.

- C processing is evident in certain speech patterns. Cs take the "scenic route" while speaking, often finding themselves heading off in a direction different from the original sentence. Cs produce definite breaks in sentence structure while they speak, which manifests as interruptions and switching gears.

- C profiles will give the listener the context of how the meme being transferred was generated—in other words, they take the long way around to get to the point, giving a lot of background information in the process.

- C people are more concerned with the "why" and "what" of a situation than they are with "how" something is done. This reflects the generalization-building infrastructure of the Right Perceptual Cortex.

Some examples of Deterministic processing in people:

- D people use procedural information in consciousness and are aware of the steps in executing a meme. If they must stop in the middle of a task, they cannot start again at the point where they left off; instead, a D must start over.
- D processing is evident in speech patterns as well. A D does not like to be interrupted and will start over from the beginning of the thought if they are. Ds also speak more fluently and with more purpose because their speech is confined to one thought at a time, which they will finish before starting on a new one.
- A D will not give the context of the situation when speaking, but will instead give the "how" of how something works—in other words, they get to the point right away.
- D people are more concerned with the "how" of a situation than with the "why" and "what." This reflects the procedure-building, abstracting processing of the Left Procedural Cortex.

Making the steps

Together, the C/D and I/E dichotomies make up the cognitive processing steps of CI explore, CE try, DI evaluate, and DE implement. These are the four steps of evolution, and we have seen that they hold true for both the genetic and the memetic replicators. To evolve genes, natural selection works to adapt a species to an environment; to evolve memes, the human brain invokes consciousness to process possible responses to triggers in the environment.

Though the cognitive processing steps are descriptive of the location of capacities on the map and in the brain, their main

Table 3: "Quick Glance" C/D Differences

Contextual	Deterministic
Generalizations	Abstractions
Try it	Aim it
Spontaneous	Planned
Approximate	Precise
Interruptions okay	Hates interruptions
"Scenic route"	Articulate and direct
What, who, where, why	*How*
Episodes	Processes
Observe	Deduce
Explore	Predict
Speculate	Reason

purpose is to represent the movement inherent in the HDM describing transactions. The steps are the dynamic processing that happens within the infrastructures of the modes. On the map, they are always represented as an arrow of processing moving from one capacity to another along either the C or D pathways:

Figure 24: The contextual (C) pathways

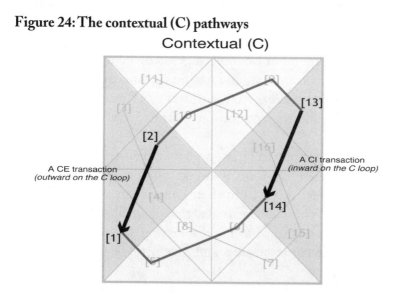

Figure 25: The deterministic (D) pathways

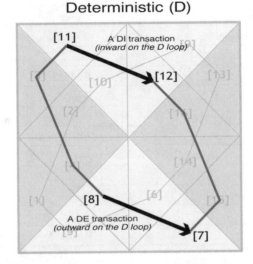

The CI step moves from an action-taking capacity to its result in a world-model capacity within the contextual, right cortex. The DE step moves from a world-modeling capacity to its result in an action-taking capacity within the deterministic, left cortex.

For some people, the entrance pathway to their consciousness is CI explore. A CI is aware of the process of taking in information, no matter in what mode they function. Awareness allows the individual to manipulate and refine the processing so that it happens at the highest efficiency. For example, a person who operates as a CI within the SF mode is very good at finding and exploring experiences in the world, whereas a CI within the NT mode is very good at finding and exploring connections within hierarchical patterns of information.

But CIs are not particularly good at implementing—they are not aware of their DE process, and so when it happens, it happens without direct input from their consciousness. A CI would rather go where consciousness sits, that is, exploring and finding connections instead of trying, evaluating, and implementing, which sit outside consciousness and give little or no feedback to the individual.

The steps in people

Examples of each of the cognitive processing steps in people:

- CI individuals gather and explore information. A CI tends to be laid back and accepting of the world and situations. Things come to a CI; this person does not tend to make things happen.
- CE individuals try possibilities. A CE will manipulate the environment, check for how the environment has been changed, and then manipulate it again.
- DI individuals evaluate and perfect sequences created by the CE try process, abstractions, and memes. DIs edit, coach, and teach.
- DE individuals implement sequences, abstractions, and memes. DEs implement the output of procedural sequences and hierarchies.

Feeling and Thinking

The string processing of the ST mode lacked the emotional tracking of the SF mode, giving rise to the Feeling/Thinking dichotomy in the HDM.

The Feeling/Thinking (F/T) dichotomy is determined by whether an individual consciously processes one episode at a time for F, or processes multiple combinations for T. For the F person, consciousness is applied to episodes and sequences that have been checked by the emotional system and therefore tagged, making feelings and emotions part of the generation and manipulation of memetic information. For the T person, consciousness is worked on string memes and hierarchies that cannot be checked or tagged, making the generation and manipulation of memes free of emotional content.

Also for the F, the emotional tags attached to an episode are used to match that episode with others, effectively allowing the F to "file" memories by the *feeling*—the specific combination of emotions generated in that episode. Ts lack the emotional tags, so they do not make matches in this way.

On the HDM, Feeling and Thinking are represented by a division bisecting the map:

Figure 26: Feeling and Thinking on the HDM Model

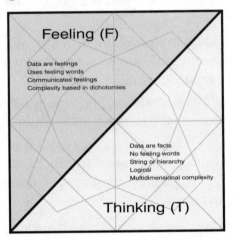

Some examples of Feeling processing in people:

- An F person remembers the feelings that were part of an initiating episode and will transfer those emotions to the new episode.
- An F will use emotional words in their speech.
- Feelers tend to label all of their thoughts either "good" or "bad"; that is, "this feels good" or "this feels bad."
- A situation will hit a Feeler "in the gut" or "right in the heart."

Some examples of Thinking processing in people:

- A T person does not transfer emotional content between episodes.
- A T will use objective terms such as "I think" or references to logic in their speech.
- A Thinker will look for how a situation fits together as opposed to how it makes him feel.

Table 4: "Quick Glance" F/T Differences

Feeling	Thinking
Feelings part of thoughts	Feelings not in thoughts
Single *now* processing	Complex processing
Uses feeling words	Does not use feeling words
People-oriented	Thing-oriented

Sensing and iNtuitive

The new ability to abstract also created a new dichotomy of Sensing/iNtuitive (S/N). This dichotomy indicates whether a person's consciousness sits within the sensing or the intuitive world models. S people are sensing and perception-oriented; their consciousness deals first with the sensations that their bodies are generating. N people are intuitive and language-oriented; their consciousness deals first with the abstractions that label a perception.

On the HDM, sensing and iNtuitive are also represented by a line bisecting the map:

Figure 27: Sensing and iNtuitive on the HDM map

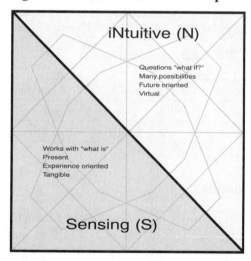

Some examples of sensing processing in people:

- S people are body-oriented; SFs process physical memes and STs process memes of fine manipulation, such as the control of the hands or financial bookkeeping.
- S people are concerned with the *now;* they process information as it comes in and match it to past episodes or features of string memes.
- Their past orientation leads them to look for stability in situations.

Some examples of intuitive processing in people:

- N people are language-oriented; NFs process words and communication between people, and NTs process logic.
- N people are concerned with the "what if" of a situation; they process hierarchies consciously and search out connections between abstractions.
- Their future orientation leads them to search out new possibilities in a situation.

Table 5: "Quick Glance" S/N Differences

Sensing	iNuitive
"All I know is…"	"Could it be that…"
Present	Future
What is	What could be
Practicalities	Possibilities
Tangible	Virtual and symbolic

Making the modes

Together, the S/N and F/T dichotomies make up the cognitive processing modes of SF, ST, NF, and NT. The modes correspond to the evolutionary advances in the *Homo* genus and appear on the individual level with the four levels of development in today's children.

Like the cognitive processing steps, human consciousness also picks a mode and sticks with it. But while the steps act to shape *how* a person processes, the modes act as the container holding the process, producing the point of reference for the person. For example, a DE implementing in the SF mode will produce whole episode, perception-based output and specialize in implementing physical memes. On the other hand, a DE implementing hierarchies in the NT mode will produce multipronged, logic-based output and specialize in implementing abstract intellectual memes.

Figure 28: Map of cognitive processing modes

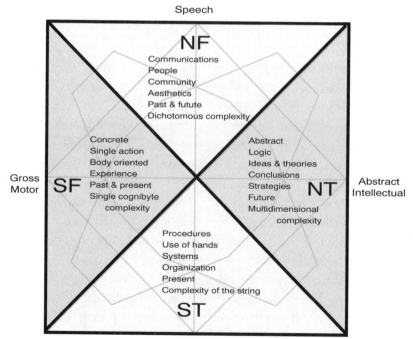

Combining step and mode into the HDM

As we defined earlier, the capacities are brain activities; they are areas of processing performed on the information the brain has at that time. The capacities break down as follows:

Table 6: Breakdown of Capacities

	right cortex		left cortex	
	action-planning	world-modeling	action-planning	world-modeling
SF	[1] Signal	[2] Match	[3] Contrast	[4] Control
ST	[5] Sign	[6] Feature	[7] Sorting	[8] Routine
NF	[9] Combination	[10] Harmony	[11] Preference	[12] Association
NT	[13] Strategy	[14] Pattern	[15] Logic	[16] Structure

The numbering and naming system for the capacities was devised by Dr. Walter Lowen and is detailed in his book *Dichotomies of the Mind*. When Dr. Lowen devised the system, he numbered them in the order in which they develop in children, placing the action-taking capacities before the world-modeling capacities.

This follows from Piaget's work (as detailed in Appendix A: Child Development), where he listed development of the transactions in infants as proceeding through CI explore, CE try, DI evaluate, and then DE implement during the first, sensorimotor, SF stage.

All transactions contain both an action-taking capacity and a world-modeling capacity. As we have seen, the difference between an Externalizing and Internalizing *transaction* depends on the order in which these two capacities are activated.

The first cognitive processing step to develop is CI explore, which is an Internalizing transaction. In order for this transaction to proceed, it needs the action-taking capacity of [1] **Signal** to produce a "subject." Then, the world-modeling capacity of [2] **Match** acts as the "verb." Moving from [1] **Signal** to [2] **Match**, the capacities produce the CI transaction within the SF mode.

To produce the second development as described by Piaget, the baby engages the second cognitive processing step of CE try. In order for this transaction to proceed, the world-modeling capacity of **[2] Match** produces the "subject." Then, the action-taking capacity of **[1] Signal** acts as the "verb." Moving from **[2] Match** to **[1] Signal**, they produce the CE transaction within the SF mode. The development of the Deterministic DI evaluate and DE implement transactions follow the same sequence.

In the following sections, we describe the capacities and the transactions they produce. The description of each transaction contains two examples, one describing the transaction's appearance in child development, and another describing how this transaction is used by a fully developed adult mind.

The diagram on the left illustrates where the four SF capacities sit within the brain, with the front capacities occurring in the action-taking areas and the back capacities occurring in the world-modeling areas. The arrows indicate transaction movement.

The diagram on the right illustrates where these capacities sit on the HDM map. The thicker lines and arrows indicate the transactions. Each transaction is labeled with its letter designator and cognitive processing profile name. We will investigate the profiles in more depth in the following chapter.

Figure 29: The four SF capacities

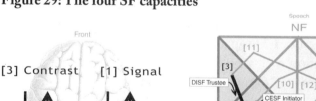

The SF capacities

The four SF capacities operate within the SF memory database, which is an organizational method based on episodic memory first developed in *Homo habilis*. This mode associates one perceptual episodic memory with one procedural sequence, forming a one-to-one link between perception and action. In essence, SF matches a *now* with the meme needed to react to that *now*.

This is primarily a physical mode that deals with the memes of the body. It is gross-motor, and first develops in children as Piaget's sensorimotor stage of development.

Signal

[1] **Signal** is the action-taking capacity of the SF mode that operates within the right cortex. **Signal** allows the brain to indicate to other people that the individual has recognized a relationship between the current *now* and a past experience.

Match

[2] **Match** is the world-modeling capacity of the SF mode that operates within the Right Perceptual Cortex. This capacity allows the brain to compare a current perception to past experiences and determine whether the "signal" has been previously experienced. In this capacity, the brain is capable of matching whole *nows* of perceptual information with whole remembered episodes that include a satisfactory response to the presented trigger.

Transactions

CISF: Moves [1] **Signal** to [2] **Match.** "Matching" (verb) the "Signal" (subject).

CESF: Moves [2] **Match** to [1] **Signal.** "Signaling" (verb) the "Match" (subject).

First development: **[1] Signal** and **[2] Match** are the first two capacities to develop in the sensorimotor stage of infancy.

- **CISF** is used when a newborn "matches" current "signals" (physical indicators) of being *hungry* with past states of *hungry*. The infant will match to the best past remembered episode. These episodes will normally include instinctive responses such as crying, that will help the infant get his or her needs met.

- **CESF** is used when a newborn "signals" that he has "matched" the current *hungry* state to a past experience. For most infants, communicating recognition of a need like *hungry* manifests as more deliberate behaviors such as finger-sucking and the "hungry cry."

As an adult: **[1] Signal** and **[2] Match** become useful to adults in sales situations or in situations where the person needs to make a quick, physical response.

- **CISF** is used when an adult "matches" current "signals" in the environment to the best previously learned body action to suit the current situation. This is particularly important for people who work with their bodies in professional situations such as fire fighting and athletics. CISF is the core transaction of the **CISF Doer** profile, detailed on page 145.

- **CESF** is used when a salesperson "signals" that he has "matched" the current needs of the customer with past experience, allowing the salesperson to say "I know just the right product for you!" The salesperson takes action to indicate to the other person that he has made a match. CESF is the core transaction of the **CESF Initiator** profile, detailed on page 149.

Contrast

[3] **Contrast** is the action-taking capacity of the SF mode that operates within the left cortex. Once signals are matched and context is created, the next capacity uses the brain's ability to employ differences. This capacity classifies recognized and matched signals as good or bad, or harmful or helpful and selects appropriate actions. Using **contrast** allows the brain to implement the correct response to satisfy a need.

Control

[4] **Control** is the world-modeling capacity of the SF mode that operates within the Left Procedural Cortex. Control is the brain's ability to generate a simple plan of action to affect a desired outcome. Control is, simply stated, motor control of the body. With this capacity, the brain recognizes that the very similar but discretely different nows of each repetition of an action are CE try attempts at the same response. Control perfects those attempts and stores the best as a gross-motor, body-oriented meme.

Transactions

DISF: Moves [3] **contrast** to [4] **control.** "Controlling" (verb) the "Contrast" (subject).

DESF: Moves [4] **control** to [3] **contrast.** "Contrasting" (verb) the "Control" (subject).

First development: [3] **contrast** and [4] **control** are the second two capacities to develop in sensorimotor stage of infancy.

- **DISF** is used when an infant chooses the one response to an object that is beneficial while rejecting another response that is not. The infant is "controlling" the "contrasts" between the responses by using this transaction to choose which is most beneficial. For example, moving the arms one way may enable crawling, but moving them in another does not.

- **DESF** manifests when an infant begins to learn how to move her hand to grasp an object. *Grasping* is a desired outcome in many discretely different triggering *nows* and shows that the infant is able to "contrast" between those nows to choose the best physical "control" for the situation. DESF responds correctly in each situation via his or her body memes stored in this area.

As an adult: [3] **contrast** and [4] **control** become useful while evaluating and performing physical memes.

- **DISF** is used by adults to perfect and evaluate physical memes. Adults will "control" the "contrast" while learning specific physical memes to be used at specific times, such as how a nurse should dispense medicine. DISF is the core transaction of the **DISF Trustee** profile, detailed on page 153.

- **DESF** allows an adult to implement the correct response to a here-and-now situation. This ability allows the adult to control the situation by responding in the manner most likely to satisfy the current need. This "contrasting" the "control" produces precision in response and is valuable to managers and coaches. DESF is the core transaction of the **DESF Classifier** profile, detailed on page 158.

The ST capacities

The ST capacities and transactions operate within the ST memory database and are based in the ability to produce string memes. Each sequence in the string becomes a point of matching, or a feature. The new string meme enables more refined processing, and the ability to match not just whole perceptual snapshots, but feature-to-feature as well. From feature-matching comes a new level of capacities.

This is primarily a physical mode that deals with memes for

using the hands and for the procedures of production. It is fine motor control and first developed in *Homo erectus*. It emerges today as Piaget's preoperational stage of child development.

As with the SF diagrams, the diagram on the left illustrates where the four ST capacities sit within the brain, with the front capacities occurring in the action-taking areas and the back capacities occurring in the world-modeling areas. The arrows indicate transaction movement.

The diagram on the right illustrates where these capacities sit on the HDM map. The thicker lines and arrows indicate the transactions. Each transaction is labeled with its letter designator and cognitive processing profile name. We will investigate the profiles in more depth in the following chapter.

Figure 30: The four ST capacities

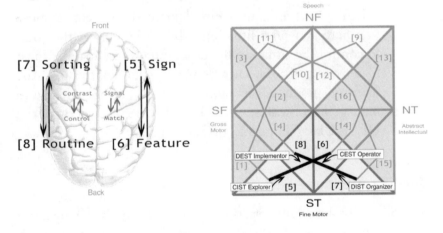

Sign

[5] **Sign** is the action-taking capacity within the ST mode that operates within the right cortex. Like the **signal** capacity, the **sign** capacity also indicates that a relationship has been recognized between the current situation and a past experience recalled from

memory. However, **sign** is more complicated and not limited to recognizing the total similarity of two entire *nows* of experiences. Instead, **sign** indicates the appreciation of relationships based upon the features within the experiences. This uses the string meme processing of the ST mode, providing a much richer and more complex tool.

Feature

[6] **Feature** is the world-modeling capacity of the ST mode that operates within the Right Perceptual Cortex. This capacity is the brain's ability to recognize a single feature within an experience. A feature is generally a single bit of perceptual information that combines with other bits to make the whole snapshot. As a capacity, **feature** denotes a complex matching process that involves recognizing the similarity between a feature of the current experience and a feature of a past experience recalled from memory. These features are most often derived from visual perceptions.

Transactions

CIST: Moves [5] **sign** to [6] **feature**. "Recognizing the features" (verb) of a "Sign" (subject).

CEST: Moves [6] **feature** to [5] **sign**. "Signing" (verb) the "Features" (subject).

First development: [5] **sign** and [6] **feature** are the first two capacities to develop in the preoperational stage of toddlerhood.

- **CIST** manifests as a toddler begins to "recognize the features" of similar "signs." For example, a toddler will distinguish between the "big red ball" and "little blue ball."
- **CEST** manifests as a toddler begins to "sign" that he "recognizes the features" of similar but distinct objects. The child may have two balls, but as CEST begins to function, the child will be able to indicate that he understands that one ball is the "big red ball" and other is the "little blue ball."

As an adult: [5] **sign** and [6] **feature** provide richer, more detailed processing of information about the environment.

- **CIST** identifies routines. This transaction is used particularly by middle managers who must recognize the "features" of a situation ("sign") and identify the necessary response that allows the company to continue to run smoothly. CIST is the core transaction of the **CIST Explorer** profile, detailed on page 164.
- **CEST** performs procedures with the hands and is particularly useful to people in the building trades. CEST allows people to use their hands to "sign" that they can manipulate the "features" of a situation. CEST is the core transaction of the **CEST Operator** profile, detailed on page 168.

Sorting

[7] **Sorting** is the action-taking capacity of the ST mode that operates in the left cortex. Like the **control** capacity, the **sorting** capacity also allows the implementation of a plan of action to affect a desired outcome. However, **sorting** is a more complicated process linking a series of actions derived from a complex of features. This linking is the part of the processing needed to build string memes, and it generates extended procedures.

Routine

[8] **Routine** is the world-modeling capacity of the ST mode that operates in the Left Procedural Cortex. This capacity is the brain's ability to link together a sequence of individual action directives, perfect them, and integrate them into an extended, procedural string meme. This string is stored in memory as part of the fine motor, hand-eye coordinating database and can be implemented at a future time when it is needed.

Transactions

DIST: Moves [7] **sorting** to [8] **routine**. "Making a routine of" (verb) the "Sorting" (subject).

DEST: Moves [8] **routine** to [7] **sorting**. "Sorting" (verb) the "Routine" (subject).

First development: [7] **sorting** and [8] **routine** are the second two capacities to develop in the preoperational stage of toddlerhood.

- **DIST** manifests as a toddler begins to learn sequences such as grammar and manners, thus "making a routine" of the "sorted" procedural memes.

- **DEST** manifests as a toddler begins to implement sequences of behaviors, that is, picking up and putting away toys, sequencing words, using a fork, and so on. In this transaction, the toddler is "sorting" which "routine" is best to use in the given situation.

As an adult: [7] **sorting** and [8] **routine** are used when dealing with procedural memes.

- **DIST** is used in creating a manufacturing procedure. The person is "making a routine" to "sort" how to produce the needed products. DIST is the core transaction of the **DIST Organizer** profile, detailed on page 172.

- **DEST** is used when implementing a manufacturing procedure. The person is "sorting" which "routine" should be implemented at that time. DEST is the core transaction of the **DEST Implementor** profile, detailed on page 176.

The NF capacities

With *H. sapiens sapiens,* intuitive processing created a new set of capacities in the brain. These are the metaphor-making capacities that use the NF mode memory database. Within the NF mode, the brain links sensory perception with intuited, abstracted information. In essence, the abstracted information links all of the sensory information that it describes together and stands in for it in consciousness.

Because of the one-to-one relationship of sensed information to intuited information, the NF mode is also feeling. This adds another point of reference to the information being matched and allows NFs to make links via the feelings and emotions contained in the relevant episodes.

The NF capacities and transactions are primarily intuitive and deal with the connections between "what is" and abstractions and generalizations. This mode is of language and people, and first develops as Piaget's concrete operational stage of development.

As with the SF and ST diagrams, the diagram on the left illustrates where the four NF capacities sit within the brain, with the front capacities occurring in the action-taking areas and the back capacities occurring in the world-modeling areas. The arrows indicate transaction movement.

The diagram on the right illustrates where these capacities sit on the HDM map. The thicker lines and arrows indicate the transactions. Each transaction is labeled with its letter designator and cognitive processing profile name. We will investigate the profiles in more depth in the following chapter.

Figure 31: The four NF capacities

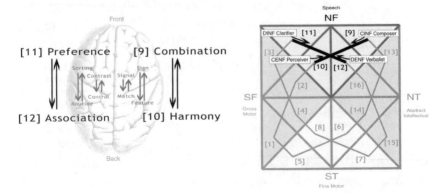

Combination

[9] **Combination** is the action-taking capacity of the NF mode that operates in the right cortex. This capacity is the brain's ability to engage the intuitive model to generate "what if" possibilities. In this capacity, the brain "imagines" combinations of elements that might not normally be thought of as belonging together. **Combination** is the first engagement of hierarchical processing and uses generalizations to link together otherwise unlinkable episodes.

Harmony

[10] **Harmony** is the world-modeling capacity of the NF mode that operates in the right cortex. Like **match** and **feature**, the **harmony** capacity matches current experience with past memories. However, **harmony** is more sophisticated in that it is a value judgment determining if the elements being matched balance and harmonize with each other. This goes beyond identifying one element matching to another; it engages the emotional system, along with all of the genetic and memetic imperatives that carry weight within it, to render an aesthetic judgment.

    Harmony, in essence, is the root of the NF metaphor. Through **harmony**, a person weighs the incoming information about one item and matches to the information of a different, remembered item. The aesthetic judgment comes into play while determining if both items form a pleasing pair and have balance.

Transactions

    CINF: Moves [9] **combination** to [10] **harmony**. "Harmonizing" (verb) the "Combinations" (subject).

    CENF: Moves [10] **harmony** to [9] **combination**. "Combining" (verb) the "Harmony" (subject).

    First development: [9] **combination** and [10] **harmony** are the first two capacities to develop in the concrete operational stage of childhood.

- **CINF** manifests as a child begins to create metaphors on her own. The child is "harmonizing" different elements into a "combination." For example, a child will begin to understand how to use use shading in artwork to signify mood.
- **CENF** manifests as a child begins to use her imagination in play. The child is "combining" her interaction with the environment by using different "harmonies" of possibilities in play. For example, playing house involves bringing different children together in different roles. The children will organize and reorganize themselves, depending on what combinations they need at the time.

As an adult: [9] combination and **[10] harmony** are used when creating art and interacting with other people.

- **CINF** is used by an adult while producing metaphoric and pleasing art. An artist "harmonizes" different elements into a "combination" or metaphor so that she can transfer an intuitive episode to the audience. CINF is the core transaction of the **CINF Composer** profile, detailed on page 182.
- **CENF** is used by an adult while thinking of different possible scenarios. Party planners "combine" the different "harmonies" of people and possibilities for an event. CENF is the core transaction of the **CENF Perceiver** profile, detailed on page 186.

Preference

[11] **Preference** is the action-taking capacity of the NF mode that operates in the left cortex. **Preference** deals with sorting elements as either "good" or "bad." Unlike the either/or behavior of the **sorting** transaction described earlier, **preference** deals with gradations of "goodness." In **preference**, the world is not merely black-and-white, but a continuous spectrum of dark and light gray. This is a reflection

of the hierarchical nature of intuitive model processing and represents a more sophisticated way of making choices because vastly more information is processed using abstractions and generalizations.

Association

[12] **Association** is the world-modeling capacity of the NF mode that operates in the Left Procedural Cortex. Like **control** and **routine**, this capacity provides the means for developing procedures for guiding behavior. In this capacity, the brain perfects and stores memes in the social interaction and communication database. **Association** uses hierarchical processing to associate symbol to meaning, which is crucial to language. It is the home of the human hierarchies of communications, most fully recognized in talking, but also in our recognition of visual and design language. This capacity includes the constructs of grammar and the symbolic hierarchical structure, including abstractions and generalizations.

Transactions

DINF: Moves [11] **preference** to [12] **association**. "Associating" (verb) the "Preferences" (subject).

DENF: Moves [12] **association** to [11] **preference**. "Giving preference to" (verb) the "Associations" (subject).

First development: [11] **preference** and [12] **association** are the second two capacities to develop in the concrete operational stage of childhood.

- **DINF** manifests as a child begins to understand that words can have several meanings. For example, "orange" means both a fruit and a color, thus the child "associates" a particular "preference" in a particular situation.

- **DENF** manifests as a child begins to grasp the nuanced nature of language, allowing him to give "preference" to various "associations" and to say the same message in the best possible manner. DENF is particularly evident in children who can debate well or who have a particular affinity for acting.

As an adult: [11] preference and **[12] association** are used when dealing with the complexities of language and social interaction.

- **DINF** evaluates and perfects the use of words and other communication media. This allows the adult to "associate" the correct "preference" at the correct time. DINF is the core transaction of the **DINF Clarifier** profile, detailed on page 191.
- **DENF** uses communication models to influence social activities. In an adult, DENF gives "preference" to the correct "association" to deal with a particular situation. DENF is the core transaction of the **DENF Verbalist** profile, detailed on page 196.

The capacities of the NT mode

The NT mode manifested with the formalization of logic. The NT memory database associates one intuited meme with an entire hierarchy, in much the same way as the ST database associates one meme with a procedural string. NT, though, works entirely in the intuitive model and manipulates only abstractions and generalizations in consciousness.

The NT mode is abstract intellectual and represents Piaget's formal operational stage of development. The full acquisition of NT capacities and transactions is predicated on an individual's assimilation of logic. Not all humans are exposed to an education that includes logic, so not everyone fully develops these capacities.

As with the SF, ST, and NF diagrams, the diagram on the left illustrates where the four NT capacities sit within the brain, with the front capacities occurring in the action-taking areas and the back capacities occurring in the world-modeling areas. The arrows indicate transaction movement.

Figure 32: The four NT capacities

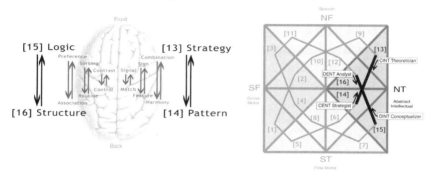

The diagram on the right illustrates where these capacities sit on the HDM map. The thicker lines and arrows indicate the transactions. Each transaction is labeled with its letter designator and cognitive processing profile name. We will investigate the profiles in more depth in the following chapter.

Strategy

[13] **Strategy** is the action-taking capacity of the NT mode that operates within the right cortex. Like the **combination** capacity, **strategy** also deals with combining and the generating possibilities out of odd elements. However, in this capacity, the brain uses logic to access linkages deep in the intuitive model, giving the generated possibilities more depth and allowing them to be formed into a plan of action. A strategy is more complex than a combination of possibilities and represents a hierarchical structuring beyond that which is produced in conjunction with the emotional system.

Pattern

[14] **Pattern** is the world-modeling capacity of the NT mode that operates within the Right Perceptual Cortex. Again, this capacity is yet another way of matching in order to identify and recognize current experience. **Pattern** is logic-driven and responsive to visual

stimuli. Its job is to detect patterns in a complex display of information, taking a rich array of information and looking for differentiating criteria useful for classification. Pattern looks for identification and clarification of where an element sits in the hierarchy by using logic to sort connections. The **pattern** capacity allows the brain to recognize order and disorder.

Transactions

CINT: Moves **[13] strategy** to **[14] pattern**. "Finding a pattern in" (verb) the "Strategy" (subject).

CENT: Moves **[14] pattern** to **[13] strategy**. "Strategizing" (verb) the "pattern" (subject).

As an adult: **[13] strategy** and **[14] pattern** are put in place during the formal operational stage of child development. They manifest in adolescence and adults.

- **CINT** manifests when an adolescent begins to "find the pattern in" the "strategy" of how the world fits together. This allows the person to understand and identify the linkages between how one event in the environment influences another. Pattern is everywhere—in pictures, events, and data, and it is this capacity that allows humans to recognize it. CINT is the core transaction of the **CINT Theoretician** profile, detailed on page 202.

- **CENT** manifests when an adolescent begins to use "patterns" to develop "strategies." This allows the person to recognize formal laws of nature. For example, it is the difference between recognizing that all objects fall to the earth and understanding the physics that describe those falls. These strategies are not rigid, but offer possible schemes for proceeding. This transaction, since it is contextual, will constantly reprocess and regenerate schemes as new data comes in. CENT is the core transaction of the **CENT Strategist** profile, detailed on page 206.

Logic

[15] **Logic** is the action-taking capacity of the NT mode that operates in the left cortex. This capacity provides the brain's ability to sort information contained in the deep structures of abstract, hierarchical memories. Through implementing logic, this capacity generates logical conclusions.

Structure

[16] **Structure** is the world-modeling capacity within the NT mode that operates in the Left Procedural Cortex. Like **control, routine,** and **association,** this capacity provides a deterministic organizing schema. However, **structure** organizes the highly abstract, underlying framework that describes reality. It is in this area that the brain "sees" the laws of nature and the abstract languages of math and logic that humans use to describe it. The **structure** capacity perfects and stores the memes used to develop abstractions and reasoning.

Transactions

DINT: Moves [15] **logic** to [16] **structure.** "Structuring" (verb) the "logic" (subject).

DENT: Moves [16] **structure** to [15] **logic.** "To apply logic to" (verb) the "Structure" (subject).

As an adult: [15] **logic** and [16] **structure** are put in place during the formal operational stage of child development. They manifest in adolescence and adults.

- **DINT** manifests as an adolescent begins to "structure" the "logic" of the world. With this transaction in place, a person can formulate a conceptual structure by applying logic to reliable data. DINT is the core transaction of the **DINT Conceptualizer** profile, detailed on page 210.

- **DENT** adolescents and adults use this transaction to generate logical conclusions that can be applied to solve current problems and needs. DENT applies "logic" to the "structure" within the world. DENT is the core transaction of the **DENT Analyst** profile, detailed on page 214.

When all sixteen capacities and transactions are included together on the same diagram, they can be represented on the brain in the following way:

Figure 33: All sixteen capacities together

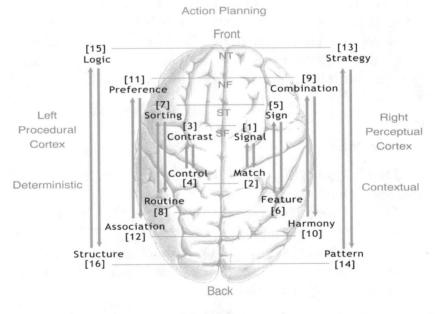

On the model, they are represented as triangular areas within each mode:

Figure 34: All 16 capacities on the HDM

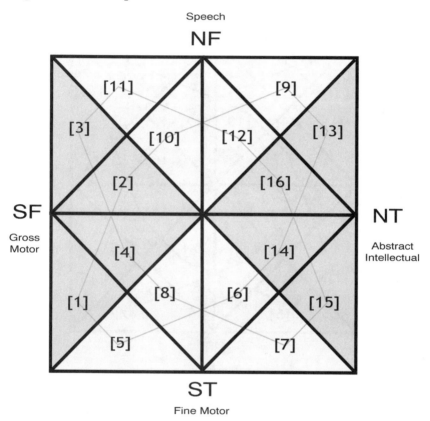

When the C and D pathways are added, and all the transactions represented, the fully developed model is represented as so:

Figure 35: The fully developed Human Dimensions Model

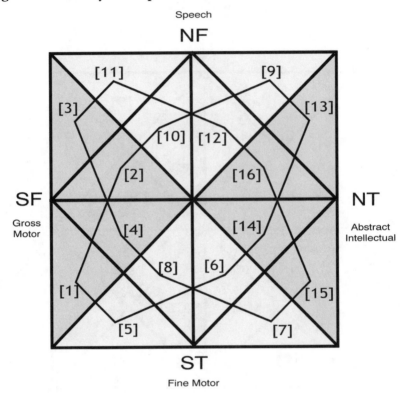

On this model are the sixteen transactions within which human consciousness can operate. Each is different from the others, and we will look at how they differ in the next chapter.

Summary

- A *capacity* is the brain's capability to process information using one of the four cognitive processing steps within one of the four cognitive processing modes. Capacities "make" information.

- A *transaction* is the dynamic interaction between two of the capacities.

- A transaction is a behavior and generates an episode using the first capacity as the "subject" and the second capacity as the "verb."

- The steps and modes of the HDM form four dichotomies, which are divided into two groups. First are the *Contextual/ Deterministic* and *Internalizing/Externalizing* dichotomies of the cognitive processing steps. Second are the *Sensing/ iNtuitive* and *Feeling/Thinking* dichotomies of the cognitive processing modes.

- Consciousness fully uses only one transaction.

- Internalizing/Externalizing were the first transactions, and appeared with Australopithecus. The I/E dichotomy is observable in higher mammals today.

- I/E represents purpose in action. Internalizers take action to position themselves to acquire the best input for model-building; whereas Externalizers use the model to take action in the world.

- The Contextual/Deterministic dichotomy first appeared with *H. habilis* and spawned the first set of four cognitive capacities and transactions.

- Contextual people use the looping processing of the Right Perceptual Cortex in consciousness. Deterministic people use the sequential processing of the Left Procedural Cortex.

- The C/D and I/E dichotomies form the four cognitive processing steps of CI explore, CE try, DI evaluate, and DE implement.

- In an individual, consciousness picks a step and sticks with it, operating with full, internal awareness of that step.

- The Feeling/Thinking dichotomy appeared with the complex processing of *H. erectus* and spawned the second set of capacities and transactions.

- The Feeling/Thinking (F/T) dichotomy is determined by whether an individual consciously processes episode-to-episode for F, or processes initial episode-to-string or -hierarchy for T.
- Fs have access to and use emotional tagging as a sorting system for memories; Ts do not.
- A *feeling* is the specific combination of emotions generated in that episode.
- The Sensing/iNtuitive dichotomy appeared with *H. sapiens sapiens* and spawned the third set of capacities and transactions.
- The S/N dichotomy determines whether an individual's consciousness sits within the sensing or the intuitive models.
- S people are sensing and perception oriented; their consciousness deals first with the sensations that their bodies are generating. N people are intuitive and language-oriented; their consciousness deals first with the abstractions that label a perception.
- The appearance of the NT mode did not create a new dichotomy, it generated the final set of capacities and transactions.
- Together, the S/N and F/T dichotomies make up the cognitive processing modes of SF, ST, NF, and NT. The modes correspond to the evolutionary advances in the *Homo* genus and appear today on the individual level with the four levels of child development.

8

THE PROFILES: DIFFERENTIATION

Overview

Consciousness involves the work of capacities and transactions. There are three conscious transactions: *Competence, play,* and *toil.* The competence transaction operates fully in consciousness, and the person is aware of the work of the "subject" capacity, the "verb" capacity, and the flow of information between the two. The play operates in semiconsciousness and the person is aware of the work of the capacities, but not the effort of the transaction. Toil operates in semiconsciousness also, and the person is aware of the "subject" capacity and the work of the transaction, but is unaware of the "verb" capacity and the results it generates.

Play is the start of the *creative track,* which checks the validity of the work done by the *competence track* as well as provides a way to generate unexpected results. The competence track includes the competence transaction and the toil transaction. Other transactions fill out the tracks, but they are unconscious and play a lesser role in molding a person's cognitive processing profile.

DIFFERENTIATION

As we discussed previously, consciousness is a meme processor based on language. Its purpose is to process change and ambiguity via the intuitive model and to generate new memes to deal with new situations. The intuitive model is a virtual mind-space where possibilities and outcomes are "run through" quickly and without harm to the individual, very much like how computer simulations are used today.

"Running through" possibilities involves capacities and transactions. An individual's cognitive processing uses eight of the sixteen possible transactions, and will separate itself into a main *competence track* and a supporting *creative track*. If the individual has a difficult task to complete and he must create a new memetic response, information will be processed along both tracks over a period of time until the person generates a solution. Examples of such tasks include generating new designs for a product; creating real and believable characters for a story; or learning how to play basketball on a certain court.

Both tracks start with the capacity where input enters consciousness. From this point, the main *competence transaction* takes the information and does the immediate response processing. The competence transaction occurs completely in consciousness, and the person is conscious of all the work done, including the work of the "subject" capacity, the "verb" capacity, and the flow of information between the two.

In the light and film emulsion metaphor, the "subject" capacity of the competence transaction will make a "picture" with only a specific type of information. For example, if the individual's competence transaction includes [1] signal, this capacity will make an action-taking picture in the SF mode. If the information coming in to the individual is abstract intellectual and highly intuitive, then [1] signal can't grab onto it, and it floats by and is lost to consciousness.

In this way, the competence transaction filters what information comes into consciousness. The changes and ambiguities that a person perceives; what parts of a conversation are salient, or what facts are intelligible, will be different depending on the individual's competence. This shapes both what it works with and the memories it produces.

Conscious awareness of the competence transaction allows higher quality work in that transaction, leading to better matching to responses already in memory. Control comes with awareness of process, and the individual can arrange the details of her thinking. It is easier to stop and consider what you are doing when you are aware of doing it.

Also, as a person uses her competence, it generates the episodes that fill that person's memory database. This creates a feedback loop—the more the competence is used, the more it formats potential matches in memory. The more matches in memory, the more reinforcement of the conscious processing that can match to them. This funnels information through the competence transaction and supports its use.

From the end of the competence transaction, cognition will continue to process information. The output of the competence becomes the input into the next transaction used, which is the *toil transaction*. Toil drops out of consciousness, with the person not having any conscious awareness of the work done by the "verb" capacity. This leaves awareness of the start of the transaction, and the effort of the flow of information, but it does not leave the person with any sense of generating a result. This is not satisfying, and an individual will tend to procrastinate this process.

On the other side of the competence transaction is the *play transaction*.[13] The play is the first transaction of the creative track, and uses the same conscious input as the competence. It moves, though, into a different memory database than the competence transaction and gives cognitive processing a "check" for the competence transaction.

But, because play sits in a different memory database from the competence transaction, it is underused in that it does not do the immediate matching work and does not contain as many possible matches. This increases the likelihood that the creative track will come up with something unexpected and "creative" because it has to "reach" more to find matches.

To increase the attraction of using the creative track and to counterbalance the lack of matches in its database, human cognition engages the emotional system to make using play "fun." The emotional enjoyment of using play allows a person to stay in it as their consciousness does the extra work necessary to "reach" for the unusual possibilities.

The play transaction is less conscious than the competence. The "fun" of using the play masks the extra work of moving information from the "subject" capacity to the play's "verb" capacity. This drops awareness of the flow of information out of consciousness. But, it also speeds up the work along the creative track as the emotional system turns desire toward working in play. This, along with the procrastination in toil, synchronizes the two tracks so that they can work in concert.

Competence, toil, and play make up the three transactions that occur within consciousness. From these three transactions, information will circulate into five other unconscious transactions, and then back out again into consciousness. The other five transactions create the epiphany moments where a solution presents itself to consciousness "out of the blue."

When the creative and the competence tracks work in con-

---

13. In Lowen's text, "play" is the mode, and "perseverance" is the transaction. We prefer "play" for the transaction because it is more descriptive.

cert, they share information and generate new and novel memetic responses. When a person is allowed to use both tracks, then that person can produce the highest quality memetic output that person is capable of creating.

The other five transactions do not occur in consciousness, and they are not necessarily all used to solve a particular problem. They support the three main conscious transactions, which form a person's cognitive processing profile.

The cognitive processing profiles are labeled according to their competence transactions. When a transaction is a play or a toil, it manifests differently for that person than it would if it were his competence transaction. Within the profile, play and toil are used by the competence in a subordinate role.

Figure 36: Example of consciousness in the CINF Composer profile

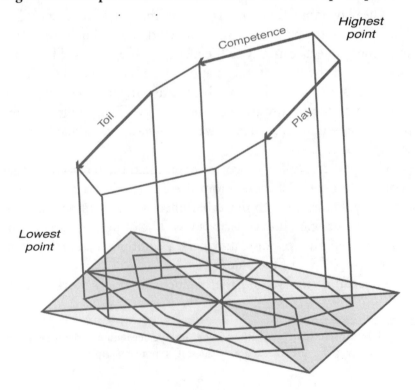

Different shapes of minds

Without full conscious awareness of "subject," "verb," and the flow of information between them, consciousness cannot refine the process of thinking. This is why people can achieve greater success using their competence transactions than they can with either play or toil.

A person's point of view is formed on his competence transaction. All memetic information that is manipulated by the individual's mind is passed through the competence transaction. All filters are shaped by the capacities on which the transaction sits. The competence transaction is the "lens" on the camera that focuses the entire "picture."

There are sixteen different lenses, each corresponding to a competence transaction and anchoring a cognitive processing profile. The differences in the profiles become particularly clear when different people are asked the same question, such as "What is common sense?" Answers range from "recognizing your needs" to "using logic to understand how the world works." When people think about the question, they answer with what it means for each of them to have common sense—in other words, how they understand the world around them.

All of the answers to the common sense question can be classified as "what people do when thinking." They are all processes, and they are the work done in consciousness. But, they are not all the same process—the ability to recognize needs does not tell you how the world works.

These differences in point of view, in how the world is perceived through the lens of consciousness, impact how a person interacts with others, how he learns, how well he performs certain kinds of tasks, and so on. Knowing that there are differences in people impacts all areas where people interact, from the grocery store to the doctor's office. And knowing the differences comes down to recognizing the transactions.

The Analyst, an example of how a profile works

An Analyst is a DENT, a person who cognitively processes *D*eterministically in an *E*xternalizing transaction, all within the i*N*tuitive *T*hinking mode:

Figure 37: DENT Analyst competency transaction

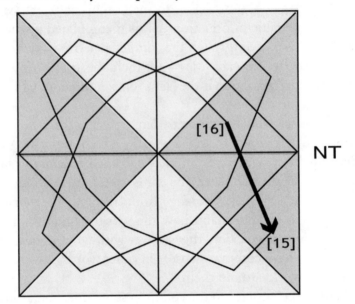

NT

For the Analyst, conscious work starts on the inside of the model at the **[16] structure** capacity. It is in this area that the brain "sees" the laws of nature in the abstract languages of math and logic humans use to describe it. This capacity forms the "subject" of the Analyst's transaction and forms a picture of the underlying structure of the world.

The Analyst transaction moves outward, externalizing toward the **[15] logic** capacity. Here, the brain is capable of sorting information by using logic to generate and apply abstract processes to existing problems. This capacity forms the "verb" of the Analyst's transaction and logically sorts the information provided to it from the **[16] structure** capacity.

The DENT Analyst transaction takes the already modeled abstractions and hierarchies and implements them by forming firm, logical conclusions, and sends them outward, into the world.

In contrast with the Analyst, the DINT Conceptualizer uses the same two capacities on the HDM, but works from the outside inward:

Figure 38: DINT Conceptualizer competency transaction

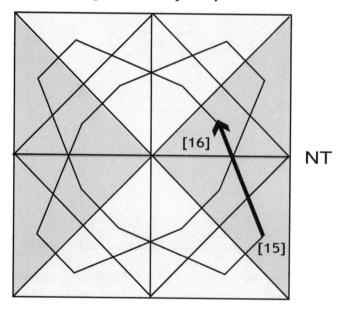

The DINT Conceptualizer transaction takes data, which is formed into a logical picture by the **[15] logic** capacity, and creates abstractions and hierarchies in **[16] structure**. The Conceptualizer internalizes, evaluating and perfecting logical structure in order to form a better conceptual model.

The Analyst's play transaction

Play occupies the fringe around the start of conscious work for the individual and is the transaction that starts the creative track. The DENF Verbalist is the play transaction for the Analyst:

Figure 39: DENT Analyst play transaction (DENF verbalist)

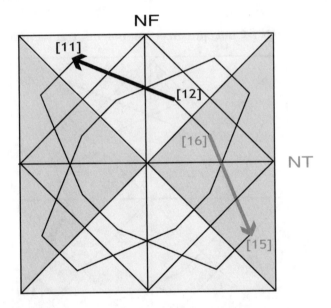

In the competence transaction, people hold themselves accountable for conscious output. For example, Analysts strive to be right; for them, producing correct conclusions is what they do, and if the result is wrong, then they are not thinking in the correct manner. In the play transaction, though, a person does not hold himself accountable for the result. Analysts might always strive to be right, but they really don't care if they are not verbalizing in the best possible manner.

In the play transaction, a person has no awareness of the movement of the transaction. Without this awareness, operating in the play transaction gives no sense of fatigue. A person can continue with this activity almost indefinitely. For an Analyst, this means that they can talk continuously, without getting tired.

Cognition also uses the play transaction to verify output from the competence transaction. If output continues to be coherent when run through the alternate memory database of play, then that work is valid and processing can continue to run in concert along both the competence and creative tracks. For the Analyst, verification comes from using his DENF Verbalist transaction to talk and lecture; for the Conceptualizer, verification comes from utilizing his DIST Organizer transaction to organize information by drawing graphs and diagrams with the hands.

The Analyst's toil transaction

The toil is a continuation of the competence's effort into the next transaction. The toil occupies the other fringe of the stage of perception where work ends. For the Analyst, toil is the Organizer:

Figure 40: DENT Analyst toil transaction (DIST organizer)

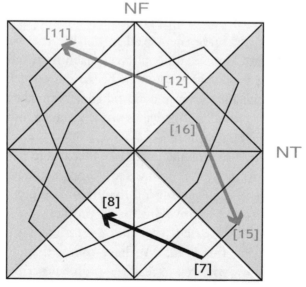

In the DIST Organizer transaction, the Analyst orders the logical conclusions generated by his competence. The inherent procrastination of this transaction slows up its work, giving play time to do its creative work of finding an unexpected result. Ultimately, as cognition continues to process and the tracks work in concert, the ordering done by the DIST Organizer will finish the conscious work applied to the problem by producing the final output of the solution.

A few words about profiling

The next chapter of this section will set out in detail for the reader the meaning of the cognitive processing profiles. Profiling someone, though, and especially profiling yourself, is very difficult. As of yet, your profile cannot be assessed via a multiple choice quiz or any other self-assessment tool. In order to tease out the underlying transactions being used by your consciousness, most people need to be observed by someone trained in profiling.

Most people also have some "wannabe" traits—characteristics that they have learned in order to work around a part of their profile that does not serve them well in the life they are living. For example, some Contextual people will teach themselves to talk in a manner that sounds Deterministic because D speech patterns are more influential and easier to comprehend. Wannabe traits such as these are only partially effective as work-arounds, but can be very effective at masking a profile.

Also, because of circumstances in a life, and in particular when a person's cognitive system is stressed, some people will attempt to function more in their play or toil than their competence. This too masks the person's cognitive processing profile.

That is not to say that you cannot get a good, general assessment from using this book. We have found that if you ask five people who know you well to read the profile descriptions that follow, they will, in general, come to a consensus that matches your transactions and reveals your cognitive processing profile.

Also, a cognitive processing profile is not a personality profile. How someone processes information is a vital component of personality, but there are many other factors that go into building a person, chief among which is how an individual's Self is constructed.

The next chapter lists descriptions of the sixteen cognitive processing profiles grouped by mode. Each profile includes capacity and transaction information. Also included is a description of how consciousness manifests for that particular profile.

Summary

- Human cognition is dynamic and uses two tracks of transactions to support and check processing: The *competence track*, which includes the competence transaction and does the main processing and matching to the memory database; and the *creative track*, which includes the play transaction and serves to check the work of the competence as well as to find unexpected solutions to problems.

- The *competence transaction* is the main dynamic cognitive process of an individual, and it filters what is allowed in consciousness.

- In the competence transaction, a person is aware of the work of the "subject" capacity, the "verb" capacity, and the flow of information between the two.

- The competence is fully conscious.

- In *play*, a person is aware of the work of the "subject" and "verb" capacities, but is not fully aware of the effort of moving information between the two.

- Play is the first transaction of the creative track and starts with the same input used by the competence transaction.

- Play moves information into a different memory database than the one used by competence, thus allowing cognition to check the validity of the competence output.

- In *toil*, a person is aware of the work of the "subject" capacity and the effort of moving information between the two, but is not aware of the work of the "verb" capacity. This limits awareness of the result of the transaction.

- Toil finishes the work of the competence by outputting it again through another memory database.

- Combined, the three conscious transactions produce a person's cognitive processing profile.

- All memetic information that is manipulated by the individual's mind is passed through the competence transaction, leading to different points of view in the sixteen cognitive processing profiles.

9

THE PROFILES

Overview

The HDM describes sixteen cognitive processing profiles. Each profile is based on one of the competence transactions.

THE PROFILES

This chapter contains the cognitive processing profiles as broken down by mode. Each profile covers a two-page spread: One the left page is the profile's transactions and their diagrams. On the right page is a description of the profile, including how the profile's competence and play manifest, areas that are difficult for the profile, and sections on how they communicate, learn, and understand the world. The transaction information ties the profile to the HDM map; the description illustrates how the profiles manifest in people.

The SF profiles

The SF infrastructure functions in the *now* and produces holis-tic matching between episodes. SF individuals work with sensed information, giving them a strong sense of their body and how to use it. The basic metaphor structure of the SF is body-oriented.

The four SF profiles are CISF Doer, CESF Initiator, DISF Trustee, and DESF Classifier. The four capacities used in con-sciousness by people working in the SF mode are [1] signal, [2] match, [3] contrast, and [4] control.

Figure 41: The SF profiles

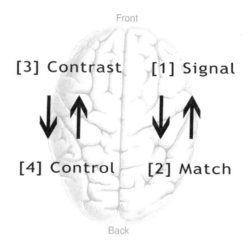

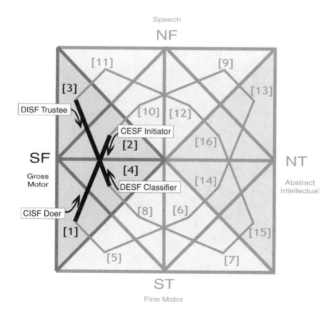

CISF DOER

Figure 42: CISF Doer

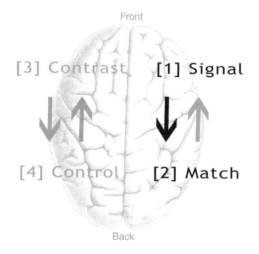

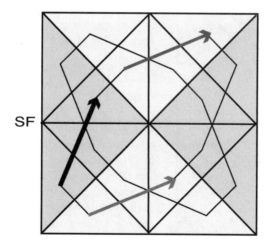

Competence Transaction

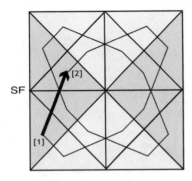

Competence Transaction

The *Doer* competence transaction moves from **[1] signal** to **[2] match**. "To match the signal" is to respond to the environment, and can be seen best in sports. While playing any fast-moving, chaotic game such as basketball, soccer, or tennis, an individual matches the tactile and visual signals of the world to the memetic responses of the body. These same skills are used by others who work closely with the tactile and chaotic world of nature, such as farmers and field guides.

Play Transaction

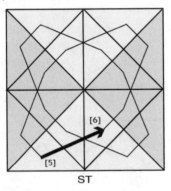

The *Doer* play transaction is in the ST mode and moves from **[5] sign** to **[6] feature**. This is the CIST Explorer transaction, which draws the features from a sign. In their play mode, *Doers* use their ST mode, fine motor control to understand the features of the world via the contact senses. This supports and reinforces the competence transaction processing.

Toil Transaction

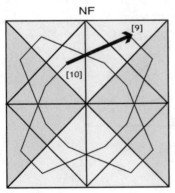

The *Doer* toil transaction is in the NF mode and moves from **[10] harmony** to **[9] combination**. This is the CENF Perceiver transaction, which uses the mixture of emotions that converge as the feeling of harmony to match up and imagine future possibilities. In their toil transaction, *Doers* are capable of "reading between the lines" when dealing with other people, but they procrastinate doing so whenever possible.

Doer *Competence*

Doers appreciate life for what it can offer at the present time. They live in "the here and now." To a *Doer,* life is full of experiences, and they move about and position themselves to be a part of as many of those experiences as much as possible. Past experience is a source of strength for *Doers,* and they see present activities as a way to enrich past memories. Their concerns do not extend very far into the future because they haven't experienced it yet. They rely on instinctual knowledge and have a natural wisdom that is often more effective than the complicated processes used by other profiles. In fact, *Doers* believe that some people make things too complicated.

Doers have a relaxed point of view. They accept life without much intent on influencing it. They are usually content and uncritical of others and themselves. *Doers* care about people and like to do things for them. While *Doers* are interacting with other people, their feelings and concerns are usually internalized. They like the freedom of spontaneity and do not tend to plan things in advance.

Play *Manifestation*

Doers enjoy working with their hands in areas such as crafts, hobbies, and playing music. They enjoy exploring the world around them, which gives them a perspective on their own personal experiences.

Areas of Difficulty

Doers tend to be shy and accepting, and have difficulty in situations where more assertiveness would be of benefit. They do not like organizing and have difficulty in envisioning future possibilities and planning accordingly. They do not like change.

Communication

Doers learn and understand in terms of actual experiences and the internal feelings created as a result. Verbal communication is much less effective. They tend to take things literally and require examples. When communicating to others, they provide their examples from the past in the form of storytelling.

Understanding and Believing

Doers understand and experience in terms of the feelings and sensations they generate inside. They match the entirety of this internal response to remembered responses, and if a relationship can be found, they understand what has happened. When confronted with new ideas, they discuss them with people in their circle of friends to get a perspective. Depending on the gut feel generated by the sharing, the *Doer* will either believe or not believe the new ideas.

Learning

Doers learn by doing and experiencing the resulting feelings. They do not learn well from verbal descriptions or other abstractions. Physical models, hands-on training, and experimentation are helpful in their education. They favor context-based learning.

CESF INITIATOR

Figure 43: CESF Initiator

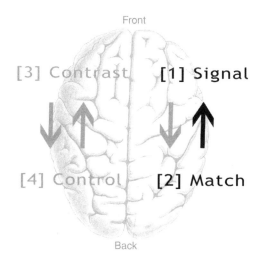

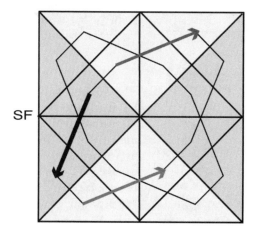

Competence Transaction

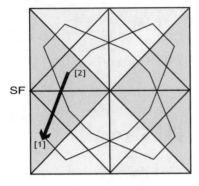

The *Initiator* competence transaction moves from **[2] match** to **[1] signal**. "To signal the match" is to notice that one thing is matched to something else, and it involves being alert to possible matches in the environment. The *Initiator's* matches may be between a need and a possibility, and, in short, may be the noticing of an opportunity. This transaction works with quick reactions and risk taking. It is beneficial in sales, some social situations, and some sports, such as certain positions on a basketball team.

Play Transaction

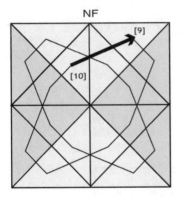

The *Initiator* play transaction is in the NF mode and moves from **[10] harmony** to **[9] combination**. This is the CENF Perceiver transaction, which uses feelings of harmony to imagine future possibilities. In their play transaction, *Initiators* are capable of "reading between the lines" when dealing with other people and use this ability to work with the public and reinforce their competence transaction processing.

Toil Transaction

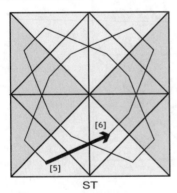

The *Initiator* toil transaction is in the ST mode and moves from **[5] sign** to **[6] feature**. This is the CIST Explorer transaction, which draws the features from a sign. In their toil mode, *Initiators* use their ST mode, fine motor control to organize their daily activities, but they will procrastinate whenever possible.

Initiator *Competence*

Initiators take action in the world of people to produce results. They are guided by their feelings and how experiences affect them. They live in the present and require that their efforts be quickly followed by rewards. *Initiators* are ambitious, independent, and energetic. They know what will work and they take charge. They often work in sales and are usually involved in a variety of sports.

Areas of Play

Initiators love being active and involved with the world of people. They surround themselves with friendships and seek acceptance in a group of like-minded people. *Initiators* like working with "the public."

Areas of Difficulty

Initiators are pragmatic, tend to take things literally, and have difficulty examining gray areas. They can be overpowered by their feelings. Negative feelings can make it difficult for them to make decisions. Their reaction to change has a quality of sadness to it because they feel change as a loss.

Communication

Information for *Initiators* is the internal feelings generated as the results of experiences. They file experiences in memory according to these feelings.

In an emotional situation, they may need to take a "time out" in order to get a grip on their feelings before making a verbal response. They plan a way to say what they mean so that they will not upset others.

Understanding and Believing

The *Initiator's* guide for assessing information is "whatever works as quickly as possible." But, they also need to experience something in order to understand it. For less tangible information, they will accept the opinions of trusted authorities. It is difficult for *Initiators* to examine new and future possibilities because they have not yet been experienced.

Learning

Initiators are highly motivated to learn material that is practical and has an application in the near term. They are less interested in learning things that may be useful in the future. They learn from experience. Once they have seen or experienced something, they can take it from there. They cannot imagine new possibilities that they have not experienced. They prefer that the relevant pieces of information be presented in context with one another so that they can form a picture of a whole. A contextual learning approach is the most advantageous for them.

DISF Trustee

Figure 44: DISF Trustee

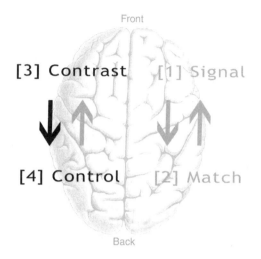

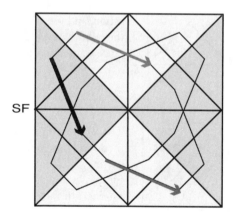

Competence Transaction

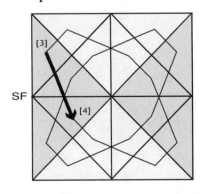

The *Trustee* competence transaction moves from **[3] contrast** to **[4] control**. "To control the differences" translates as the ability to exercise control in a situation where success or failure depends on a precise sequence of actions. This is a service-oriented profile, best exemplified by nursing, where a litany of do's and don'ts are learned in training. It is the nurses' precise ability to follow these clear-cut instructions that allows them to act in the best possible manner while helping a patient.

Play Transaction

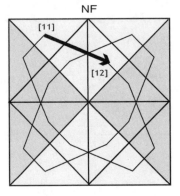

The *Trustee* play transaction is in the NF mode and moves from **[11] preference** to **[12] association**. This is the DINF Clarifier transaction, which extracts meaning from words. In their play transaction, *Trustees* are capable of learning about people through verbal communication, and use this ability to work with the public and to reinforce their competence transaction processing.

Toil Transaction

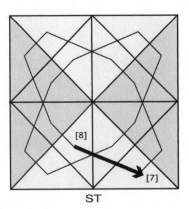

The *Trustee* toil transaction is in the ST mode and moves from **[8] routine** to **[7] sorting**. This is the DEST Implementor transaction, which creates order with routines. In their toil mode, *Trustees* use their procedural, ST mode processing to organize their world, but they will procrastinate this process whenever possible.

Trustee *Competence*

Trustees strive to do everything they do as perfectly as possible. They prefer to concentrate on a single activity and are disturbed when their concentration is interrupted. They tend to procrastinate, putting things off and having difficulty getting started. However, once started, they want to see the task to its end without interruption. When the activity is done, they find satisfaction in having done it well. They tend to follow rules and meet deadlines.

Trustees involve themselves in activities where they feel that they can be of benefit to other people. In general, their attention is directed toward the world of people rather than the world of things. They seek to be with people and want to deal with others in a way that generates good feelings. In their relationships, they are shy listeners and annoyed by people who are overly assertive and arrogant.

Thinking for the *Trustee* involves the relating of two different ideas or experiences partly through the feelings associated with each. The thought process involves a series of such comparisons and *Trustees* are consciously aware of the steps in the process. Things make sense to them when they seem to work out in a positive way.

Physical activity is an important component of any process in which a *Trustee* is involved. They become proficient in the types of sports activities that require a high degree of practice and perfection.

Areas of Play

Trustees enjoy learning about people. They have a strong sense of the past and are often interested in the study of history and genealogy.

Areas of Difficulty

Areas of difficulty are associated with *Trustee's* need for perfection in the actions they perform. They tend to be critical of their own performance, and they never quite measure up to their own high standards.

In their relationships with others, there is anxiety about whether their performance is meeting the expectations of the people around them. As the name implies, *Trustees* are very trusting and can be easily misled or taken advantage of by others. Their careful and prolonged rethinking of choices makes making decisions difficult and can result in lost opportunities.

Communication

Trustees are very down-to-earth people and rely heavily on their own past experience. Each experience generates a feeling that becomes a major part of the memory of that episode. Therefore, the *Trustee* makes the best use of information that is presented in the form of examples that can generate internal feelings, such as anecdotes. In turn, *Trustees* tend to communicate to others using the same methods, providing examples and their feelings about them.

Understanding and Believing

In order to understand a new situation or experience, the *Trustee* will attempt to match the feeling that an experience generates with feelings that she remembers as part of past episodes. If feelings match well, then the new experience is successfully filed in memory and the appropriate associative links form. The successful completion of this process is experienced as "understanding."

The process of believing is based on the tendency to trust other people. When confronted with new information, the *Trustee* will believe that information if the source is a person they trust. As a result, *Trustees* usually believe most of what people tell them.

Learning

Since *Trustees* prefer to deal with tangible information resulting from an actual experience, they tend to learn better from practical examples than from hypothetical situations or theoretical concepts. It is important to them to perform some kind of physical activity related to the learning process, such as taking notes or making diagrams. They will take notes of their own even when notes on the course material are supplied for their use.

DESF CLASSIFIER

Figure 45: DESF Classifier

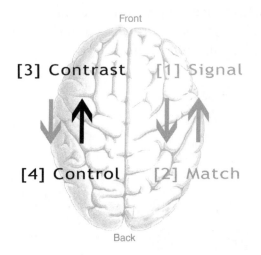

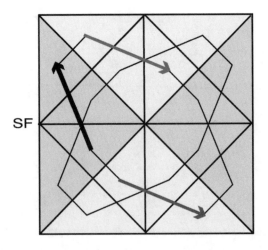

Competence Transaction

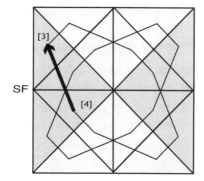

The *Classifier* competence transaction moves from **[4] control** to **[3] contrast**. "To make an either/or choice about control" translates as the ability to use a decision based on the dichotomous choice presented to manipulate the external world.

Play Transaction

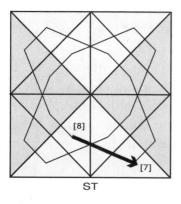

The *Classifier* play transaction is in the ST mode and moves from **[8] routine** to **[7] sorting**. This is the DEST Implementor transaction, which creates order with routines. In their play transaction, *Classifiers* are capable of implementing procedures, and they use this ability to reinforce their competence transaction processing.

Toil Transaction

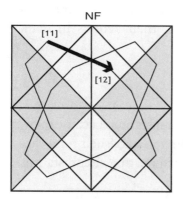

The *Classifier* toil transaction is in the NF mode and moves from **[11] preference** to **[12] association**. This is the DINF Clarifier transaction, which extracts meaning from words. In their toil mode, *Classifiers* can manage people, but they will procrastinate in this area whenever possible.

Classifier *Competence*

Classifiers manage and control the actions of people. They like having people rely on them to determine what actions to select as appropriate for the current situation. They like challenges and pride themselves on managing crisis situations in a way that benefits the people affected. They have strong feelings about right or wrong actions based on commonsense rules consistent with the cultural norms. They decide and act quickly, expect others to do the same, and become impatient with anyone who slows them down.

Classifiers like being busy and "are always on the move." They like physical activity, are usually athletic, and play sports. In this context, they often exercise control by coaching teams. They are emotional people and have a tendency to blow up when things go wrong, though they work to control their responses in order to more appropriately deal with other people.

Classifiers also need people and want to be around them. They prefer simplicity in life and like to go "back to basics." They like structure and stability, are not comfortable with change, and firmly adhere to the conventional rules of the culture for their behavior and their expectations for the behavior of others.

Areas of Play

Classifiers are good at getting things done, are impatient, and get satisfaction in seeing immediate results. They are practical and adopt existing procedures to support their actions in managing people's activities.

Areas of Difficulty

They must closely monitor their communications because their emotions blurt out. They so firmly adhere to established rules that they are unable to make adjustments for extenuating circumstances.

Communication

Classifiers prefer to receive tangible information with practical examples. Abstract possibilities and ideas do not interest them. Their speech pattern is clear and articulate and conveys feelings as well as objective information. When speaking, they have to suppress and control their emotional output. Otherwise, the emotional content prevails. This results in what can be described as "my mouth goes faster than my brain and words come out without thinking."

Understanding and Believing

Classifiers understand in terms of how their actions and the actions of others generate order in the world of people and the *Classifier's* own needs. To believe in the value of new approaches, they must match the new idea to accepted cultural rules.

Learning

Classifiers learn by successfully selecting actions that deal appropriately with people. Common sense and life experience are the best teachers.

The ST profiles

The ST matches the features of an initial episode to the features of a remembered episode that contains the beginning of a string of sequences. Each sequence in the string follows directly after the one before it and contains no contextual or emotional information.

ST individuals work with fine motor control, giving them a strong sense of their hands and how to use them. These profiles are also very visual, which they combine with string meme processing to create a high level of hand-eye coordination. The basic metaphor structure of the ST is hand-oriented.

The four ST profiles are CIST Explorer, CEST Operator, DIST Organizer, and DEST Implementor. The four capacities used in ST are [5] **Sign**, [6] **Feature**, [7] **Sorting**, and [8] **Routine**.

Figure 46: The ST profiles

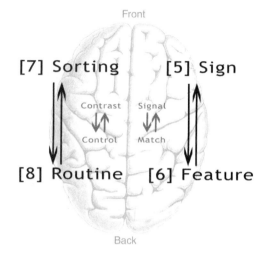

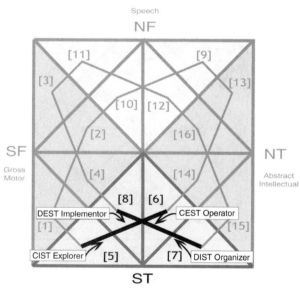

CIST EXPLORER

Figure 47: CIST Explorer

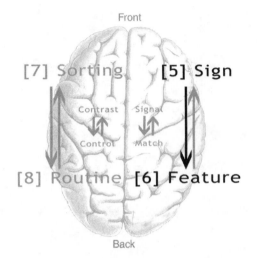

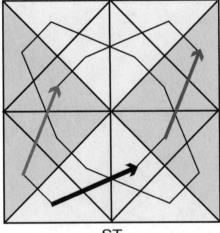

Competence Transaction

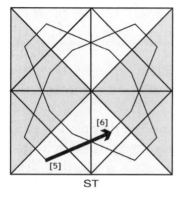

ST

The *Explorer* competence transaction moves from **[5] sign** to **[6] feature**. "To feature the sign" takes the ST input source—the eyes and hands—and extracts and labels the information. This type of processing enables tactile scanning such as that done by artisans, craftsmen, and sculptors. *Explorers* also tend to become middle managers; they are good at extracting the features of a complicated management situation and prioritizing their approaches. "Prioritize" is a preferred word in their vocabulary.

Play Transaction

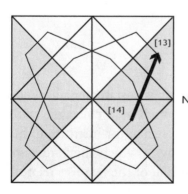

SF

The *Explorer* play transaction is in the SF mode, moves from **[1] signal** to **[2] match**, and is the CISF Doer transaction. In their play transaction, Explorers are able to position themselves to experience the environment, and they use this ability to reinforce their competence transaction processing.

Toil Transaction

NT

The *Explorer* toil transaction is in the NT mode, moves from **[14] pattern** to **[13] strategy**, and is the CENT Strategist transaction. In their toil transaction, *Explorers* are able to devise strategies and prioritize the features they have sorted with their competence, but they will procrastinate whenever possible, especially on making decisions.

Explorer *Competence*

Explorers investigate things in the world around them. Their memory is a rich collection of the features derived from everything they encounter. They move from one episode to another, briefly extracting points of interests. As a result of exploring, they develop a holistic sense of their world. They also arrange their activities according to a system of priorities.

Explorers like to see things get done, but they tend to procrastinate their decisions and actions. They soon learn to rely on others for guidance and implementation. As a result, they delegate readily and become efficient general managers who see the "big picture." *Explorers* are practical, down-to-earth people who value these qualities in others. They have a relaxed and positive attitude toward life.

Areas of Play

Explorers enjoy experiencing physical activities of all kinds; sports, outdoors, and the like. Doing these activities gives them a "feel" for the world around them.

Areas of Difficulty

Explorers deal with tangible things. If necessary, they think about future possibilities and select strategies leading to methods for assigning priorities for accomplishing tasks.

Communication

Explorers want "facts." To them, a fact is a statement backed by the authority of a source they trust, such as a colleague with a good track record or an authoritative person or institution. Such facts become features of the episode with which they are associated. *Explorers* communicate to others all of the features related to experiences similar to the situation under discussion, in a rich but loosely organized manner.

Understanding and Believing

Explorers add the features extracted from a new experience to their storehouse in memory. If the features fit somewhere and links to other memories can be established, they understand the new experience. In order to believe new information, they depend on their own gut feel as well as on the opinions of trusted colleagues and other authorities.

Learning

Explorers are constantly adding to their sense of "the whole" and prefer that all facts or features be presented in context with one another. *Explorers* depend heavily on visualization of features, and they are more receptive to information presented in the form of pictures and diagrams. Context-based learning is preferred.

CEST Operator

Figure 48: CEST Operator

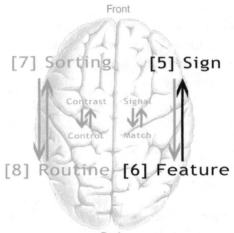

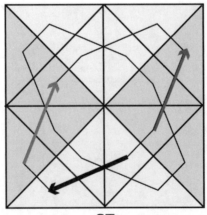

Competence Transaction

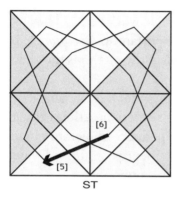

The *Operator* competence transaction moves from **[6] feature** to **[5] sign**. The *Operator* manipulates things in the world via their exceptional hand-eye coordination. In this transaction, "signing the feature" translates as the ability to make actions based on the features of the environment. The *Operator* cognitive processing profile is also the profile that literally signs features, and mimes actions with their hands. Please see Appendix C: The Operator in Action for an example of an *Operator* miming.

Play Transaction

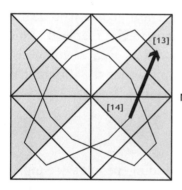

The *Operator* play transaction is in the NT mode, moves from **[14] pattern** to **[13] strategy**, and is the CENT Strategist transaction. In their play transaction, *Operators* are able to devise strategies for manipulating the world, and they use this ability to reinforce their competence transaction processing.

Toil Transaction

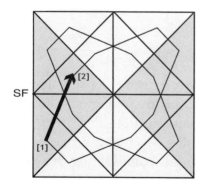

The *Operator* toil transaction is in the SF mode, moves from **[1] signal** to **[2] match**, and is the CISF Doer transaction. In their toil transaction, *Operators* are able to match holistic experiences instead of using features, but will procrastinate whenever possible.

Operator *Competence*

Operators act on the world of physical objects where they fix broken things and improve designs to make them work better. They like to learn what makes things work. It is important to *Operators* to be in control of their work and be free to select the methods they need to accomplish their tasks.

Operators think in sharp visual images that they are able to recall with great clarity and detail. From each experience, they extract the important features and then file the experience in memory in terms of those features. Different visual experiences are linked together on the basis of the features they have in common.

Areas of Play

While *Operators* are basically very practical people who deal with tangible things, they also like to select strategies that lead to methods for accomplishing mechanical tasks as well as methods for improving designs. They enjoy learning about the different ways people go about fixing and designing things.

Areas of Difficulty

Operators have difficulty in understanding people's feelings and why people behave the way they do. They are wary of the motives of others. They resist change and like to stick to existing methods that they have selected previously. They do not like organizing.

Communication

In communicating with others, *Operators* exhibit a unique and expressive style. While interactions involving feelings and human relationships generate very little enthusiasm from the *Operator,* a description of a mechanical methodology, such as a surgical procedure, is greeted with much more enthusiasm. During this kind of communication, the *Operator* uses her hands to perform the action at the same time the process is being described verbally. The *Operator* appears to be actually seeing the objects being described. The hand motions depicting manipulation of the objects are very different from the hand motions used by other types of people for emphasis. This communication is a "show and tell" process intended to train the observer on the method described by the *Operator*.

Understanding and Believing

Given a new situation, *Operators* extract key visual features and match those features with combinations remembered from past experience. To the extent to which the combination of features can be matched to memories, the *Operator* understands the new experience. When exposed to a new methodology, the process of believing what will work involves searching for a strategy to explain the new methodology and to make it reasonable. If a strategy can be discovered that yields the new method, then the *Operator* will believe that the method will work.

Learning

Operators prefer that new information be presented visually so that they can extract the important features. Further, if the new information is accompanied by an explanation of how it works, it will make it easier for the *Operator* to develop the strategy necessary to believe it. They understand new information in the context of its applications and prefer a context-based learning style.

DIST ORGANIZER

Figure 49: DIST Organizer

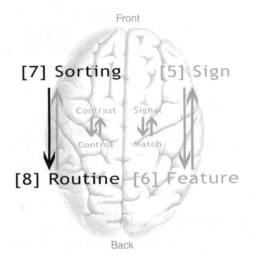

ST

Competence Transaction

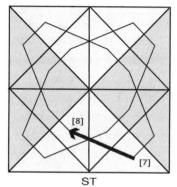

ST

The *Organizer* competence transaction moves from **[7] sorting** to **[8] routine**. This transaction puts into routine the sorting of actions in the world—it develops a system for organizing. *Organizers* are dedicated to efficiency and order.

Play Transaction

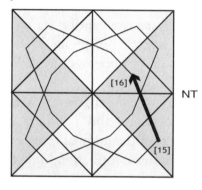

NT

The *Organizer* play transaction is in the NT mode, moves from **[15] logic** to **[16] structure**, and is the DINT Conceptualizer transaction. In their play transaction, *Organizers* learn about concepts that apply to their work, and they use this ability to reinforce their competence transaction processing.

Toil Transaction

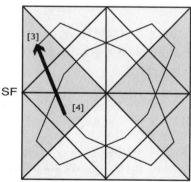

SF

The *Organizer* toil transaction is in the SF mode, moves from **[4] control** to **[3] contrast,** and is the DESF Classifier transaction. In their toil transaction, *Organizers* are good at making dichotomous decisions, but they will procrastinate whenever possible.

Organizer *Competence*

Organizers build procedures to organize everything they can, including time management, things, procedures, numbers, information, and even conversations with friends. *Organizers* are driven by a need for order in their lives, and they seek perfection.

Organizers need to be prepared. They plan for anything that happens in their lives. They develop systems and procedures and don't like these to change. They can generally manage changes that are planned well in advance, but they are upset by unexpected occurrences.

Organizers are proficient at procedures for managing numbers and other sorts of information, including accounting and computer programming. They like routines and enjoy learning new ones. *Organizers* prefer to do one thing at a time until it is finished and are disrupted by interruptions. They tend to procrastinate in decisions and in initiating actions. However, once given a deadline, they usually get things done on time.

For *Organizers,* thinking is a very visual experience. Mental images are as sharp as the original experiences and "photographic" in quality, though they lack the context of the original experience. *Organizers* rely on visual recall to access information, and they clearly see the structure in which it is stored.

Areas of Play

Organizers enjoy learning about the concepts that apply to things and procedures in their life. Because they have a good concept of how things work, they are good at fixing things.

Areas of Difficulty

Organizers generally have difficulty interacting with people in social relationships. They do not want to meet or talk to people they do not know well. They do not experience feelings in their normal thought processes and do not understand what is going on with people who do.

Communication

Organizers are most receptive to well-ordered, tangible information. They interpret information literally. They are shy and tend to listen and communicate only after being given the opportunity to think things through.

Understanding and Believing

Organizers require well-structured data from which they can generate an organizing procedure. The procedure "makes sense" if it can be related to other procedures already in memory. These procedures are represented visually. Once new information is understood in this manner, it is tested by developing a concept of how it works. Belief is dependent on the successful development of the concept.

Learning

Organizers develop their own internal procedures for structuring information and tend to reorganize the material presented to them in lectures. Having done so, the material becomes a visual imprint in memory. They prefer to learn one thing at a time in depth. They do not favor context-based learning.

DEST Implementor

Figure 50: DEST Implementor

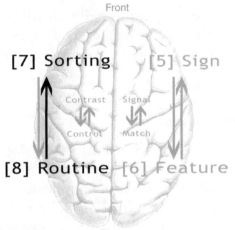

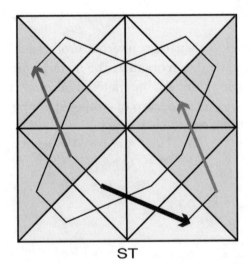

Competence Transaction

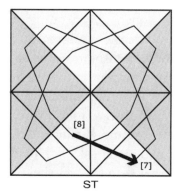

ST

The *Implementor* competence transaction moves from [8] **routine** to [7] **sorting**. "To sort the routines" is to create order when given routines. It is an action-oriented transaction with a heavy reliance on hand-eye coordination, details, and a preoccupation with things.

Play Transaction

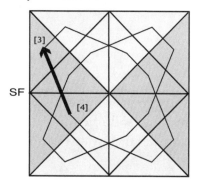

SF

The *Implementor* play transaction is in the SF mode, moves from [4] **control** to [3] **contrast**, and is the DESF Classifier transaction. In their play transaction, *Implementors* can make quick, dichotomous decisions, which they use to support their competence transaction processing.

Toil Transaction

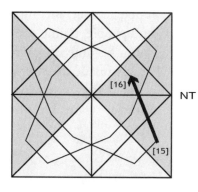

NT

The *Implementor* toil transaction is in the NT mode, moves from [15] **logic** to [16] **structure**, and is the DINT Conceptualizer transaction. In their toil transaction, *Implementors* are capable of learning concepts about the world and things, but they will procrastinate whenever possible.

Implementor *Competence*

Implementors are good at getting things done and generating order. When given an objective and a procedure for attaining it, they aggressively complete the task in an orderly fashion in the shortest possible time. *Implementors* are very impatient and get a lot of satisfaction in seeing immediate results. They can function totally independently of others and can be relied upon to follow through. They prefer to finish one task completely before starting another.

Implementors are down-to-earth and practical, and tend to focus on the things the way they are rather than the way they could be. They like structure and stability, and are uncomfortable with change because change throws everything out of order. They have difficulty in coming up with new approaches and rely on procedures generated by others.

Areas of Play

Implementors like physical activities. They are usually athletic and play sports. They are energetic, fast-moving, and often impatient with people who move more slowly and get in their way. They need to keep busy all the time.

Areas of Difficulty

Implementors judge people in terms of competence and incompetence. As supervisors, they tend to command people, telling them exactly what to do and when to do it. They can become impatient with fellow workers who work more slowly and impede their progress, in which case they prefer "to do it myself." They are reserved with their feelings and often are not perceived as warm by other people.

Communication

Implementors prefer to receive tangible information with practical examples. To them, abstract ideas seem irrelevant and a waste of time. They are fast-talking, concise, and speak without frills, communicating well-ordered data to others.

Understanding and Believing

Implementors understand in terms of how things may be used to generate order and achieve results. To believe new things, they need the "hands-on" experience of physically completing tasks.

Learning

Implementors learn through experiencing success in applying procedures and routines. An apprenticeship situation suits them best.

The NF profiles

The NF matches whole, initial perceptions to whole abstractions, giving the emotional system access to the information being processed and facilitating emotional tagging. NFs work with language and the movement of language from person to person. They are people and metaphor oriented. The basic metaphor structure of the NF is communication.

The four NF profiles are CINF Composer, CENF Perceiver, DINF Clarifier, and DENF Verbalist. The four capacities used in NF are [9] **Combination**, [10] **Harmony**, [11] **Preference**, and [12] **Association**.

Figure 51: The NF profiles

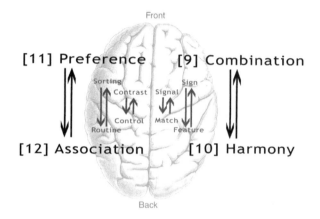

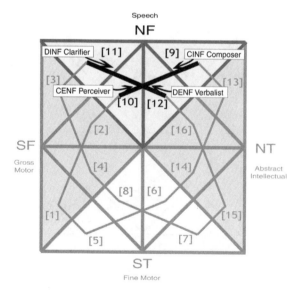

CINF COMPOSER

Figure 52: CINF Composer

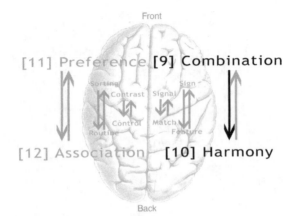

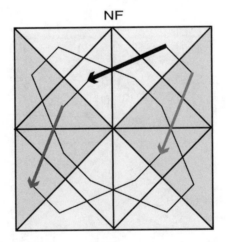

Competence Transaction

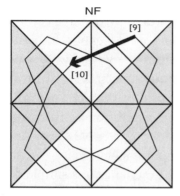

NF

The *Composer* competence transaction moves from **[9] combination** to **[10] harmony.** *Composers* bring harmony to the many and varied combinations of symbols and possibilities available to the NF mode. The *Composer* is the essence of the artist and storyteller, as well as the therapist who helps another find the harmonious path out of a bad situation.

Play Transaction

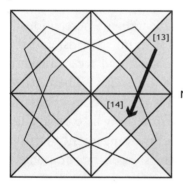

NT

The *Composer* play transaction is in the NT mode, moves from **[13] strategy** to **[14] pattern,** and is the CINT Theoretician transaction. In their play transaction, the *Composer* is capable of creating theories to explain the NT combinations generated by their competence, and they use this ability to support their competence transaction processing.

Toil Transaction

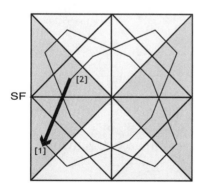

SF

The *Composer* toil transaction is in the SF mode, moves from **[2] match** to **[1] signal,** and is the CESF Initiator transaction. Using their toil transaction, *Composers* often become salespeople who are laid back and thoughtful.

Composer *Competence*

A *Composer* takes possibilities and creates unpredictable combinations that generate beauty, harmony, and good feelings. Experience serves to stimulate beautiful possibilities.

Composers are very concerned about others, and all of their activities are directed to impact the world of people. Their gift to people is beauty. They create aesthetic expression in the form of art, literature, and poetry as well as in more tangible areas such as gourmet cooking and composing computer languages.

Composers try to translate complex experience to a simple dualism of good or bad. They are usually spiritual people fascinated by the possibilities for good or evil. They are very sensitive to cues from their surroundings.

Thinking for a *Composer* is a collection of perceptions and impressions including the memories of sights, sounds, and information. They play with it, move it around, and try to make new combinations. *Composers* see images and patterns. These patterns can be used in two ways, one of which is as identifiers where things are fitted together or taken apart. The other way is to build a larger picture from the components. There is an arrangement to this process, and the arrangement is beyond the sum of the components.

Composer's primary processes require latitude for free expression and spontaneous response; they avoid highly structured situations demanding orderliness and attention to details. *Composers* don't like things that are predictable because predictability limits and eliminates future possibilities.

Areas of Play

Composers enjoy thinking about philosophical and theoretical ideas, which helps them explore life's mysteries. It is this process that gives *Composers* tools to manage abstract intellectual activities.

Areas of Difficulty

It is more difficult for a *Composer* to deal with pragmatic realities like the "here and now." *Composers* procrastinate opportunities. They have lots of ideas but have difficulty implementing them.

Communication

Composers imagine possibilities that are beyond everyday living experiences and interactions. For a *Composer,* precise articulation is difficult since thoughts are holistic and not structured in linear strings of words. Their thoughts are better expressed in metaphoric language in which the style of communication conveys more than the actual content.

Understanding and Believing

A *Composer* understands an experience in terms of the good or bad feelings it generates. This primary feeling sense is then supported by an exploration of the possible theories that might explain the experience. While the *Composer* understands in terms of the feelings that are experienced, she must discover a theoretical basis to support it in order to fully believe it.

Learning

Composers learn best in an environment where elements of the material are presented simultaneously in a context with one another. They are more concerned about the links that bind the material into a single experience and will learn more quickly when possible links are presented along with the material itself. Otherwise, they must either search for a pattern of linkages elsewhere or create ones for themselves. A contextual learning approach is the most advantageous for this kind of person.

CENF Perceiver

Figure 53: CENF Perceiver

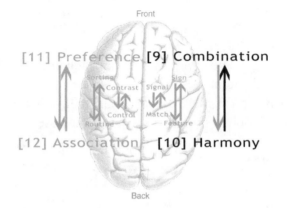

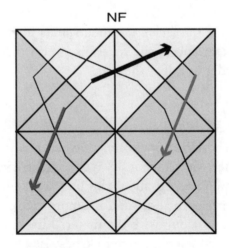

Competence Transaction

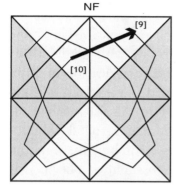

The *Perceiver* competence transaction moves from [10] harmony to [9] combination. *Perceivers* act on the world of people by using their inner sense of harmony and aesthetics to bring together unexpected combinations of people and things. For example, they promote events, the arts, and the like.

Play Transaction

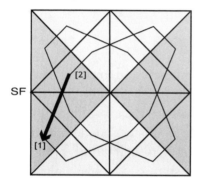

The *Perceiver* play transaction is in the SF mode, moves from [2] match to [1] signal, and is the CESF Initiator transaction. *Perceivers* use their play transaction to convince people. This is effective in the areas of management and sales. They are careful that these efforts are beneficial to everyone involved.

Toil Transaction

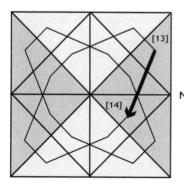

The *Perceiver* toil transaction is in the NT mode, moves from [13] strategy to [14] pattern, and is the CINT Theoretician transaction. In their toil transaction, the *Perceiver* tries to explore the complex relationships resulting from their generation of possibilities in support of their competence.

Perceiver *Competence*

As the name implies, *Perceivers* are very sensitive to the world around them. They have a "feel" for it all and perceive harmony and disharmony in all its elements. In dealing with people, they use this process to sense the feelings of others and develop an empathy with them. They are especially concerned and involved in relationships among the people in their lives. They are also sensitive to the aesthetic harmony of the physical environment around them. Using these perceptions as elements, *Perceivers* combine them in unique and unexpected ways to generate new possibilities. They match up people who have complementary interests, create new and innovative businesses, and produce special events. They are aggressive promoters of things that they feel will be of benefit to people.

Areas of Play

In addition to the facility for generating new and unexpected possibilities, *Perceivers* have a practical side. They are quick to try out new ideas and decide which ones will produce practical results that benefit themselves and others. It is this added capacity that gives them the power to produce changes in their world. They like changes and become easily bored in a status quo. Hence, they are good at starting things, but have difficulty in maintaining a repetitive activity. They usually rely on others for that kind of support. *Perceivers* are physically active and energetic.

Areas of Difficulty

They use abstract theoretical ideas when necessary. Though this is an area of difficulty for the *Perceiver*, when they do dig into the abstract, they are able to take those ideas and humanize them, thus connecting the abstract to the world of people.

Communication

Perceivers are especially attentive to "vibes" in any communication to them. They have less interest in information content that does not have a feeling component since the feelings provide the basis for understanding and remembering the information.

Their communication with others is full of feelings and exciting possibilities. However, *Perceivers* have some difficulty in finding the words to support the thoughts they are trying to communicate. They know what they want to say in their head, but precise articulation does not automatically take place. Under circumstances where good articulation is important, they will tend to speak slowly in order to give themselves the time for the words to come before saying them.

Understanding and Believing

Perceivers develop a memory rich in episodes, both those that have happened and those imagined as might have happened. Each one of these episodes is associated with a feeling that it generated. This feeling is used to identify the experience in memory. When a new experience generates a new feeling the memory is searched for episodes that previously generated similar feelings, and are then matched with the current experience on that basis. If the match is successful, the *Perceiver* understands the new situation on the basis of the past experience. While the past experience may be very different from the current one, the feelings are the same, and that is what makes sense. This is what enables the *Perceiver* to generate unexpected combinations.

After understanding something in this manner, a *Perceiver* usually must try it out to see if it can be applied in a practical way. If new information does not appear to have any practical significance, the *Perceiver* might understand it, but he will not believe in it. To a *Perceiver*, "practical" means that something will work and be of benefit to people.

Learning

Perceivers learn best when the information is presented in a total context that includes the applications for which the information is intended. They prefer that the presentation provide an experience for them, whether it be in words or pictures. Examples help, and a little humor makes the experience more memorable for them. They favor context-based learning.

DINF CLARIFIER

Figure 54: DINF Clarifier

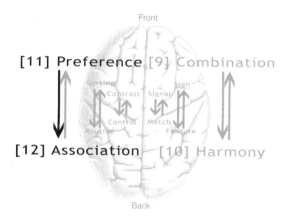

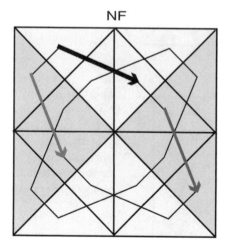

Competence Transaction

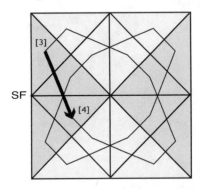

The *Clarifier* competence transaction moves from [11] **preference** to [12] **association**. This transaction extracts the right associations between the abstractions being discussed and the words that symbolize those abstractions. The *Clarifier* transaction involves precise evaluation of procedures for communication.

Play Transaction

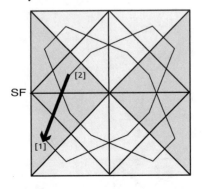

The *Clarifier* play transaction is in the SF mode, moves from [3] **contrast** to [4] **control**, and is the DISF Trustee transaction. In their play transaction, *Clarifiers* perfect and simplify their evaluations.

Toil Transaction

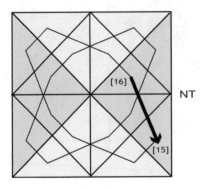

The *Clarifier* toil transaction is in the NT mode, moves from [16] **structure** to [15] **logic**, and is the DENT Analyst transaction. In their toil transaction, when necessary, *Clarifiers* develop intellectual conclusions arising from their competence evaluations.

Clarifier *Competence*

Clarifiers are most concerned with the accuracy of communications in general and in spoken and written language in particular. To *Clarifiers*, words are so powerful that they seem to have a life of their own. Choosing the right words is important to accurately communicating substance and evoking feelings.

To assist in understanding and preparing communications, *Clarifiers* examine experiences on the basis of the feelings that are generated internally. They carefully dissect the experience into components and weigh the goodness or badness of each one, thereby achieving an understanding of the experience in terms of feelings. The result is an aesthetic critique, and *Clarifiers* can be found in action as critics of arts, culture, and literature.

Clarifiers are focused on the world of people, observing their behavior in interactions and providing people with feedback to help them obtain clear understandings. *Clarifiers* are often teachers, specializing in English, other languages, and history. They are nonassertive, good listeners, and tend to involve themselves in activities that they feel can be of benefit to other people.

Areas of Play

Clarifiers strive to do everything as perfectly as possible. They prefer to concentrate on the things they are doing, one at a time, and are disturbed when that process is interrupted.

Areas of Difficulty

Clarifiers have a strong need to know in advance what is coming up in order to be able to prepare for what they need to do. Planning and preparation play a large role. They carefully deliberate and rethink choices. This makes decision-making difficult for them and can result in lost opportunities. When necessary, *Clarifiers* can analyze their evaluations generated from using their competence, and then draw conclusions about what is going on in the process.

Communication

The manner in which *Clarifiers* take in information was discussed
with their primary transactions. They communicate to others in a
careful precise way, assuring that the meanings will be understood
and the feelings experienced accurately. During a conversation,
Clarifiers are often dissatisfied with the words chosen in an expression and will interrupt themselves with the phase "in other words,"
and then restate the meaning using other words. This behavior is
unique to *Clarifiers* and signals their internal process.

In communicating to others, *Clarifiers* tend to present the bad
points and good points of experiences. They usually start with
the bad points. Listeners often misinterpret the communication
as being "picky," negative criticism and respond defensively. This
leads *Clarifiers* to be even more careful in their communications in
order to not disturb the feelings of others.

Understanding and Believing

Clarifiers depend heavily on past experience to understand new
situations. They store information in memory on the basis of how
things are said or done and the feelings these actions evoked. They
extract this kind of information out of new experiences, and understanding involves matching those new feelings with those remembered. A successful match "rings true" and generates the perception
of understanding. Believing it requires the additional step of assessing how other people around them have responded to the same or
similar situations. *Clarifiers* depend heavily on the assessment of
others in whom they have trust.

Learning

Clarifiers depend upon structure and orderliness in the learning
process. Clarity and organization of the lectures and other materials is important to them. They prefer learning one subject at a time.

They tend to evaluate the material presented based upon its impact on helping people. *Clarifiers* rely heavily on note-taking and tend to rewrite their notes over again several times in order to make them perfectly clear.

DENF Verbalist

Figure 55: DENF Verbalist

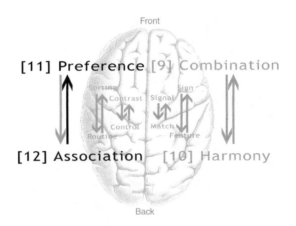

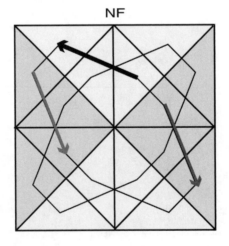

Competence Transaction

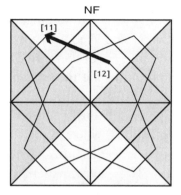

The *Verbalist* competence transaction moves from [12] association to [11] preference. This transaction selects the best words to express meaning, or in short, it articulates. *Verbalists* speak, and they speak well.

Play Transaction

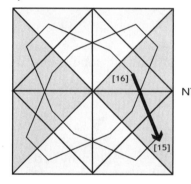

The *Verbalist* play transaction is in the NT mode, moves from [16] structure to [15] logic, and is the DENT Analyst transaction. In their play transaction, *Verbalists* analyze the information that they have articulated and draw logical conclusions.

Toil Transaction

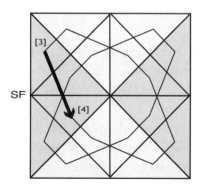

The *Verbalist* toil transaction is in the SF mode, moves from [3] contrast to [4] control, and is the DISF Trustee transaction. In their toil transaction, *Verbalists* perfect and simplify the language chosen for communication and bring into play body gestures for emphasis.

Verbalist *Competence*

Verbalists influence others through convincing communication. They communicate with words, gestures, and personal appearance. They are composed and have a presence about them. In communication, their emphasis is on content and style more than on concepts.

Verbalists are concerned about people, individually and collectively. They like to be active in organizations, where their communication skills enable them to provide leadership. They are strong-willed, organized, and persistent. They are impatient with people who do not express themselves well. *Verbalists* are future-oriented.

Areas of Play

Verbalists enjoy thinking, analyzing, and drawing conclusions that help in the communication process.

Areas of Difficulty

Verbalists take charge of situations, which can seem pushy to others. Also, though *Verbalists* are good leaders, they rely on others for the invention of novel solutions.

Communication

The communication style of *Verbalists* was described as their primary transaction. They communicate to others forcefully and clearly, assuring that they will be understood. Verbal communication is presented in the form of a lecture.

In addition, *Verbalists* have strong emotions that naturally form a part of their communications to others. They must work to suppress this emotional content in circumstances requiring that they appear totally objective.

Understanding and Believing

Verbalists are attracted to new ideas, from which they extract meanings. They put the meanings into words and articulate them. If the articulation feels right, they understand the idea. They then analyze what they have said, drawing a conclusion. If the conclusion makes sense, they believe the idea.

Learning

Verbalists prefer material presented in words, verbally and in writing. They are more receptive if the information is logical and clear. They tend to concentrate on one subject at a time and master it. They do not react well to fragments of information blended into a contextual framework.

The NT profiles

The NT matches abstractions to abstractions and uses logic to build deep hierarchies of information. Like the ST, the matching function of the NT is not available to the emotional system for tagging. NTs work with abstract ideas. The basic metaphor structure of the NT is logic.

The four NT profiles are CINT Theoretician, CENT Strategist, DINT Conceptualizer, and DENT Analyst. The four capacities used in NT are **[13] Strategy**, **[14] Pattern**, **[15] Logic**, and **[16] Structure**.

Figure 56: The NT profiles

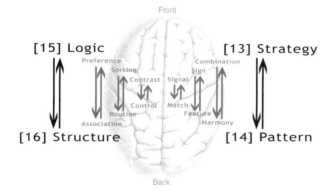

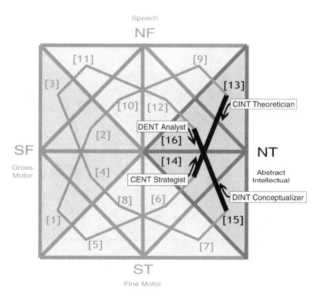

CINT THEORETICIAN

Figure 57: CINT Theoretician

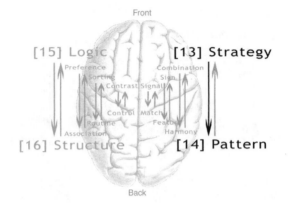

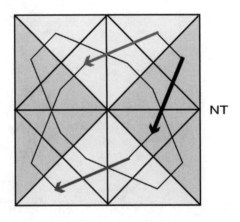

Competence Transaction

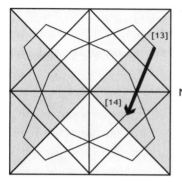

The *Theoretician* competence transaction moves from **[13] strategy** to **[14] pattern**. "To find the pattern by using strategy" means that this transaction searches for regularities that explain a particular set of data. In other words, it means generating a theory that unifies possibilities.

Play Transaction

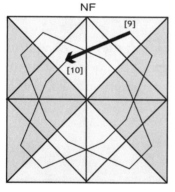

The *Theoretician* play transaction is in the NF mode, moves from **[9] combination** to **[10] harmony**, and is the CINF Composer transaction. In their play transaction, *Theoreticians* use their aesthetic sense to check the "elegance" of a theory.

Toil Transaction

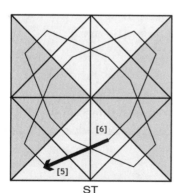

The *Theoretician* toil transaction is in the ST mode, moves from **[6] feature** to **[5] sign**, and is the CEST Operator transaction. In their toil transaction, *Theoreticians* are capable of understanding the features of any routine. This is useful in activities such as performing experiments to support their theories.

Theoretician *Competence*

Theoreticians explore the world of ideas. Their desire to learn new things is their source of energy. They extract from perceptions abstract patterns that they experience as images. As a result of this experience, "ideas seem to just come." These ideas are abstract, future-oriented, theoretical, and combine all related experience to provide a holistic picture of the world. Their process has a passive quality, expressed in the "I look for opportunities that open up rather than pushing open my own doors."

The *Theoretician* primary process requires latitude for free expression and spontaneous response, leading them to avoid highly structured situations. They tend not to like deterministic models that predict limited outcomes because this type of predictability restricts future possibilities.

Once *Theoreticians* come up with ideas, they are done. Implementation and maintenance of the idea is of no interest to them. They would much rather think and come up with another new idea.

Areas of Play

Theoreticians enjoy the world of aesthetics and are interested in music, arts, and literature. They often play musical instruments and frequently attend concerts and performances. Their aesthetic sensibility supports their primary transaction in that they use their feelings to check out the "elegance" of a new theory.

Areas of Difficulty

Theoreticians avoid situations demanding orderliness and attention to details. It is more difficult for a *Theoretician* to deal with pragmatic realities, "the here and now."

Communication

Theoreticians are interested in a wide range of ideas in many fields, and they are not constrained by relevance or application. They envision possibilities that are beyond everyday living experiences and interactions. For a *Theoretician,* precise articulation is difficult since thoughts are holistic and not structured in linear strings of words. Their verbal patterns are characteristically wandering and exploring. *Theoreticians* have an easygoing and nonjudgmental quality about them.

Understanding and Believing

For *Theoreticians* to understand new ideas, they must identify abstract patterns that can be matched to patterns previously remembered. An important attribute of such patterns is their symmetry. Patterns with more symmetry are more easily detected and more significant. If the current pattern can be matched with one in memory, the *Theoretician* understands the new information because "it fits." Believing it requires an additional step in which the pattern is subjected to an aesthetic evaluation that generates a feeling. If the feeling is one of beauty or elegance, the *Theoretician* will believe the pattern or the theory.

Learning

Theoreticians learn best in an environment where the different ideas associated with the subject are presented simultaneously in context with one another. They are concerned with the manner in which the ideas link together into a single pattern and they will learn more quickly when relationships are presented along with the material itself. Otherwise, they must either search for a pattern of linkages elsewhere or create one for themselves. A contextual learning approach is the most advantageous for them.

CENT Strategist

Figure 58: CENT Strategist

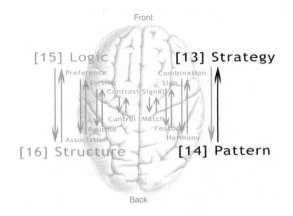

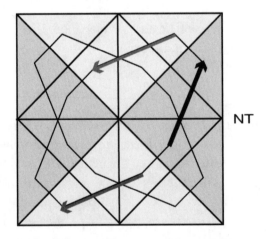

Competence Transaction

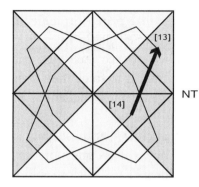

The *Strategist* competence transaction moves from **[14] pattern** to **[13] strategy**. "To strategize the pattern" means to find a strategy that will produce the desired result. This is an investigative transaction that looks for clues that lead to the attainment of goals.

Play Transaction

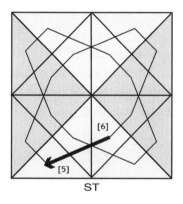

The *Strategist* play transaction is in the ST mode, moves from **[6] feature** to **[5] sign**, and is the CEST Operator transaction. In their play transaction, *Strategists* use hands-on activities to try and test out their schemes.

Toil Transaction

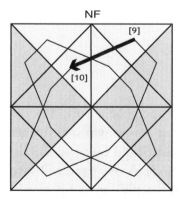

The *Strategist* toil transaction is in the NF mode, moves from **[9] combination** to **[10] harmony**, and is the CINF Composer transaction. In their toil mode, *Strategists* are tentative in social situations.

Strategist *Competence*

Strategists develop flexible, multidimensional plans for achieving long-term goals. They are abstract intellectuals, able to envision possible futures not yet experienced. They can see the entire context of their lives and set goals and benchmarks to track their progress. They are aggressive and full of energy, seeking challenges and striving for control of their future.

   Strategists are very visual. They look at clues, but these clues are only of interest if they form a pattern. They will ask questions such as: "What is the reasoning behind this idea?" and "How should we proceed in light of the patterns noted?"

Areas of Play

Strategists enjoy working with their hands, especially when the things they are working with fit in with their future plans. They use "hands-on" approaches to try different ways of working. They also enjoy other activities using their hands, such as cooking.

Areas of Difficulty

Strategists have difficulty in understanding people's feelings and why people behave the way they do. Since *Strategists* apply their strategizing to their relationships with people, they assume that other people are strategizing, too. This can make *Strategists* suspicious of others.

Communication

Strategists are interested in how things and people work. They enjoy the challenge presented by figuring out how new things operate.

   It is important to a *Strategist* to understand *how* a person thinks and not necessarily *what* a person thinks. A *Strategist* will investigate into another person's thinking by listening to that person's reasoning, by asking how he arrived at a conclusion, and by observing the person as they talk. The *Strategist* pieces together these clues to accomplish the understanding they seek.

In their interactions with others, the *Strategist* is direct and assertive. They formulate abstract intellectual strategies for achieving future goals.

Understanding and Believing

Strategists rely on data containing clues that form patterns. If the pattern can be matched to one that is remembered, the *Strategist* generates a plan. This success leads the *Strategist* to experience a sense of understanding. If elements of the generated plan can be shown to work in the hands of the *Strategist,* the original information can then be believed. In short, for the *Strategist,* believing new information ultimately requires that it can be used to affect the future.

Learning

Strategists learn in order to take actions that are relevant to their future plans. Hence, they like to have information in the same context as the applications and future possibilities. A context-based learning environment is favorable to their learning.

DINT CONCEPTUALIZER

Figure 59: DINT Conceptualizer

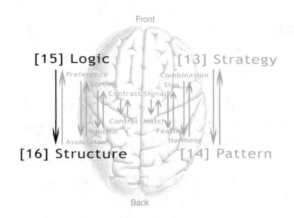

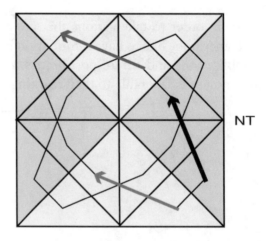

Competence Transaction

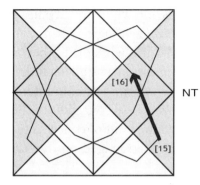

The *Conceptualizer* competence transaction moves from **[15] logic** to **[16] structure**. "To find structure in the logically sorted data" is to perfect, organize, and create abstract intellectual memes or concepts.

Play Transaction

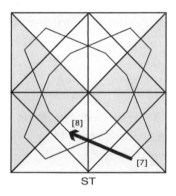

The *Conceptualizer* play transaction is in the ST mode, moves from **[7] sorting** to **[8] routine**, and is the DIST Organizer transaction. In their play transaction, *Conceptualizers* are capable of organizing routines, and do so by using their hand-eye coordination to produce diagrams.

Toil Transaction

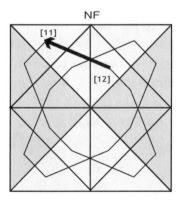

The *Conceptualizer* toil transaction is in the NF mode, moves from **[12] association** to **[11] preference**, and is the DENF Verbalist transaction. In their toil transaction, *Conceptualizers* are capable of being articulate, but will procrastinate and plan as much as possible any speaking they must do.

Conceptualizer *Competence*

Conceptualizers are abstract intellectuals for whom reality lies in their thought processes. To the *Conceptualizer*, logic is truth, and they are driven by a need for logical order in their world. They are always on the lookout for ideas to increase their understanding. Using their process, they translate logical information into internal concepts that explain how the idea works. These concepts are then tested for a "fit" with a remembered structure built of concepts previously generated. The new concepts are then judged on the basis of that fit.

 Conceptualizers tend to be private people, quiet and reflective. At times they struggle to perfect some aspect of the world upon which they focus their attention. They are honest, idealistic, and often dissatisfied with the current state of affairs. They are very visual and concerned with design.

Areas of Play

Conceptualizers enjoy organizing, and using a pencil or pen to do so is so important that it becomes part of their work style. They enjoy other activities involving organizing using their hands.

Areas of Difficulty

Conceptualizers generally have difficulty interacting with people in social relationships. They do not want to meet and talk to people whom they do not know well. They sometimes avoid answering the telephone because they never know who's going to be on the other end. They do not experience feelings in their normal thought processes and do not understand what is going on with people who do. They do not naturally reach conclusions quickly and are irritated by people who do.

Communication

Conceptualizers are on the lookout for abstract logical ideas to test. They translate these ideas into procedural concepts. Being abstract and visual, they prefer information in the form of diagrams depicting conceptual structures. Emotional communication is difficult and tends to erupt with sudden intensity.

Conceptualizers do not like extended verbal communications with people and prefer to communicate in writing. They can lecture if well prepared in advance, but they cannot verbalize well until preparation is complete. They have a faculty for ironic humor, which helps them deal with other people.

Understanding and Believing

The process of understanding for *Conceptualizers* was described in the first paragraph, and is determined by the degree of "fit" into a conceptual structure. However, believing new information requires the additional step of organizing it on paper, often in a complex diagram.

Learning

Conceptualizers process logically sorted information and prefer that lectures and texts be in that format. If not, they attempt to find logical relationships in the material. They have more difficulty with rote memory. They like to concentrate on one thing at a time and understand it in depth. The classical curriculum in which each basic science is taught separately best fits their learning style.

DENT ANALYST

Figure 60: DENT Analyst

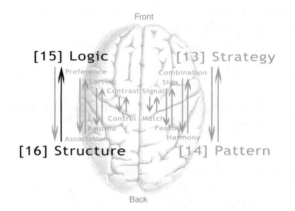

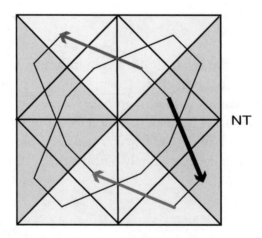

Competence Transaction

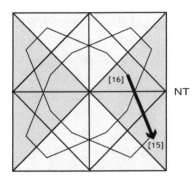

The *Analyst* competence transaction moves from [16] **structure** to [15] **logic**. "To logically sort structures" means to be able to analyze by applying logic to a structured set of data. One example of where this skill applies is in making medical diagnoses.

Play Transaction

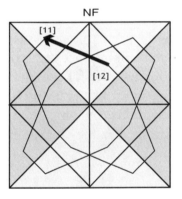

The *Analyst* play transaction is in the NF mode, moves from [12] **association** to [11] **preference**, and is the DENF Verbalist transaction. In their play transaction, *Analysts* will talk through their work and use this to support their competence transaction processing.

Toil Transaction

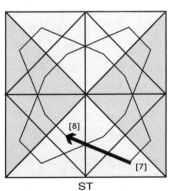

The *Analyst* toil transaction is in the ST mode, moves from [7] **sorting** to [8] **routine**, and is the DIST Organizer transaction. In their toil transaction, *Analysts* are capable of organizing routines, but will procrastinate doing so.

Analyst *Competence*

Analysts generate unique solutions to difficult problems. They are especially attracted to problems that have defied previous attempts at solutions by others. Rather than using conventional approaches involving the gathering of additional data to add to the work of finding the solution, *Analysts* tend to restructure the problem in terms of its abstract basic principles, free of any context. They then reframe the problem into a new context that yields a solution more easily. Essentially, they look at the problem from a new angle.

This process can happen quickly and does not usually require much additional data. If the problem can be clearly defined, a solution is usually immediately forthcoming in the form of a logical conclusion. *Analysts* are compelled to implement their solution to the problem. They have little interest in maintaining routine procedures after their first implementation.

It is very important to the *Analyst* to be right, since being right provides the primary internal reward for a successful completion. When an *Analyst* learns a new discipline or attacks a new problem area, she is inclined to learn it in depth and become highly proficient. *Analysts* usually have many interests, but they pursue each one in a single-minded "intense" manner.

Areas of Play

Analysts like to translate complex concepts into simple language and present it in an articulate manner. They tend to adopt a lecturing style of communication and present their material clearly, logically, and conclusively. They enjoy people, are outgoing, and like to share ideas and become exposed to new possibilities.

Areas of Difficulty

Because the *Analyst* thinking process results in rapid conclusions, they occasionally produce incorrect results due to insufficient collection of data. The communication process also generates some difficulties. Because the conclusions presented are not usually derived from conventional techniques of collecting and analyzing data, they sometimes do not seem credible to research-oriented listeners. The strong verbal conclusive style of presentation often appears arrogant to the listener.

Communication

Analysts are continually scanning for new possibilities from which they can generate basic principles and concepts to add to their repertoire. Their memory structure is a hierarchy of such operations. In this hierarchy, the linkages enable the development of abstract principles that unite the principles into a complex structure. When an *Analyst* is stuck on a problem, she will welcome possibilities from others. They use these possibilities to generate new contexts to examine.

Analysts communicate to others with logical, abstract conclusions. When the communication is in writing, it is usually succinct and objective. When the communication is verbal, it is usually in the form of a lecture with strong emphasis to convince others.

Understanding and Believing

Analysts are most interested in inputs containing new ideas and possibilities. From these, they extract operating principles that they translate into concepts and then store in long-term memory. When confronted with a new idea, *Analysts* will derive a concept and attempt to match it with concepts previously remembered. If a match of concepts can be obtained, they will understand the new idea.

Analysts translate the concept into words and articulate it verbally. They listen to themselves and get a feeling about what has been said. If the feeling is positive, they will believe the new idea.

Learning

Since *Analysts* remember in terms of operating principles, they are more interested in how things work than in what things are or what they do. The more basic principles taught in a curriculum, the more readily *Analysts* will learn. If the curriculum is more context-based, then the material cannot be readily processed and the *Analyst* must first work to extract from the material any unifying principles she can detect. *Analysts* prefer educational curricula that initially delve deeply into basic principles, followed by examining practical applications to help provide them with useful tools.

10

THE PROFILES: COMMUNICATION

Overview

Communication is the transfer of memes between individuals. Communication takes place in three stages: *awareness, understanding,* and *belief.* "Awareness" is the fit of the new information into the "subject" capacity of the individual's competence transaction, and is moderated by the Self. "Understanding" is the work of the competence transaction to process the new information. "Belief" is the authorization of the new meme via a reason that connects it to the emotional system.

COMMUNICATION

One of the essential functions of a replicator is transmission. With humans, memes transfer via three steps: awareness, understanding, and belief. These three steps manifest as the three stages of *communication:* getting the attention of and alerting an individual that a new meme is coming his way; the presentation of the new content; and the supporting argument.

In the previous chapter, each cognitive processing profile included paragraphs on these three steps. "Communication" covers the awareness as well as how the profile "shapes," transmits, and receives memes. "Understanding" covers how each profile understands and fits new memes into the memory databases. "Believing" covers how each profile makes memes "stick," or how individuals with that profile complete the process of communication and memetic transferal.

Anyone who has ever written a term paper is intimately familiar with the three steps of communication—the introduction, the thesis, and the supporting evidence. The support—the *reasons* why a thought is valid—takes up the vast majority of the words generated in any presentation.

Reasons are memes used by a memetic organism to authorize and justify behavior. They are hierarchically organized in modern groups and combine together to make the social "language" of a culture. The rule-set of reasons within a memetic organism are what hold it together and give its members a common base for authorizing how to act.

Reasons give support for behaviors. Where "queuing in line" is a behavior, the reasons *why* we do it—social order; politeness, and so on, are the motivators for that behavior. These reasons are abstractions made from the social interactions an individual has experienced in the past, and they guide the person in how to behave in future situations.

Tying a communication to the reason rule-set of a memetic organism ties it to all of the accepted behaviors of that group via the hierarchical organization of abstractions. It also ties the new meme to the hierarchical prioritizing system within the Self and allows the individual to place the communication in reference to other social interaction. The ties that bind in the new meme to the memetic infrastructure of the individual and the culture must be strongly set or the person will discount the meme.

Advertising, too, brings each of the three steps into consciousness of every person in modern culture as well—ads shout "Hey you!"; present their pitch; and then back it with a myriad of reasons for why you should buy the product. Reasons also form the majority of the overall content as the ad tries to tie the product into an individual's accepted beliefs and behaviors.

In order to bring about acceptance to tie the new meme into all that is believed by the individual, the three steps engage consciousness. Each step uses consciousness differently: *Awareness* requires that the new meme "fit" the input capacity of the individual's competence transaction. Awareness also involves the getting and holding of attention, which is refreshed constantly. *Understanding* requires processing by the competence transaction and builds as reasons are processed, adding links and matches to past episodes and abstractions for the individual. *Belief* requires the addition of a positive emotional tag associated with the meme. These tags are the "good feelings" we get from correct social behavior, and the "bad feelings" we get when we violate a social norm, such as cutting in line. Once tagged, the new meme can be acted upon.

Awareness

At its basic, genetic level, awareness starts when an animal's attention is placed on the contextual trigger that has the most potential to affect the animal's needs, that is, the predator hiding in the grass or the mouse running in front of the cat. Once attention is caught, the animal tracks the trigger from one perceptual episode to the next.

For humans, the contextual trigger that carries our attention from one episode to the next can be anything from the movement of a ball in a game to the flow of math in particle physics. Also, a person has supporting factors that influence what gets her attention at any given moment. These can include a need to conform to verbal "pay attention!" commands from teachers and parents, or heightened sensitivity to environmental movement and noise.

But these supporting factors can only increase or decrease the range of triggers being attended to during a given moment. What gets into the person's consciousness, though, lies at the center of attention. Consciousness, which is built on the structure of the person's cognitive processing profile, picks up inputs at that person's starting capacity for her competence transaction.

Each profile carries a distinctive input capacity. There are four types of *inputs* that enter into the HDM map, each at a corner. They are "feelings," "links," "order," and "actions." These four inputs feed the capacities that cluster around them (Figure 61).

On the HDM map, the inputs are descriptive of which dichotomy is dominant in a particular profile's cognitive processing modes. For example, the CINT Theoretician competence transaction is in NT and the play transaction is in NF. Both transactions start from the same input, which is "N" in both, and the "N" dominant input is "links." For profiles with "T" dominance have competence and play transactions that share the Thinking way of matching, the input is "order." For profiles that share a competence and play in "F," the input is "feelings." "Actions" is the input for "S" dominant profiles.

Figure 61: Inputs and capacities around them

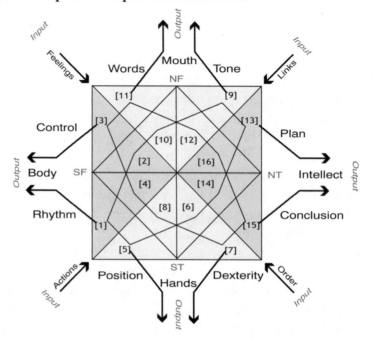

If the input "fits" the shape of the capacity, then it is easier for that individual to pay attention to the information. For example, a CENT Strategist's input is in the bottom right corner of the model and is "order." Strategists look for order—they search for clues that reveal the pattern within the context. This is the essence of the [14] **pattern** capacity when used as the input—attending to clues.

The "order" input is opposite the "feelings" input, which is in the upper left corner of the model. The opposite side of the model from the competence transaction is unconscious and does not come into consciousness at all. For the Strategist and the other three cognitive processing profiles that use "order" as their input, feelings are as far from fitting into their input capacity as an input can get. A Strategist is, in effect, clueless about other's feelings.

This means that for Strategists, feeling-laden inputs such as subtle body language, shifts in vocal modulation, and the like, are lost to them. Even when labeled and presented as descriptions of states, feeling-laden information doesn't "fit," and doesn't stick with the Strategist. No matter how hard the Strategist may try to focus attention, feelings do not fit their conscious input capacity, and slip away.

On the other hand, "order" inputs do fit. A Strategist will notice and hold in attention clues that, when put together, form a pattern. Forensic detective work is an excellent example of a Strategist putting together clues—details, no matter how small, are attended to and placed together as part of the puzzle. All inputs are data points and are either physical like fingerprints left at a scene, or logical, like the modeling done to determine the trajectory of a bullet. All of these inputs are cold, hard evidence devoid of feelings.

Attention, too, can be signaled in other ways. A captive audience such as a classroom of students may have no choice but to attend to the information presented. This does not mean that all of the kids want to do so, or that they would have done so on their own. The kids involved in such situations may actually be attending to the social need to pay attention. Using this social need to focus, the students are picking out the bits and pieces that fit their input capacity so that they can learn and fulfill their social need. Unfortunately, if the information presented only partially matches their input capacity—or doesn't match at all—attention will be spotty and learning will be difficult.

Noncaptive audiences, such as those watching television or walking by a billboard, need more assertive alert signals than those provided by a teacher. Advertising relies on several genetic, deep-seated attention grabbers that are hardwired into humans as instincts that we cannot ignore, no matter how hard we try. Loud, sudden noises grab attention, which is why television advertisements tend to start with a "bang." Yellow and black together signal danger in nature (a black panther with yellow eyes, stinging insects) and grab attention, which is why these two colors are used in combination in road signs and in print ads. Red is a physiologically stimulating color, which is why cars in commercials tend to be red. Sex gets attention, too, and when used as a reason illustrated in a thirty-second narrative for a product, holds attention long enough for the new meme to enter into consciousness.

Attention, once grabbed, is the first part of awareness. Awareness is the production of a "subject" by the starting capacity of the competence transaction. Once in consciousness, the information is labeled in the intuitive model and becomes the "subject" in the person's competence transaction.

In consciousness, the manifestation of the intuitive model language may not be a stream of words. For a contextual C, it will manifest as generalizations generated in the Right Perceptual Cortex. These generalizations can be images, movements, hand-eye coordination, or feelings. Not all deterministic D profiles "think" in words, either. A sensing S individual will be more conscious of the movements generated by the language than the language itself.

Understanding

Once awareness occurs, the individual's consciousness performs his competence transaction on the information. In this process, the meme's specific content is processed by the competence. In doing this, the "verb" capacity performs its function on the information.

For example, a CEST Operator processes by moving from capacity [6] **feature** to capacity [5] **sign**. The Operator manipulates things in the world via his ability to make actions based on the features of the environment. In doing so, the Operator must literally process all new information by manipulating it with his hands, thus the miming of actions. The manipulation is the action of "signing" and manifests as miming, which is a very important part of Operator communication. Miming allows the individual to connect the new information to known procedures for operating other tools or devices.

"Understanding" is the cognitive processing we have described throughout this book. Understanding is a two-pronged event—on one side, it is the matching process of human cognition as it ties new information into the database of that individual's life. Second, this matching generates the flip side of understanding—the language the brain uses to do the matching. This language is the individual's internal metaphor structure. In the case of the Operator, miming is his expression of the ST fine-motor way of generating metaphor.

Also, the person who originally generated the meme engaged his competence transaction when creating the communication. In doing so, he created a metaphor to carry the meme, and this metaphor reflects the creator's competence transaction. If the generator's profile is significantly different from that of the receiver, then the metaphor that enters the receiver won't match and subsequently won't make it into consciousness.

For example, the Operator is watching a special program about the emotional heartbreak of the students in a school who are having one of their favorite programs cut. No information about *how* the program is being cut is presented, nor is there information that *shows* the kids engaging in the activity. The producers of the story, whose inputs are at "feeling," generate metaphors driven by emotions. To the Operator, the story is nothing more than a bunch of weepy-eyed kids. It is, in effect, *unintelligible*.

In another example, to the Strategist, the story is also unintelligible even though clues are presented. The clues, though, aren't clues that can be woven together with the Strategist's metaphor.

On the other hand, if the story had been presented with images of the student's engaging in their activity and information pertaining to how that activity would be affected, then the Operator would have had a metaphor onto which to grab. The metaphor could then be related to the Operator's past experience. If a match is made, then the new information is intelligible, and understanding occurs.

For the Strategist, if the larger context were described, then usable clues would have been available, and the Strategist could build a pattern by linking clue to clue in the complex, hierarchical structure of the NT metaphor.

For a viewer whose input is at "feeling," though, the story makes perfect sense. A CENF Perceiver will understand immediately the injustice of the situation and may very well use his competence to create a harmonious solution that would benefit both the kids and the school.

Belief

If a meme is to be believed, it must be connected to the accepted memes within the individual's Self. A modern Self will include the memes of several memetic organisms. These memes are prioritized by the person's social allegiances and usually will not interfere with each other. For example, the high laws of the person's civic memetic organism ("I am an American so I do not steal") do not conflict with the moral laws of the person's religion ("I follow the Ten Commandments").

In order for these memes to carry weight, they must be tied to the emotional system. This "secondary" emotional system is the brain's way of making needs out of cultural rules and helps humans organize as memetic organisms. It is a newer, frontal lobe adaptation that taps into the much older emotional system.

This "tapping," like everything else the brain does, can be turned into an abstraction. Positive secondary emotional system tags—tags that reinforce a behavior—are the basis of the **true** abstraction. Negative tags—tags that discourage a behavior by reinforcing a bad emotional response—are the basis of the **false** abstraction.

True and **false** are not intrinsically necessary for belief. They are essentially bits of logic overlaid upon the emotional system to allow the "language" of logic access to emotional tagging. They are the abstractions under which reasons sit, forming hierarchies of what is **true** and "right," and what is **false** and "wrong." Without logic, belief comes with good tags; with logic, belief comes with **true** reasons.

A reason is tagged as **true** and connected into the secondary emotional system where it becomes one of the memes that make up the Self. This does not necessarily mean that it will be acted upon—a meme tagged **true** within the domain of one memetic organism may still be secondary to memes tagged **true** within a memetic organism that the individual holds in higher priority.

In order for the meme to become incorporated, it must have a reason that facilitates secondary emotional system tagging. If the reason comes from an accepted authority (someone from a memetic organism high in the Self priority and who always carries a **true** tag) then it is tagged **true** all of the time. For example, with children, this type of tagging happens with teachers and parents.

Secondary emotional system tagging occurs through matching with remembered memes that have been tagged **true**. For example, for an NT, if the new meme fits with the other memes of science, then it is conditionally tagged **true**. Because of the rigors of the scientific method, a **true** tag is usually reserved only for theories that have accumulated a great deal of experimental support. The more support, the closer to completely **true** the new meme becomes. Soon, it becomes a law. Evolution, relativity, and the laws of thermodynamics are excellent examples of hierarchical memetic structures that have passed through scientific scrutiny and now carry high-level, authoritative **true** tags.

Sometimes, though, the reason must influence without the support of an authoritative voice. An example of this type of influential reason is advertising that does not quote "authorities." Companies who compete for consumer dollars accompany their products with a whole host of reasons—we build better cars, we'll make you sexy, and so on.

Modifying memes in competence

Also, new memes are modified when processed by the competence transaction. The modification could be very slight, or it could be a major adjustment, depending on the information's fit with the input capacity.

For example, we will return for a moment to the Strategist who looks for clues but is clueless about feelings. To deal with this problem, a motivated Strategist can build a conscious work-around to get as close as possible to the unconscious "feeling" inputs. In doing so, the Strategist looks for and attends to clues that fit his inputs and also point to the feeling states of other individuals. The feelings of others then become useful "data." This will not make the Strategist more emotive, but will allow him to communicate better with others whose inputs are "feelings."

For the Strategist, understanding of feelings takes place because the original metaphor—the feelings of others—is modified so that it fits the Strategist's input capacity. In this case, the modification is vastly different than the original metaphor.

If information needs a large amount of adjusting to fit the input capacity, it is more open to being revised in such a way as to make it fit better with existing **true** memes, making matching to and tagging as **true** easier for the individual. In the case of the Strategist, these newly translated memes fit the NT database where they are filed as environmental clues into the complex hierarchical linkages of logic. They are no longer "feelings" as such, but have been adjusted to include abstractions that the Strategist can use to match to existing **true** memes. Without the adjustments, the memes were not in an accessible form.

Awareness, understanding, and belief are summed up in the following table:

Table 8: Awareness, understanding, and belief

	Definition	Support	How?
Awareness	Alerted to a new meme in consciousness.	Attention	Instinctive or secondary emotional system attention grabbers
Understanding	Transfer of specific content.	Metaphor	Via metaphor as created by the competence transaction
Belief	A meme worthy of action.	Reasons	Using reasons to create **true** tags

Awareness, understanding, and belief appear under other labels in many different models. Schoolchildren are taught how to structure reports and papers around the introduction, thesis, and supporting argument. Advertising and graphic design focus on grabbing attention, moving content, and fixing the desire, all in one push. Human resource managers work diligently to open channels of communication, exchange ideas, and support those ideas with approval from the management.

The following table holds some examples of awareness, understanding, and belief as they appear in daily communication.

Table 9: Examples of awareness, understanding, and belief

	Example 1	Example 2	Example 3	Example 4
Awareness	Title and cover design of a nonfiction book.	"Teaser" scene before the credits of a TV program.	Manager says that the company is not working at its full potential.	Teacher says, "These ten items on why you shouldn't smoke will be on the test."
Understand-ing	Comprehending the information presented.	Theme as carried by the program's content.	Work group designs a method to increase productivity.	Student learns the items taught.
Belief	Adding the theories presented to your model of how the world works because of a) the book's authoritative voice, or b) clear and well-reasoned presentation.	Making changes in your life to mirror the theme based on examples in the program, i.e., "It worked for the guest."	The method is approved by management and implemented by staff.	Student is able to connect the reasons given to his "database" and never touches a cigarette in his life.

Just "because"

When a new meme is tied to a reason through grammar by words such as "because," it appends the meme and the episode built from it. The reason becomes part of the new meme through abstractions and generalizations, and everything attached to that reason also becomes part of the new meme as well.

Reasons, like any other input, must fit the input "subject" capacity. Emotional reasons do nothing for people with "order" inputs, and orderly reasons do nothing for people with "feeling" inputs.

This is one reason why a well-framed argument will contain multiple reasons—the more varied the reason-set, the more likely one will stick with the listener. When reasons stick, they add an emotional tag to that meme.

Reasons are the most prevalent type of behavior control meme in modern culture. They are many, varied, and omnipresent. They are the cultural rule-sets of our memetic organisms, and they allow, via language, the transmission of secondary emotional system information. Reasons are the supporting argument for all new memetic information, and without a good reason, a new meme may be added to the accumulating pile of human musings, but it will not be acted upon in science or society.

Memetic organisms and communication

Belief facilitates the growth of influence of a memetic organism. When an individual accepts an outside reason, then the new memetic organism gets a foothold in new territory. Religions practice this all the time when they convert nonbelievers.

Within memetic organisms, communication moves memes between member A and member B. The reason-set is ubiquitous within the memetic organism—everyone knows and lives by the same set of rules. As modern humans, we move in and out of different memetic organisms as we move through our days. For example, when at work, we follow the rules of work. When at home, we follow the rules of home, and so on. In order for a meme to move within a memetic organism, it must be supported by at least one of the ubiquitous reasons of the memetic organism. If it is not, it is rejected.

When member A tells member B a new idea, member B is alerted to the new meme and attends to it, bringing it into awareness. Then member B processes it with her competence transaction, understanding it. Member A then offers a reason for why this new idea is good, and if that reason is supported by members B's knowledge of the memetic organism's reasons, then member B will accept the new meme.

At this point, member B may continue to process the new meme with her competence and other transactions, adding to, trying out, editing, or implementing it depending on her cognitive processing profile. The meme expands and becomes more complete before B shares it with member C. In this way the meme flows through the memetic organism, growing and expanding, becoming more refined and usable as it goes.

This process will stop if the meme runs into a reason that cuts off its access to a **true** emotional tag. The boss may say "I don't like this," thus removing authoritative support. Or, the meme may run up against compliance laws of a bigger, stronger memetic organism, like the government. Or, it may mutate into something that falls outside of the company's mission statement.

But, if the meme holds its good reasons and continues to grow and expand, as it moves from members A to B to C to D, it takes those reasons with it. Every time the reasons land in the consciousness of the next person, they are processed, reinforcing and refreshing their use within that individual and within the memetic organism.

Such reinforcing and refreshing is what keeps the reasons ubiquitous. Everyone in the memetic organism knows the reasons because they are constantly used, reused, and emblazoned on the memory of every individual. In this way, they help strengthen the bonds between the individuals by adding to the coherence of the memetic organism.

In the next chapter, as we look at the different communication styles of the different cognitive processing profiles, we will follow a meme as it flows through the inputs and outputs around the different cognitive processing profiles of an organization's members.

Belief systems

Each individual's Self is built from memes he has tagged **true**. Without a **true** validation, a meme is just a story that lacks the emotional backup and motivation from the secondary emotional system.

Without that emotional connection, the meme can never be harnessed as a need and can never motivate the individual to act.

An individual may know and understand a huge number of memes but may believe only a few of them. This system of beliefs may be constrained to the teachings of a single memetic organism, leading the person to function in a manner that mimics consciousness without a Self. The teachings of the dominant memetic organism become the first priority in as many situations as that organism can control behavior, that is, at work, at home, shopping, and so on. Phases such as "What would Jesus do?" facilitate single social-organism domination by pulling the rules of that organism into consciousness in situations that would normally not be matched to religious episodes.

For individuals whose beliefs are tightly constrained, the dominant memetic organism's rank as first priority takes up considerable space within the Self. At times when the individual finds himself in situations not covered by the dominant memetic organism, for example, when driving in traffic or choosing breakfast cereals, the individual will use other memes from other memetic organisms as prioritized within the Self. But these memes are always of lower priority and may be replaced if the dominant memetic organism takes an interest in such situations. Some examples of memetic organisms that can inspire such adhesion are religions, corporations, or, at the most extreme and harmful level, cults.

In cases where the individual is functioning essentially without a Self, his belief system is closed. *Closed belief systems* have a very limited number of **true** abstractions allowing new matches into the believed section of the memory database. Basically, a new meme must come from an approved authority or it is **false**, and the approved authorities are severely restricted by the memetic organism to which the individual adheres.

But closed belief systems are not limited to those lacking a Self. Highly rational NTs who are very conscious of the prioritizing work of the Self can mark an entire field of study as **false** without a second thought. This can happen because of a bad experience, exposure to bad data, or exposure to a faulty execution of the scientific method, all of which remove the credibility of the source.

False designations can also happen because new data, no matter how good it is, does not fit with already held beliefs. When an individual has placed years and years of his life into a career researching one particular phenomenon, and new data appears that the individual believes contradicts that work, it can throw that individual's entire Self into disarray, causing psychological pain. In such cases, a **false** designation is a survival response.

Opposite a closed belief system is an *open belief system*. In this kind of system, the individual has many **true** abstractions. An individual with an open belief system is constantly changing and accommodating new ideas.

It is possible to have a belief system that is too open. Without some controls, everything will be **true**, and the individual will be paralyzed by the guilt generated by having too many competing **true** memes from too many memetic organisms. People who accommodate too much can find themselves spending their lives pulled in too many directions, never saying no, and losing their Selves in a sea of contradictions.

Each of the cognitive processing profiles in the previous chapter contains paragraphs looking at that profile's style of awareness, understanding, and belief. In the following chapter we will put a "face" on much of what we have talked about and follow a meme through the many and varied communications styles in a fictional organization.

Summary

- *Awareness, understanding,* and *belief* are the three steps manifest as the three stages of *communication:* getting the attention of and alerting an individual that a new meme is coming her way; the presentation of the new content; and the supporting argument.

- *Awareness* requires that the new meme "fit" the input capacity of the individual's competence transaction. Awareness also involves the getting and holding of attention, which is refreshed constantly.

- *Understanding* requires processing by the competence transaction and builds as reasons are processed, adding links and matches to past episodes and abstractions for the individual.

- *Belief* requires the addition of a secondary emotional system tag of **true**. Once **true**, the new meme can be acted upon.

- Consciousness, which is built on the structure of the person's cognitive processing profile, picks up inputs at that person's starting capacity for her competence transaction.

- Each profile carries a distinctive input capacity. It is here, at this capacity, that information is grabbed and placed in consciousness.

- If the information "fits" the shape of the capacity, then it is easier for that individual to pay attention to the information.

- Attention, once grabbed, is the first part of awareness. Awareness is labeling a "subject" and making that information available to be acted upon by the action capacity of the competence transaction.

- Once awareness occurs, the individual's consciousness performs her competence transaction on the information.

- This is the matching process of human cognitive processing as it ties new information into the "database" of that individual's life.

- This process also generates the language the brain uses to do the matching. This language is the individual's internal metaphor structure.

- If an incoming metaphor does not match the internal metaphor of the receiver, then the information will be *unintelligible*.

- If a meme is to be believed, it is tagged as **true** and connected into the secondary emotional system where it becomes one of the memes that make up the Self.

- Reasons are the supporting argument for all new memetic information. Without a good reason, a new meme may be added to the accumulating human musings, but it will not be acted upon in science or society.
- Belief facilitates the growth of influence of a memetic organism.
- The reinforcing and refreshing of reason is what keeps the reasons ubiquitous within a memetic organism.
- An individual may know and understand a huge number of memes, but may believe only a few of them.
- *Closed belief systems* have a very limited number of **true** abstractions.
- In an *open belief system*, the individual has many **true** abstractions. An individual with an open belief system is constantly changing and accommodating new ideas.

11

PROFILES: INPUTS AND OUTPUTS

Overview

Each cognitive processing profile has one *input* and two or three *outputs*. An input is delineated by which dichotomy is dominant in the cognitive processing profile's mode. For example, if the competence transaction is NT and the play transaction is NF, then N is dominant and the input is "links." If the competence transaction is externalizing and has a "verb" capacity in an action-taking area of the brain, then the competence output is externalized and affects the world. The play will also be externalized. If the competence transaction is internalized, then so is play, and the individual will produce world-modeling output that he will use to further enrich his model. Therefore, cognitive processing profiles that are externalizing *do,* and profiles that are internalizing *consider.*

The differences in inputs and outputs can cause problems when two people attempt to communicate with each other. The first person's outputs must match the second person's inputs, or the second person's consciousness will not be able to latch onto the new information.

INPUTS AND OUTPUTS

Where the "subject" capacity takes in the input, the "verb" capacity produces the output for a transaction, generating new memes in consciousness. Input and output cycle through all of a person's transactions, including the conscious transactions of competence, play, and toil as well as the remaining unconscious transactions. In this cycle, the "verb" capacity of one transaction feeds the "subject" capacity of another.

Output generated by action-taking "verb" capacities affect the world outside the individual and are externalizing; output generated by world-modeling "verb" capacities affect that individual's model of the world and are internalizing. Profiles with competence transactions that enrich their world-model can still share their output with others via communication, but this sharing is tentative and can be difficult for the person to do.

And sharing, too, is also affected by how one person's outputs mesh with another person's inputs. Like the flow of information between the transactions in a person's cognition, the flow from person to person must also follow a path. Capacities do their work on particular types of information, and they cannot produce "pictures" of information if that information doesn't fit. This makes communication between people of different cognitive processing profiles difficult.

The "verb" capacity formats information so that it can be stored easily in the memory database of its transaction. For example, an NT competence transaction will produce NT-type information. When the NT communicates the thoughts she has produced, those thoughts will come out in NT language, shaped by logic and in complicated hierarchical structures. Other NTs will have less of a problem with this information as an input than an SF will, because it is formatted in a way that matches the NT memory database. An SF, on the other hand, will have difficulty matching abstract NT information to the one-to-one, here-and-now SF memory database.

For the first part of the remainder of this chapter, we will look at how the inputs and outputs map onto the HDM. Every profile has a distinct output pattern but shares a competence input with three other profiles. For the second part of the chapter, we will put this information into play and look at anecdotal descriptions of the HDM in action as people try to communicate with each other.

Inputs

The "subject" capacity is where input enters a transaction. On the model, the four capacities that cluster around each corner use the same type of input information. For example, we discussed two of the four input areas, "order" and "feelings," in the previous chapter.

The two inputs we looked at previously, "feeling" and "order," exist on opposite sides of the model from one another. They represent the F/T dichotomy shown on Figure 62.

The "feeling" input is situated on the corner of the model where the Feeling modes intersect. It represents information that fits the capacities that use F emotional awareness for matching and processing. It feeds both the SF and NF modes and services capacities [2] match, [3] contrast, [10] harmony, and [11] preference. It is the input for the CENF Perceiver, DINF Clarifier, DISF Trustee, and CESF Initiator.

The "order" input is situated in the corner of the model where the Thinking modes intersect. It represents information that fits the capacities that use T ordered awareness for matching and processing. It feeds both the ST and NT modes, and services capacities [6] feature, [7] sorting, [14] pattern, and [15] logic. It is the input for the CEST Operator, DIST Organizer, CENT Strategist, and the DINT Conceptualizer.

Figure 62: The Feeling/Thinking dichotomy

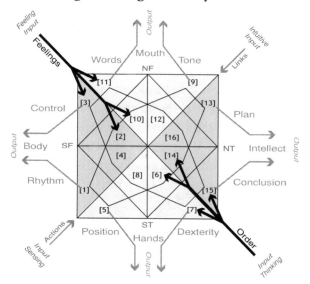

The other two inputs reflect the S/N dichotomy:

Figure 63: The Sensing/iNtuitive dichotomy

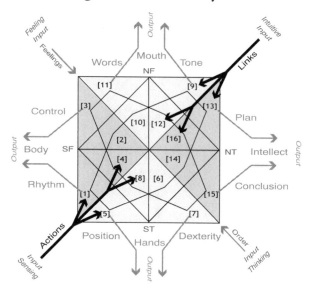

The "action" input is situated in the corner where the Sensing modes intersect. It represents information that fits the capacities that use S physical action awareness for matching and processing. It feeds both the SF and ST modes, and services capacities [1] **signal**, [4] **control**, [5] **sign**, and [8] **routine**. It is the input for the CISF Doer, DESF Classifier, CIST Explorer, and DEST Implementor.

The "links" input is situated in the corner where the iNtuitive modes intersect. It represents information that fits the capacities that use N awareness of abstractions for matching and processing. It feeds both the NF and NT modes, and services capacities [9] **combination**, [12] **association**, [13] **strategy**, and [16] **structure**. It is the input for the CINT Theoretician, CINF Composer, DENT Analyst, and DENF Verbalist.

Outputs

Outputs vary from profile to profile, but match to the mode from which they emerge:

Figure 64: Outputs match the mode from which they emerge

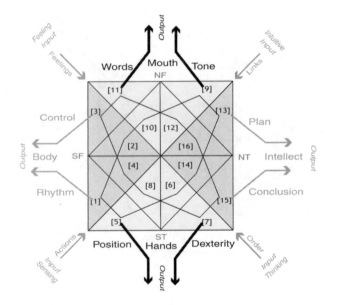

In the NF mode, output consists of words, tone, subtle body language, images, and the like. The NF mode produces outputs that facilitate the transfer of memes, that is, classic literary metaphor, acting, music, and any of the arts; other forms of control meme transfer such as religious outreach, producing harmonious workings within a memetic organism, or mental health work.

In the ST mode, output consists of physical manifestations of hand-eye coordination; for example, the crafts and trades dealing with building or tool design and construction; and the physical manifestations of string meme procedures such as computer coding, office management, scheduling, and surgery.

Figure 65: Output in the ST mode

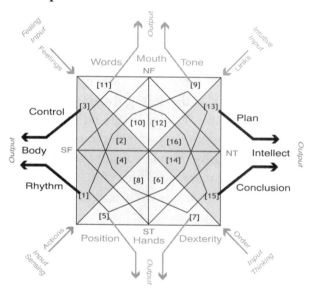

In the SF mode, output consists of the physical manifestations of body movements, for example, athletics, the controlled and exact movements needed to nurse and the reflexes needed to fly fighter jets, and the quick contextual responses needed to close a sales deal.

In the NT mode, output consists of complex, hierarchical, and abstract intellectual constructs, that is, plans, conclusions, theories, and concepts, such as academics, corporate mission statements, mathematical models, and the like.

Externalizing and Internalizing outputs

The route of an output is determined by whether the competence transaction is externalizing or internalizing. Externalizing transactions end in a "verb" capacity that produces output from the action-planning areas of the brain, which manifests as an effect on the environment. Internalizing transactions end in a "verb" capacity that produces output from the world-modeling areas of the brain, which manifests as more information to be thought about, or in other words, more input. Therefore, E transactions *do,* and I transactions *consider.*

In terms of the cognitive processing profiles, E profiles have three outputs. With the competence and the play, information comes in through the input and out at the end of the transaction as the output. With the toil, because it is an internalizing transaction, input is considered and produces more input for the transaction to consider, making that output tentative. While considering, the internalizing process is also generating more data. This enriches the world model as it is being built. The process is circular, with the input and the output reinforcing each other, never actually separated, and always meshed in a continuous accumulation of thinking.

For example, the DENT Analyst input and outputs are shown on Figure 66.

Outputs manifest differently for internalizing cognitive processing profiles. Internalizers have two tentative outputs, one along their competence and the other along their play. The output from an I's toil transaction is unconscious and does not manifest on the stage of perception for the individual. Like all toil transactions, the *result* of the transaction is unconscious.

Figure 66: DENT Analyst input and outputs

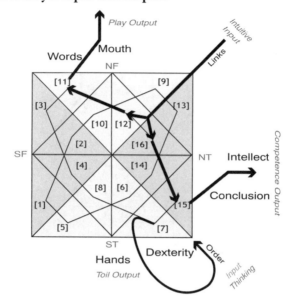

For example, the DINT Conceptualizer input and outputs look like this:

Figure 67: DINT Conceptualizer input and outputs

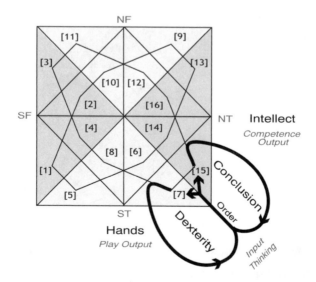

These two diagrams can be moved around the model and used for any of the profiles:

Figure 68: CESF Initiator

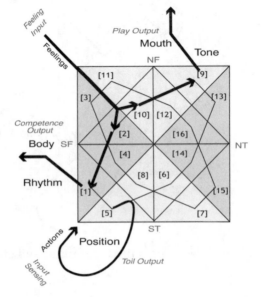

Figure 69: CINT Theoretician

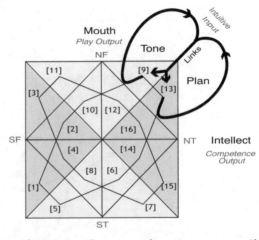

(More examples of input and output diagrams are available at www.humandimensions.net.)

Communication in action

The following anecdotes demonstrate some of the differences in people and the variety of human communication. Memetic transmission is not a simple process—on the contrary, conflicts can arise around any of the dichotomies, between opposite inputs and outputs, even in how a meme is processed in understanding. Conflicts are rarely limited to one dimension either, and instead will manifest along several lines.

In later chapters we will look more closely at how to use the HDM to evaluate and enhance communications in areas such as family, education, and corporate communications. The following anecdotes are some examples of the dichotomies, as well as the inputs, in action. All are based on real-life situations the authors have encountered while applying the HDM to corporate consultations or to friends and family. Names have been changed or avoided as a courtesy to the people involved.

Internalizing vs. Externalizing: Family Decisions

Pam is a CENF Perceiver and married to Bob, a CINT Theoretician. Pam and Bob have a strong marriage; with both being Contextual and iNtuitive, they share two of the four dichotomies. Pam's inputs are at "feelings" and Bob's inputs are at "links," and though they are not the same, Pam's competence output is usable as input by Bob. Also, since Pam's toil is in NT and Bob's play is in NF, they can "get" to each other's mode, which helps facilitate understanding.

But Pam is an Externalizer and Bob is an Internalizer. Pam *does;* Bob *considers.* When making family decisions, this can strain their relationship. Pam wants to make the decision and move on, whereas Bob wants to consider and consider and consider. For Pam, the relentless reprocessing holds up her competence transaction—it literally keeps it from completing, causing her discomfort. For Bob, making the decision too fast cuts off his competence transaction in process, causing him discomfort.

When making decisions, Pam goes with what feels right to her and moves on. Bob, on the other hand, needs the "larger picture" and will continue to gather information until a pattern emerges. On the way to the appearance of the pattern, a theory is borne about how the decision will best fit into the overall lifestyle of the family. This theory is constantly checked and rechecked against the emerging pattern of information.

Pam wants a decision now; Bob wants to continue making the decision. Neither is happy.

A solution that works well for both of them is that they have a previously agreed upon time frame for making decisions—the following evening at dinner. This, of course, is extended for decisions that take extra research such as large purchases, but works very well for smaller projects and social dates.

With a decision-making time frame set, Pam has a foreseeable end to the cliffhanger of decision-processing. Bob, too, has a deadline to which he can shape his processing and bring it to a workable end for himself.

Contextual vs. Deterministic: Marketing and Engineering

From consulting work with hundreds of different companies, we have anecdotally noted that marketing departments tend to be heavy in Contextual profiles, and in particular CENF Perceivers and CINF Composers, with an occasional CINT Theoretician. Engineering departments, on the other hand, are heavy in the Deterministic profiles, and in particular DINT Conceptualizers, DENT Analysts, and DIST Organizers.

Contextuals work moment-to-moment, taking into account the context of the environment and the changes that are happening in it. Deterministics, on the other hand, start a task according to a fixed plan and stick with it, carrying it through to the end and finishing it.

The C/D dichotomy sets up an interesting dynamic between

marketing and engineering. For example, in a firm manufacturing medical devices, marketing assesses the initial market need for a device. They then devise a rough idea of what they want and send that idea to engineering.

This, of course, follows the same pattern of processing as the brain. The Right Perceptual Cortex performs the CI function of exploring and the CE function of trying new possibilities. This is what marketing does—they determine the market need and send the possibilities to engineering.

Once in engineering, the design is perfected and implemented. These are start-to-finish, deterministic processes that once started are no longer bound to market context. The engineers, once they begin to implement production, are glued to a plan that is delineated by specified steps, including parts shipment arrivals, testing, and approvals. Once the device is in the pipeline, it progresses forward in implementation, no matter what happens in the market context.

But, for marketing, the market context is in consciousness. Marketing may become aware of a new medical industry show for which they need the device three months ahead of schedule, or they may become aware of a change in design that would better fit the current market.

When these changes happen, marketing will come to engineering and ask for modifications. Often, engineering will *try* to make the changes, but ultimately will be unable to do so in a timely manner because engineering is deterministic—the plan is the process and the process is the plan.

Channels of communication clog and frustrations build between marketing and engineering. The solution is to be conscious of the differences between the contextual and deterministic processes.

Marketing, though not detail-oriented, must do thorough research and map out market trends in advance. This way they can give engineering the most complete picture possible. When the inevitable changes occur, engineering must work to accommodate the context as much as possible by, for example, running processes in parallel to condense the time frame to completion. If the changes cannot be made, engineering must be honest about the unworkable situation with marketing.

When marketing and engineering employees happen to have opposite inputs such as a CENF Perceiver operating at "feelings" and a DINT Conceptualizer operating at "order," communication can be doubly difficult. The Perceiver has a "feel" for the market and will communicate that feeling via talking. The Conceptualizer, on the other hand, understands the order inherent in the design and will communicate it visually as a diagram. Because of the opposite inputs, a lot of content will be lost during face-to-face communication, and the employees may be better off communicating in written words.

Feeling vs. Thinking: Loyalty and Business

CENF Perceivers tend to be the entrepreneurial spirits behind innovative start-ups: they are the ones with the ability to bring together all of the disparate elements needed to get a new venture off the ground.

When a person puts considerable time and effort into a new venture, that venture becomes very important to that individual. For an NF Feeler, that importance manifests as feelings.

Start-ups are taken over all of the time, and sometimes not in a friendly manner. For Jim, a Perceiver who poured his heart and soul into his new medical venture, a takeover came, and Jim was forced out of his own company. This left him with very bad feelings toward the new owners.

Jim's friend, David, is a product designer and a CENT Strategist. When Jim founded a new venture, David went with him to the new company, leaving behind the old venture with its new owners.

For Jim, any thought or contact with the old business generates bad feelings and a negative reaction. He expects everyone around him to react the same way—that they would also *feel* how poorly the original deal was handled. From this common feeling would come loyalty.

But Strategists, as we have seen, are clueless about feelings. For David, the old business is just that—business. It generates no bad feelings or consequential feelings of loyalty. So when the old company came to David and offered freelance design work, David accepted. To David, the process of work was understandable, not the feeling of loyalty.

Jim could not understand David's disloyal actions and became very angry. Jim and David's relationship became strained. By understanding how each of their cognitive processing profiles works, they were able to comprehend why each of them responded in the manner they did, and it helped in future situations.

Sensing vs. iNtuitive: Authority

At another medical device company, Jan, the head of engineering and a DINT Conceptualizer, was having difficulties moving product proposals past Wayne, the new senior vice president of technology. The proposals included not just newfangled devices, but also the entire product line for the company. Subsequently the company faced financial difficulties, and a very frustrated Jan was ready to quit.

The new VP, Wayne, had come in from a firm in Dallas and was new to everyone at the company. As a CIST Explorer, his consciousness explored and prioritized the "actions" of his input. These are, ultimately, physical string memes that he can perform, and not at all the order and logic inherent in a Conceptualizer's output.

Wayne could not use the information as presented by Jan. It was unintelligible to him because Jan's output did not fit his input. Wayne, as a CI, has a hard time making decisions anyway, and when faced with something unintelligible, decisions became impossible.

To solve their problem, in a one-page report Jan laid out what she wanted to do, the reason why, and the authority to support it from well-established labs that had completed research supporting the usefulness of the proposed device. She appended the report with her data for her own satisfaction, but it was not included directly in the report. This format provided Wayne with an authorized action—what, why, and the voice giving the **true** tag. The presence of the authority effectively made the decision for him, and he was able to move on to his next action.

Summary

- On the model, the four capacities that cluster around each corner use the same type of input information.
- Outputs vary from profile to profile, but match to the mode from which they emerge.
- Externalizing transactions produce output from the action-planning areas of the brain, which manifests as an effect on the environment. Internalizing transactions produce output from the world-modeling areas of the brain, which manifests as more information to be thought about, or in other words, more input. Therefore, E transactions *do*, and I transactions *consider*.
- Externalizing profiles have three outputs. With the competence and the play, information comes in through the input and out at the end of the transaction as the output. With the toil, because it is an internalizing transaction, input is considered and produces more input for the transaction to consider, making the output tentative.
- Internalizing profiles have two tentative outputs, one along their competence and the other along their play.

12

PROFILES: APPLICATIONS

Overview

By applying the HDM and the information it contains about how humans communicate, many areas of interaction can be improved, including task distribution and communication in a work environment, family relations, education, and marketing.

COMMUNICATION APPLICATIONS OF
THE HDM

L earning to profile is an interactive activity; it takes hands-on training with other people in the context of actual, situational cognitive processing. It also takes considerable practice to master. For that reason, we cannot give the reader the tools needed to profile with any margin of accuracy from this book alone.

We can, though, give you some examples of how the HDM has been applied to different areas of life. The anecdotes of the previous chapter illustrated a few applications within the corporate world as well as one within family dynamics. In this chapter we will look more closely at understanding your own cognitive processing competence, family dynamics, education, corporate dynamics and team-building, and marketing.

Know thyself

If you have not done so already, have five people (or more, if needed) who know you well carefully read the cognitive processing profiles listed in chapter 8. Generally, they will come to a consensus that matches your profile. Do not be surprised if your profile does not match your expectations. The memes within the Self are strongly centered on how you believe you *ought* to process and can do much to mask your ability to look inward and see how you *actually* process.

Understanding your own processing will also help you come to terms with your own weaknesses. Everyone has "gaps" in their ability to learn and produce. Some obvious examples are the differences in the modes, such as NFs who are naturally empathic toward the people around them but aren't good with sequential procedures and manual techniques, and STs who are good with sequences but not at interacting with people. There are smaller, profile-specific gaps as well—gaps that are not general enough to be considered "okay" or "common" by the mainstream.

For example, CINT Theoreticians have difficulty being practical. They tend toward flightiness and forgetfulness. This is not only a curse when it is time to find the car keys, but also in educational and professional circumstances when the Theoretician is expected to apply the material he has learned. Application to "real life" does not happen readily in Theoretician consciousness, and this can, unless recognized and understood, affect self-esteem.

Flightiness is a weakness that, in mainstream thinking, can be changed if the individual just "works hard enough." But if you are a Theoretician, and you spend your life trying to be more "conscientious" and more "practical" like you *ought* to, it can wear you down. Knowing and understanding your weaknesses can help free you from their grasp.

Knowing yourself can also help you identify when your weaknesses complicate your life. A good example of this type of interference is a Theoretician trying to do accounting. This is not to say that a Theoretician can't do accounting, just that it will be fatiguing for the Theoretician as he tries to build work-arounds to do something the CINT brain is not set up to do. The best thing to do in this situation is ask for help.

On the flip side of weaknesses is the understanding of your strengths. Theoreticians, for all of their flightiness, operate in the profile that discovers the underlying principles of their chosen field. Without Theoreticians, many of the discoveries of science would not happen.

Know thy family

One observation of particular interest that has come out of the profiling interviews done by Human Dimensions Inc. is that people do not tend to marry someone of the same profile. Different profiles balance each other, though profiles that are too different cannot communicate well with each other.

Because of profile differences within marriages, translating from one spouse's outputs to the other spouse's inputs is necessary. The farther away from each other a couple's profiles are, though, the more translation is needed and the more difficult communication will be within the marriage.

The following matrix illustrates the variation in communication between the profiles. The matrix provides insight into the matching and mismatching that occurs when a person with one profile attempts to communicate with someone of a different profile. It is applicable to all communications situations, including the family, educational, and corporate situations we will be examining later in this chapter.

Figure 70: Communication Matrix

Communication Matrix — TO

FROM	Analyst	Clarifier	Classifier	Composer	Conceptualizer	Doer	Explorer	Implementor	Initiator	Operator	Organizer	Perceiver	Strategist	Theoretician	Trustee	Verbalist
Analyst	2	2	0	0	2	0	0	0	0	1	2	1	2	1	0	2
Clarifier	2	2	0	2	0	0	0	0	1	0	0	1	0	0	2	2
Classifier	0	2	2	0	0	1	0	2	2	1	2	1	0	0	2	0
Composer	1	2	0	2	0	0	0	0	2	0	0	2	0	2	0	1
Conceptualizer	2	0	0	0	2	0	0	0	0	1	2	0	1	2	0	2
Doer	0	0	1	0	0	2	2	1	2	0	0	2	0	0	2	0
Explorer	0	0	1	0	0	2	2	1	0	2	2	0	2	0	0	0
Implementor	0	0	2	0	2	0	1	2	1	2	2	0	1	0	2	0
Initiator	0	0	2	2	0	2	2	1	2	0	0	2	0	0	1	1
Operator	1	0	1	0	0	2	2	2	0	2	1	0	2	2	0	0
Organizer	0	0	2	0	2	0	2	2	0	1	2	0	1	0	0	0
Perceiver	1	1	1	2	0	2	0	0	2	0	0	2	0	2	0	2
Strategist	2	0	0	2	1	0	2	1	0	2	0	0	2	2	0	1
Theoretician	1	0	0	2	2	0	0	0	0	2	0	0	2	2	0	1
Trustee	0	2	2	0	0	2	0	2	1	0	0	1	0	0	2	0
Verbalist	2	2	0	1	2	0	0	0	1	0	0	2	1	0	2	2

On the matrix, profiles that intersect at a "2" are able to communicate intelligibly. Profiles intersecting with a "1" are more prone to misunderstandings. Profiles intersecting at a "0" have so little in common with their conscious processing that communication is difficult. However, it is possible to develop work-arounds to enable the communication.

On the matrix, the fact that a communication between two people with different profiles might work well in one direction does not imply that communication in the other direction will also work well. For example, the communication matrix shows that communication from a DENT Analyst to a DIST Organizer has a value of 2, which is very good. On the other hand, communication from the Organizer to the Analyst has a value of 0, which is very poor.

The Analyst and Organizer communication gap can be illustrated by a firsthand experience of Dr. Kahn's. This particular scenario has occurred twice, and in both cases the relationship was between an Analyst supervisor and an Organizer assistant. The logical information provided by the Analyst was easily sorted by the Organizer into tangible, orderly sequences. The Organizer would use the output of the Analyst to generate the necessary procedures to accomplish the needed objectives of the team. On the other hand, the Analyst had little interest in these procedural sequences, and when the Organizer ran into problems, it was difficult to get the Analyst to pay attention. Furthermore, the Internalizing disposition of the Organizer made it difficult for that person to speak out.

These situations occurred because the output for the Analyst's toil transaction loops back into the "order" input of the Organizer, while the outputs of the Organizer do not match the "linking" N inputs of the Analyst:

Figure 71: Analyst-Organizer communication gap

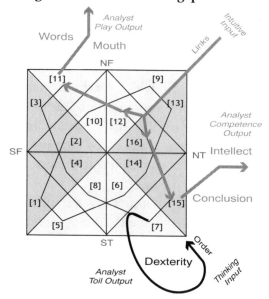

And is the same cognitive process the Organizer uses in the competence transaction:

Figure 72: The competence transaction of the Organizer

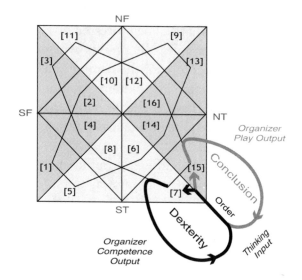

The overlap allowed the Organizer to use her competence transaction to process the output of the Analyst, leading to a 2 rating for communication from Analyst to Organizer. But, the Organizer's output did not match the Analyst's input at all. This led to a rating of 0 from Organizer to Analyst.

In both situations in which Dr. Kahn encountered this condition, this difficulty in communication was managed by scheduling a weekly meeting where the Analyst would listen quietly while the Organizer meticulously enumerated current concerns. This meeting provided an artificial disciplined structure to enable communication across a natural barrier.

The same sort of dynamics happen in families as well. If the parent is an Analyst and the child is an Organizer, the child will have no problem understanding and organizing duties within the family, but will have a difficult time getting the parent to "listen."

Another aspect of family dynamics to consider is that the odds of a child having the same profile as a parent is quite low. Counting the likelihood of any of the profiles appearing in a child as equal, the odds of hitting the same roll of the genetic dice with a child is 16:1, meaning that about only 6 ¼ percent of the population shares its profile with a particular offspring.

Different processing leads to different inclinations. Importance is placed on what can be processed by a person's competence transaction. For example, NF parents will not understand their ST child's desire to program the computer and build mechanical models instead of joining the drama club and volunteering with the church group. Or an artistic NF child may find her practically minded ST parents quite unsupportive of her desire to play guitar and write poems.

Understanding that different profiles manifest different viewpoints and pursuits can go a long way to increasing tolerance in a family. Knowing where the differences lie will also smooth family interactions.

Children and the HDM

Children do not come into this world fully developed—they must learn how to move their bodies, how to talk, and how to be part of the multifaceted world of human memetic organisms. Children, as we have discussed, progress through the four stages of development, starting with the SF gross-motor skills as babies and progressing to the NT logic skills as adolescents.

The pliable brain of a human child soaks up information and configures itself to best handle the languages and memetic organisms with which the child lives. Along with the progression through the four stages of development, the child has genetic underpinnings that determine the child's ultimate cognitive profile. As the child grows and her brain increases in ability to handle the memes at each level of development, consciousness "slides" around. When the child reaches the level corresponding to her profile, consciousness locks in. This is differentiation.

Before differentiation occurs, the child's profile appears "slippery." For example, NT children who have not yet developed to the level of abstract reasoning use ST, or in some cases NF, processing. In such cases, without logic, the child cannot fully *think* like an NT until her cognitive development reaches abstract processing in adolescence.

In order to differentiate into a profile, the child must be exposed to the memes that support that profile as well as have a brain mature enough to handle those memes. SF children differentiate first, usually quite young. NT children differentiate later, usually in their teens. Occasionally an NF or NT prodigy will differentiate earlier than their peers and show artistic or logic-based skills quite young.

Unlike the fully configured brains of adults, children continue to develop and build capacities and transactions, and in a literate, multimemetic organism culture, those capacities will extend into the NT mode. Even children whose profile is apparent by age five are still learning, and their brains are still maturing.

This is why it is important to expose kids to a variety of activities. A child will benefit greatly from having been exposed to and assimilated NT memes that allow abstract processing; memes that, for the non-NT, will be unconscious or semiconscious for her as an adult. A child exposed to SF memes will benefit from learning gross motor skills and sports activities. For the non-SF adult, these memes will provide a balance and greatly improve the individual's poise and understanding of her body. A child exposed to ST fine-motor control and procedural, sequential processing give the individual greater expression with her hands as well as better overall organizational skills. And, a child exposed to NF community, arts, literature, and social interaction memes will give that individual better social skills and understanding of metaphor as an adult.

As parents and teachers, it is important when working with children not to shun activities that teach memes outside of the adult's conscious modes. An NT family will have more books than baseball mitts, but when one mode is held above the others, minimizing exposure to the other modes, the kids may, in the long term, have limitations and self-esteem problems that could have been avoided.

Education

Educators have long understood that there are different types of learners in the world—physical learners, abstract learners, visual learners, kids who need to work through a problem with their hands, kids who do better learning in groups and from other kids, and so on. There are many, many different classification systems available to teachers and parents, many of which overlap and most of which don't fit well.

One of the problems with these systems is that classification by overlapping traits such as "visual learner" do not actually look at *how* the children are learning. All Contextual profiles are "visual" to some degree, and the "order" input profiles—DINT Conceptualizer, CENT Strategist, DIST Organizer, and CEST Operator—

are particularly "visual" in their learning. None of these profiles learn in the same way and will glean in their way what they need from the visual information presented to them.

A complex visual representation of data will mean nothing to a profile that is not set up to process complexity. For example, the complex diagrams generated by DINT Conceptualizers are concise and ordered, but they tend toward high complexity and can be inaccessible to most other profiles, and even other NTs.

Like all other areas of communication, education comes back to a focus on the inputs and outputs of the students. An example of how the differences in profiles affect learning is illustrated by a survey conducted by Human Dimensions Inc. of freshman at a major university medical school.

Studying medicine

The survey provided the students with useful tools to help them better ingest and understand the education they were about to receive at the medical school. Profiling the students also provided the faculty with insights on how to improve curriculum.

The analysis revealed that certain students easily learned and retained information given to them in the format provided by one type of class, while they struggled to understand information in a different format from another class. Other students also had similar difficulties, but with different classes. These learning behaviors were predicted by the HDM using the cognitive processing profile of each student.

Coursework during the student's first year of medical school included a course in anatomy and another in physiology. The anatomy course was "hands-on," and the students learned by performing dissections of human cadavers. The physiology course was abstract and provided a conceptual understanding of the underlying mechanisms of normal and abnormal life processes.

During the interviews, students were asked about their ability to readily understand the information presented in each of these courses. The following anecdotes describe the responses from two of the students.

The first student, a DINT Conceptualizer, reported that understanding the conceptual information in the physiology class was easy and required no further effort to generate comprehension. Anatomy, though, was a different situation. The Conceptualizer found that it was difficult to dig out the conceptual infrastructure underlying anatomy class work and had to spend additional library research time after each class to even begin to understand.

The second student, a CIST Explorer, reported that anatomy was easy since he could touch the body and thereby know it. Physiology, though, was so difficult to grasp that the student simply matched each concept to a remembered cartoon. Then, during an examination, that student recalled the cartoon in order to restate the physiological concept. While this did not generate conceptual understanding, it was relatively effective for passing the examination.

By helping the students understand their cognitive processing profiles, they gained an understanding of themselves that helped them discover their best way to learn. Later this knowledge could be applied to their clinical activities, specialty selection, and patient relations.

Profile distributions at the medical school

One observation of interest concerning the distribution within the freshman class is that there was not a concentration of particular profiles. This is not the case in other disciplines. Engineering, for example, tends to be predominantly Deterministic STs and NTs, with the STs concentrating on mechanical engineering and the NTs concentrating on electrical and chemical engineering. The Arts tend to concentrate in the opposite direction with CINF Composers and CENF Perceivers.

In medicine, though, the distribution is holistic and not sex-dependent. The following graphs show the breakdown of cognitive processing profiles within the class:

Figure 73: Entire medical school class

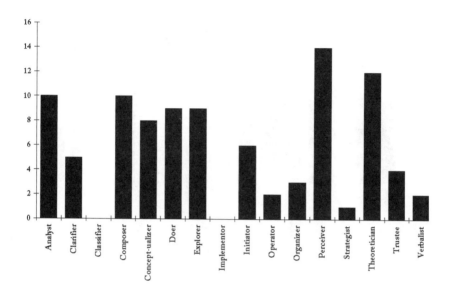

Figure 74: Medical school class women

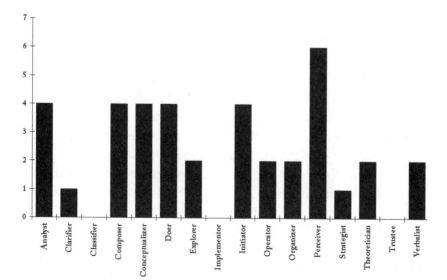

Figure 75: Medical school class men

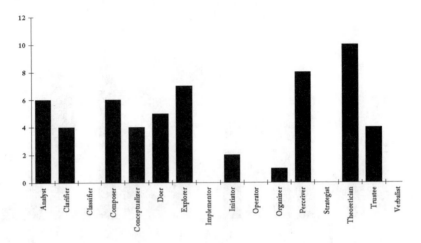

Ultimately the selection of medical specialties by medical students is strongly influenced by their cognitive processing profiles. The anatomy and physiology anecdote above reveals the processes that will influence the student's specialty selection. For example, the N symbolic processes used by the first student serve well in the thinking of practitioners of internal medicine and psychiatry in which it is important to detect and understand the underlying processes responsible for pathologies. On the other hand, the "see it" and "touch it" S sensory processing displayed by the second student serve well in the practices of surgery and ophthalmology.

Is not surprising that surveys using the Myers-Briggs Type Indicator (MBTI) confirm that only the N types find satisfaction in the practices of internal medicine and psychiatry and only the S types find satisfaction in the practices of surgery and ophthalmology. These surveys were conducted on over four thousand physicians who had been in practice at least ten years[14] and included a look at the

14. Over four thousand medical students took the MBTI in the early 1950s, and were then followed up in the 1960s and 1970s. For more information, please see McCaulley, M. H. (1977) *The Myers longitudinal medical study (Monograph II),* and McCaulley, M. H. (1978) *Application of the Myers-Briggs Type Indicator to medicine and other health professions (Monograph I).*

physicians' level of satisfaction with their chosen specialty.

We have translated the Myers-Briggs typology used for the study, into the HDM nomenclature for presentation here. The Myers-Briggs Type Indicator (MBTI) parallels the HDM very closely in mode designators, and uses the same terminology. The MBTI, though, uses different terms and meanings for the steps. For a more detailed comparison of the MBTI to the HDM, please see Appendix B: Comparing the Myers-Briggs Type Indicator and the HDM.

On the graphs, a (-) indicates negative satisfaction with the chosen specialty and a (+) indicates positive satisfaction. A blank indicates that few or no physicians with these profiles went into that specialty.

Figure 76: Satisfaction with chosen specialty

Internal Medicine

	ST	SF	NF	NT
CI	–	–	+	+
DI	–	–	+	+
DE	–	–	+	+
CE	–			+

Family Practice

	ST	SF	NF	NT
CI	+	+		
DI		+		
DE				–
CE		+		

Surgery

	ST	SF	NF	NT
CI	+			
DI	+	+	–	–
DE	+	+	–	–
CE	+			

Neurology

	ST	SF	NF	NT
CI	–		+	+
DI	–		+	+
DE	–			
CE	–			+

Psychiatry

	ST	SF	NF	NT
CI	–	–	+	+
DI	–	–	+	+
DE	–	–	+	+
CE	–	–	+	+

Anesthesiology

	ST	SF	NF	NT
CI	+	+		
DI	+	+		
DE			–	–
CE			–	–

Ophthalmology	ST	SF	NF	NT
CI	−	+		−
DI	+	+		
DE	+	+		
CE	−	+		

Dermatology	ST	SF	NF	NT
CI	+	−		
DI	+	−		
DE	+	−		
CE	+	−		

Applying the HDM to the "real world"

Human Dimensions Inc. has verified the HDM's capability for prediction by studying the cognitive processing profiles of over one thousand subjects under a variety of controlled circumstances. The methodology used by Human Dimensions Inc. to determine a person's cognitive processing style includes a thirty to forty-minute interview that is videotaped to record verbal responses and body activity. Following the interview, the tape is reviewed and analyzed.

The interview consists of a set series of open-ended questions designed to elicit specific verbal responses indicative of the type of information processing used by the subject. For example, the interviewer will look for "to the point" speech indicating a D, or "scenic route" speech indicative of a C. This kind of interview is unique in that it is oriented toward process being used to generate those answers and not the content of the answers themselves.

In order to interpret a subject's responses, those who analyze the videotapes require special training, which includes learning to ignore the content of the responses. *What* is being said is not what is being studied; instead we compare the structure of the responses to a set of rules that look for *how* the answers are generated. This is a much nuanced process and requires understanding the Human Dimensions Model in sufficient detail to knowledgeably apply those rules. It takes about thirty hours of study and practice to train a good interviewer.

The formal studies conducted by Human Dimensions have included a study of the cognitive demographics of the customer population for a *Fortune* 100 company as well freshman class studies of two major medical schools. In addition, Human Dimensions has developed a set of consulting tools used primarily for organizational communications and team-building. These have been applied in a number of companies and universities. All of these tools include the interviewing and determination of subject profiles as part of their process. The videotapes from all of these interviews were independently examined by two (or more) reviewers and, in almost all cases, both results were identical.

It is not possible to include a training course in cognitive profile interviewing as part of this book. However, Human Dimensions is currently developing a software package that is intended to provide an accurate profiling tool for future readers.

Through the Human Dimensions Inc. studies, we have learned that the HDM can be applied to any memetic organism, from the corporate environment where they were originally tested to volunteer organizations, educational facilities, and, with some modifications, to family settings.

When applied, the tools address several areas of concern within an organization. The first area of concern, *organizational communications*, involves different departments such as, marketing, research, engineering, manufacturing, and human resources within a company; or mom, dad, eldest offspring, and youngest child in a family. In a typical corporation, these departments attract people who have specific cognitive processing profiles. In a family, households rarely have more than one member with the same profile. These differences lead to communication barriers and misunderstandings. Using knowledge of inputs and outputs in communication has been effective in identifying and bridging these differences.

Through the analysis of the natural strengths of team members, team dynamics can be altered so that the team competences better match the task requirements. In a family and in looser volunteer organizations, the tasks can be altered to better match the profiles available.

In a company, human resources departments can use the HDM

to match individual cognitive processes to job requirements. This has resulted in better vocational placement, providing improved performance and job satisfaction with significantly less turnover. Understanding vocational aptitude has also helped families deal with differing desires of parent and child.

In a corporate setting, Human Dimensions typically presents a seminar to the entire group, describing the model and its applications. This is often followed by an additional, more detailed discussion of how the HDM works for those who are interested. For academic classes in a university setting, this detailed discussion is part of the course work.

Each individual in the group engages in a profiling interview. The testing consists of a single forty-five-minute videotaped interview performed by a professionally trained interviewer, and a subsequent analysis of the videotape. During the interview, the profiler asks carefully selected open-ended questions designed to reveal the individual's cognitive processing profile.

To do the analysis, trained observers score the processes a person demonstrates based on parameters derived from the HDM. Also, the observers use physical parameters measured by automatic electronic analysis of the video and audio signals. The analysis includes assessment of twenty-four measurable parameters, including:

- Communication style
- Decision-making strategy
- Level of symbolic processing
- Organizational tools
- Complexity
- Physical measures of verbal patterns and body language

The results reveal the individual's cognitive processing profile, which includes cognitive strengths and weaknesses as well as the processes used for communication, understanding, believing, learning, and making choices, providing much more information than a simple type classification.

In the next step, the team leader identifies the competencies required in the team or for a task. The individual strengths are matched to the needs. Potential communication barriers between the individual members are identified and translation methods are proposed.

The results of the profiling and team analysis are presented at a meeting of the entire team. Discussions and exercises are used to demonstrate differences, communications, and translations.

Difficulties are not confined to departments within an organization, but exist as well between an organization, its customers, and its suppliers. In a family, difficulties may exist between family members and the school or the family and the neighbors. An analysis of the people in each of these areas is helpful to understand how information must be translated to be useful to another organization.

Another problem area was revealed with the in-depth market research study for the *Fortune* 100 company. Analysis of several different product lines showed that the styles of consumer communications significantly influenced purchasing behaviors. Problems occur when the profiles of those generating the communication materials in marketing and advertising are very different from the customer group.

Marketing and the HDM

Modern humans have a love/hate relationship with marketing. Advertisements and product information are the routes through which we acquire information about the availability of new products and services, but it is also the route through which corporations transmit memes designed to enlist allegiances within the Self.

The dynamics of economic, social, political, and individual interactions involving the memes of marketing—as well as those of narrative transmission—are quite complex. In this book we will try to point only to some of the major issues as they intersect with individual cognitive processing.

When viewed as "bad," marketing is annoying, invasive, and, at its worst, propaganda. When viewed as "good," marketing brings information to consumers so that they can process it and make decisions on what to buy. It all depends on how well the marketing fits an individual's inputs, and whether the memetic organism generating it carries **good** or **bad** emotional tags. For the remainder of this chapter, we will assume a "good" memetic organism with the intention of selling "useful" products.

Well-done marketing will:

- Enlist the conscious cognitive system by getting attention.
- Format media information to match targeted cognitive processing profiles so that it may move into awareness.
- Engage consumers enough that they process the information being transmitted, thus developing an understanding of the product.
- Provide a foundation for influencing beliefs, motivating the consumer to add a **good** tag to the product.

Attention is caught via a variety of means, several of which we have previously discussed. Color, movement, deviation from the current norm, wit, humor, and so on, all grab attention. If the attention-grabber is one that fits the input of the audience, then the information can move into awareness.

One of the major questions facing the field of marketing concerns how to understand the inputs of the target consumer group. The *Fortune* 100 study revealed that, for some products, the target group is quite narrow. For the company's new laxative product, the majority of consumers were Deterministic as well as ST.

To help the mostly Contextual members of the marketing department of the company comprehend the differences inherent in the C/D dichotomy, Human Dimensions enlisted a preselected group of 24 subjects; half were CENF Perceivers and half were DIST Organizers. This group of 24 was divided in half to form two separate focus groups of 12, with each group containing an equal number of each profile. During each of the two focus group sessions, participants were asked to examine two different illustrations concerning an under-the-sink-installed water purification system. The first illustration presented the features and benefits of such a system, and the second illustration described how the water purification system works. The participants were then asked to select which of the two illustrations best provided to them the kind of information they would need to make a purchasing decision. Copies of the two illustrations are provided on the following pages.

In both focus groups, all of the CENF Perceivers chose the first illustration communicating features and benefits. All of the DIST Organizers chose the second illustration communicating how such a system works. Clearly these two different profiles require different kinds of information for making purchasing decisions. Since the majority of the marketing people in the company were CENF Perceivers and the majority of laxative users previously had been determined to be DIST Organizers, this study clearly demonstrated the barrier in the marketing communications.

The marketing people designed the advertising and marketing information associated with the product so that it matched the inputs of their own Contextual profiles. Unfortunately, this was unintelligible to the major consumers.

On the following page is the example of a water purification system that illustrates the difference between marketing to the C *what* of a product is (Figure 76) and the D *how* it works (Figure 77).

Using the HDM, marketing and advertising professionals can:

- Target the style of advertising they use to the profiles of intended consumers.
- Develop an advertising mix for the range of profiles with which they wish to connect.
- Tailor properties of products and packaging to their intended consumer profiles.
- Select new products for profiles for which no product is currently directed.

Figure 77: *What* a purification system does: features and benefits

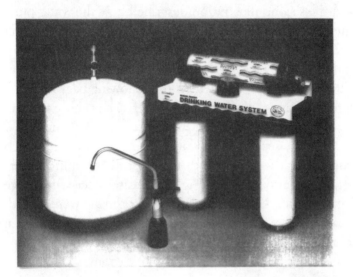

FEATURES:

- High quality drinking water
- Reverse osmosis process
- Fully automatic
- Automatic shut off to drain
- Pre and post filter included
- Attractive chrome faucet included
- Pressurized storage tank
- Operates on water line pressure

BENEFITS:

- Removes objectionable taste and odor
- Provides clean, clear, sparkling, good tasting water
- Replaces expensive, inconvenient bottled water
- Gives you better flavored beverages
- Improves flavor of foods cooked in water
- Makes better tasting, clearer ice cubes
- Provides water appropriate for low sodium diets
- Can be used for fish and plants
- Provides water for use in steam irons, batteries, humidifiers, and picture developing

Figure 78: *How* **the purification system operates**

HOW AN RO DRINKING WATER SYSTEM PROVIDES HIGH QUALITY WATER.

1. Household water is directed through a 5 micron filter for ultra filtration to remove sediment and particulate matter.

2. The water is then forced, by pressure, through a semi-permeable membrane where most of the chemicals, heavy metals, dissolved solids, bacteria, etc. are rejected and flushed to the drain.

3. A final polishing of the water is accomplished by an activated carbon absorption modified neck block filter removing tastes and odors, organic chemicals and dissolved gasses. The water passes through this final filtering process immediately before going to the faucet whether it comes direct from the unit or from the storage tank.

4. The automatic shut off control shuts down the system when the storage tank is filled and water is not being drawn. This "demand production" feature conserves water by eliminating the constant running to the drain found in some units. The control also depressurizes the membrane when not in service extending the membranes life.

Using the HDM to tailor fund-raising appeals

As a final example of using the HDM to tailor communications, we would like to share a wonderful example from one of Dr. Kahn's "Individuality and Cognition" classes at the University of Minnesota and done by student Reine Shiffman as the final class paper. This example pulls together understanding of interpersonal communication, educational goals, and marketing. The following two examples are of letters written with opposite profiles in mind. The first appeals to a CISF Doer while the second appeals to a DENT Analyst.

Designed to be intelligible to a CISF Doer, the first letter focuses on the Doer's sense of the tangible world around her; her matching to past experience through the illustration of her friend's gift; and her greater comprehension of visually offered information.

Figure 79: Fundraising appeal to a CISF Doer profile

MEDICAL HOSPITAL FOUNDATION

Mrs. Dorthea Doer
4343 43rd Street
Asheville, NC 28803

Dear Mrs. Doer:

Truly one of the privileges of my position with the Medical Foundation is the opportunity to visit with our friends and supporters. Thank you for taking the time to meet with me last week. I was exhausted after hearing of the many organizations with which you are involved! Truly, we are all enriched by your zest for life--you are an inspiration.

Like you, we wish that our emergency waiting room was as inviting as that in Crises Care Hospital. As you know, funds for the renovation of their area was a result of private gifts; indeed, it was Miriam Smith's contribution that motivated others to follow suit.

We, too, hope to establish an endowment that will provide us with the necessary funding to renovate ours. As you can see on the enclosed diagram, an endowment provides annual support in perpetuity. Never again would we have to scramble for funds when we wish to purchase a new magazine. Indeed, an initial gift of $10,000 would provide us with $550 annually. Consider the improvements that could be made!

I would like you to consider that gift. You mentioned that you had a certificate of deposit about to come due. Rather than roll it over, why not use it create the Dorthea Doer Emergency Room Endowment Fund. With this letter I have included a sample "Memorandum of Agreement" we would prepare for your signature. Of course, we will make any changes you and your advisors feel prudent.

Like your volunteer experiences, a gift of this nature would give others much comfort. I hope you will say yes. I'll call soon.

Sincerely,

Reine Shiffman
Director of Planned Giving

Designed to be intelligible to a DENT Analyst, this letter focuses on supporting the Analyst's need to know how the system of giving works. It does so by including more information, and by letting the Analyst draw his own conclusions.

Figure 80: Fund-raising appeal to a DENT Analyst profile

MEDICAL HOSPITAL FOUNDATION

Dr. Albert Analyst
810 5th Decade
Duluth, MN 55555

Dear Dr. Analyst:

Truly one of the privileges of my position with the Fairview Foundation is the opportunity to visit with our friends and supporters. Thank you for taking the time to meet with me last week.

I do hope our conversation was helpful. Once more I commend you for so thoroughly examining this problem; surely an acceptable solution is around the corner. For your perusal I am enclosing a few more articles: the piece by Lynda Moerschbaecher details the principles behind the IRS guidelines with which we are dealing; Arthur Anderson's essay provides even more insights. Perhaps by understanding them, we can discover a way to resolve your problem.

Dr. Analyst, we are privileged by your continued interest in the Medical Foundation's Peaceful Domestic Coexistence program. On behalf of those whom will benefit from your ultimate generosity, I say thank you.

I'll call you soon.

Sincerely,

Reine Shiffman
Director of Planned Giving

(More examples are available at www.humandimensions.net.)

Summary

- The HDM can be applied to any area where humans communicate, including knowing yourself, understanding family dynamics, education, corporate interactions, and marketing.

13

FINAL THOUGHTS

Mind Shapes outlines the most personal part of the Human Dimensions Model: the "cognitive" element of the sociocognitive system. By understanding yourself and the people around you, communication improves. Understanding how your brain best processes information improves self-esteem. But it also does something else—by understanding how you process and the type of outputs you generate, you can better place yourself within the context of the group.

Working best in the group is the core of the "socio" element of the sociocognitive system. Without the adaptations that allowed cognitive differentiation, human specialization and memetic organisms could not exist as we have them today, and neither would human civilization.

But civilization places demands on a person. The brain creates needs, both physical such as eating, sleeping, procreating, and avoiding pain. These support the continued living of the body. It also creates social needs such as achieving, conforming, helping. These support the continued living of the memetic organism. Straddling these two areas is the milieu in which humans exist.

And if that weren't hard enough, we don't all think the same. It is very likely that the person sitting next to you has a brain that processes information differently from yours. Even though these differences build, grease, optimize, and coordinate the wheels of civilization, they place emphasis on different memes supporting different social needs in different areas. And when neighbors have different agendas, dissonance propagates.

The key to dealing with this dissonance is to understand the differences. Like any other human endeavor, better understanding leads to refined responses, which in turn decrease the "noise" in the system. Better understanding of human differences will ultimately lead to clearer and more efficient communication, which will decrease the time and energy needed to transmit as well as comprehend memes. This should reduce stress, even if it does increase the speed at which information propagates.

And, really, that is what we all want—less stress. Not understanding, and watching other people not understand, is stressful. It's wasteful and causes fights. Knowing *how* to understand relieves some of the pressure. Knowing *how* will also increase empathy.

Knowing, too, that the best-constructed memes come from cognitively diverse groups helps us build the best memetic organisms we can. Diverse groups with good communication have less internal friction and produce better output.

Less stress, less group friction, more empathy—where is this leading us? It would be very easy to paint a picture of a happy-go-lucky, love-everybody-while-running-through-the-daisies kind of utopia, but that's not realistic, nor is it feasible. What we can imagine is a world with less of the "noise" we encounter every day of our lives. No more floundering around to find a way to explain yourself. No more destruction of self-esteem as you try to behave in the manner of a profile you are not. Fewer bombardments by memes like marketing and entertainment that grab your attention but don't match your inputs, then slide on by, leaving you feeling agitated, annoyed, and just a little bit confused.

What you've learned about here—the modes, steps, profiles, inputs, and outputs—are tools designed to facilitate communication, both how you "communicate" with yourself, internally, as you process information, as well as how that processing shapes what you give to the world. What *Mind Shapes* does is filter out the cognitive noise. We also hope that this book will help you help others by giving you tools to "prefilter" what you want to communiciate, letting it arrive in the consciousness of your target smoothly and clearly.

In other words, *Mind Shapes* is essentially a how-to book. On the other hand, *Who Are We Now?*—the companion volume to *Mind Shapes*—is a big-picture book. It turns outward form the "cognitive" and focuses on the "socio," covering more deeply much of what we have examined here as well as just exactly what it is that our memetic organisms are doing, both in our heads and outside in the world.

With that in mind, you can see that *Mind Shapes* is part of a developmental process... the beginning of a journey. It is a very good place to start. Depending on your profile and your inclination, it might be enough. Or it might not. Either way, we hope that *Mind Shapes* has served you well.

Appendix A

CHILD DEVELOPMENT

From the 1920s until his death in 1980, Jean Piaget studied how children develop. During these six decades of research, he produced the theoretical framework of "genetic epistemology," the study of how knowledge develops within a human organism.

Piaget was particularly interested in the development of cognitive structures. These structures, which for Piaget were patterns of mental behavior that underlie the four stages of child development, correspond to the four modes within the Human Dimensions Model (HDM):

Age	Piaget's stage	HDM mode	Skill
0–2 years	Sensorimotor	SF	Gross-motor
2–7 years	Preoperational	ST	Fine-motor
7–12 years	Concrete Operational	NF	Verbal/Social
12–15 years	Formal Operational	NT	Abstract intellectual

Sensorimotor

The first stage of child development is characterized by the child learning a variety of sensorimotor behaviors. These behaviors are used to obtain a goal, for example, sucking to obtain food; grasping to hold an object; banging and hitting to get attention. As the child progresses through infancy, the intentionality of the child's actions increases. For example, when the baby practices kicking, he learns that kicking moves a toy and that kicking a blanket out of the way will reveal a toy.

These behaviors show that the infant is engaging in several of the cognitive processes we describe in the HDM:

- When an infant is born, he has only the genetically coded instinctual responses with which to work. A newborn literally starts from zero, with no episodes in memory of how to work within the world. The first couple of months of life are devoted to matching trigger with instinctive response and to the practice of those responses. In this period the baby builds a repertoire of actions. This subphase of the sensorimotor stage is predominantly Contextual Internalizing in that the infant is building a world model.

- Next, an infant will begin to use those actions to achieve goals, for example, kicking at a toy so that it will move. This subphase is predominantly Contextual Externalizing in that the infant is trying possible actions in the world.

- At about a year of age, the infant will start to invent new sensorimotor behaviors and exhibit trial-and-error behavior. These trials and errors aren't the looping contextual behavior of animals, though. Babies practice their skills and thus learn the best way to move their bodies to achieve their goals. This subphase is predominantly Deterministic Internalizing. It is also the first subphase where memetic processing starts to be observable.

- At the end of infancy, babies have learned to walk, and they are beginning to talk. They also have about a year and a half of experience with their world and have accumulated enough episodes and SF body memes that they begin to show clear Deterministic Externalizing behaviors. For example, a child moving from babyhood to toddlerhood may use a stick to retrieve another toy that is out of reach. The child of the example is implementing the physical meme of wielding the stick to obtain the goal of getting the ball.

The development in infancy from the CI cognitive processing step to the DE cognitive processing step supports the evolutionary development of the SF mode. Also, infancy is a time of the body and learning how to handle the body. This too correlates with the SF mode.

During this time, a human child formats her brain for running a sensing model. The child learns awareness of the body and the body's need states. The child also learns that she can produce and remember actions to deal with those states, thus introducing memetic processing on top of the genetic responses with which the baby was born.

Preoperational

Piaget's second stage of child development is "preoperational," which occurs between two to seven years of age. Piaget tracked the majority of child development in terms of a child's increasingly sophisticated use of language. Between the ages of two and seven, a child masters a large vocabulary of verbal symbols (words) and the syntax for organizing them (grammar).

At the same time, the child is associating each symbol with a "concept" of what that symbol means. This is the process of using the symbol as a category label for a hierarchy and using the process of abstraction and generalization to annotate the child's sensing model experiences with the symbol.

Also, a child's imaginative play will blossom. This type of behavior also straddles the sensing and intuitive models—the child is physically acting out intuitive episodes in order to practice them. For the child, the imagining and the acting are one in the same; there is no separation between the two. This is core consciousness, which develops before a sense of "self."

Learning language and imaginative play are intuitive model functions, and it is during the preoperational stage that a child's consciousness becomes fully operational. In essence, "preoperational" is all of the work a child does to format her brain to run an intuitive model.

Formatting the brain for consciousness is not the only growth that happens for toddlers and preschoolers, though. The intuitive model relies on hierarchical processing, but the increasing refinement of body control does not. It is also during this time that children learn to use their hands.

Grasping becomes finger play. Children learn how to manipulate small objects consistently, thus showing the brain's usage of string memes. By the age of seven, most children can buckle belts, zip jackets, and tie shoes.

But dexterity is not the only procedural learning that young children do. A big part of the cultural rule-set known as "manners" is learned now. Manners are string meme procedures that are incorporated into consciousness as the child develops language. There are many set ways of living life such as how to brush teeth, how to put on a shirt, how to clean up toys, and so on, which are all part of having "manners." Besides these rules, there are other rules of the cultural rule-set as well, such as not to talk back to adults with authority and not to pull the sibling's hair.

Developing and using these string memes are the hallmarks of the ST mode. Even as young children are building their intuitive models, they are learning and incorporating knowledge about how the world works into their budding consciousnesses using their ST cognitive processing infrastructure.

Concrete-operational

A child enters the concrete-operational stage at approximately seven years of age. Piaget so named this stage because it is at this point that children begin to form classifications, ideas, and an understanding of highly abstract concepts such as time and numbers and are able to apply these concepts to concrete, real-world phenomena.

A child in the concrete-operational stage understands object conservation, for example, that mass is conserved even if an object changes its configuration. If you fill a tall glass and a short glass with the same amount of water, a child in the concrete-operational stage will understand that both glasses hold the same volume. A child who is preoperational will say that the tall glass has more water.

Also, children in the concrete-operational stage can "serialize" objects, that is, sort a group of objects according to an abstract concept such as smallest to biggest or first to last. This ability adds a relational dimension to a child's thinking.

What object conservation and serialization show is that children in this stage are operating with a fully functioning intuitive model. They are in essence creating NF metaphors. For example, in order to understand the conversion of mass between shapes, the child must manipulate her sensed information intuitively in consciousness. This tests possible outcomes virtually.

Also at this stage, children have learned the rules of language and are able to verbalize intuitive concepts. "Inner" life fully develops for the child. The child starts working with intuitive concepts about the self as well, such as what it means to be part of a group, to be a boy or a girl, how smart they are, how good they look, and so on. Through comprehension of the NF metaphor, the child starts comparing herself to others.

This is also the time that most children fully grasp that a scary movie is "just a story" and not "real." The child begins to learn logic and the scientific method and to build the infrastructure needed to support the next stage of development.

Formal-operational

The formal-operational stage corresponds roughly to the onset of adolescence at about the age of twelve. In this stage, adolescents begin to fully comprehend that the thoughts they think are separate from the reality of the world outside their bodies. This leads to fully modeling possibilities on the stage of consciousness in the form of creating hypotheses and then testing them with the scientific method.

Studies of teens and adults in Western cultures show that not all people reach the formal-operational stage.[15] This is because formal-operational is the NT mode. If logic is not introduced before differentiation, some portion of the SF and ST population will enter adulthood with an underdeveloped NT infrastructure. Also, without the right kind of education, no one will fully reach NT, not even those who are genetically predisposed toward consciously using that infrastructure. In some non-Western cultures, formal-operational is never attained, showing the need for logic and scientific education.

Also in this stage, adolescents are coming to terms with reaching adulthood and preparing themselves for becoming a productive part of the memetic organism. Though conventional thought says that most teens break from their parents, a multitude of studies have shown that the family is still important as the child moves into adulthood.

Also, this is when most young people fully differentiate and come into their cognitive processing profile. In the modern world, the young person must navigate many memes to find what best suits his or her competence. This is not always easy and may be helped by support from a peer group with similar profiles.

---

15. "Human Behaviour," *Encyclopedia Britannica*, 2003. Encyclopedia Britannica Premium Service, September 9, 2003 (http://www.britannica.com/eb/article?eu=119312).

Appendix B

COMPARING THE MYERS-BRIGGS TYPE INDICATOR (MBTI) AND THE HDM

In 1943, Isabel Myers and her mother, Katherine Cook Briggs, created the first set of questions that would later become the Myers-Briggs Type Indicator (MBTI). Based on the work of Carl Jung, the MBTI was the first major attempt to test for the different cognitive behaviors among people. It was an important advance in understanding how people process information differently.

Impressive as it is, the MBTI is based on work done in the early twentieth century before the role of hemispheric differentiation was understood and the current brain scan technology existed. Also, at the beginning of the twenty-first century, researchers now have at their disposal considerably richer and more detailed models of systems interaction and sociological and psychological science than Jung had available at the time.

Jung's observations, though, were very insightful and right on track, but he did not have access to what he needed to figure out *why* what he was observing occurred. Ultimately this leaves the MBTI with some gaps.

The Indicator is a self-administered questionnaire created to tease out from a person's answers how they prefer to deal with the world. The Indicator compares four dichotomies. The terms and definitions used here are based on the descriptions in *Gifts*

Differing: Understanding Personality Type (Isabel Briggs Myers and Peter B. Myers):

The main MBTI dichotomy:

Perceiving vs. Judging:

- *Perceiving* includes the process of becoming aware of things.
- *Judging* includes coming to conclusions about what has been perceived.

A person will have a preference for either P or J.

Under the P/J dichotomy, two other dichotomies are arranged hierarchically:

Under Perceiving:

Sensing vs. Intuition:

- *Sensing* is a preference for dealing with information collected directly through the five senses.
- *Intuition* is a preference for sensing information unconsciously and having it appear in consciousness as a "hunch" or as "women's intuition."

Under Judging:

Feeling vs. Thinking:

- *Feeling* is appreciation, or bestowing on things a personal subjective value.
- *Thinking* is a logical process and objective.

The MBTI includes one more dichotomy that is seen as independent of P/J:

Extroverted vs. Introverted:

- *Extroversion* is a focus on the world outside of the individual.

- *Introversion* is a focus on the inner life of the individual.

The MBTI questions lead to an identification of preferences among the dichotomies and an indication of which Myers-Briggs Type an individual is.

The MBTI and the HDM

Both the MBTI and HDM use Jung as a source, with the MBTI relying solely on his work and the HDM supplementing it with the work of Lowen and others. Because of the similar starting point, there are many similarities between the MBTI and the HDM. We will look at them dichotomy by dichotomy:

MBTI	HDM
Perceiving vs. Judging	**Contextual vs. Deterministic**
Perceiving—becoming aware of the environment	*Contextual*—focused on the environment
Judging—drawing conclusions about what has been perceived	*Deterministic*—focused on the response to the environment

The correlation between P/J and C/D is not perfect. In Walter Lowen's book *Dichotomies of the Mind,* he explains that for a pairing to be dichotomous, they must be opposite but combine to form a function greater than the sum of the two. Some of the examples he uses are the thumb and the fingers; strategic and logistic planning; and men and women. All are opposites, but together they make a whole.

Perceiving and Judging as defined in the MBTI do not form a true dichotomy. Perceiving is becoming aware of the environment, and Judging is building a model about what is in awareness. Essentially, the P and J together are the Contextual Internalizing (CI) cognitive processing step. In CI explore, the brain positions the body to best take in information to build a model of the world.

MBTI	HDM
Sensing vs. Intuition	**Sensing vs. Intuitive**
Sensing—focused on what can be understood with the senses	*Sensing*—model of the world based on perceived information
Intuition—senses are unconscious and appear as a "hunch"	*Intuitive*—model of the world based on abstractions and generalizations

The S/N dichotomies of the MBTI and the HDM line up quite well. In the HDM, though, S/N is not a subdichotomy under C/D as it is under Perceiving in the MBTI.

Another difference is that the "hunch" phenomenon of the MBTI Intuition is more a function of being Contextual than it is of being intuitive. Contextual iNtuitives process generalizations consciously, and these generalizations are the "pictures" of their intuitive thinking. CINFs, CENFs, CINTs, and CENTs do not "know" how they come up with their thoughts and ideas because that process is Deterministic and not conscious for them. For the Contextual iNtuitive, thoughts "appear" as intuitive episodes.

MBTI	HDM
Feeling vs. Thinking	**Feeling vs. Thinking**
Feeling—subjective	*Feeling*—episodes include feeling information; matching episode-to-episode allows matching by feeling
Thinking—objective	*Thinking*—links between episodes used for matching; links not accessible to emotional system so feelings not used for matching

The F/T dichotomies of the MBTI and the HDM line up quite well. In the HDM, though, F/T is not a subdichotomy under C/D as it is under Judgment in the MBTI.

MBTI	HDM
Introverted vs. Extroverted	**Internalizing vs. Externalizing**
Introverted—quiet, shy, and focused on "inner" life	*Internalizing*—positions oneself to take in information and build a world model (CI) or a response to a situation (DI)
Extroverted—outgoing and interested in being with people	*Externalizing*—acts on the world by trying new possibilities (CE) or implementing memes (DE)

Introverted and Extroverted in the MBTI are about disliking and liking contact with the world of people. They do reflect a dichotomy, but not the Internalizing vs. Externalizing dichotomy of the HDM. Being Extroverted is more about being NF than it is about being an Externalizer. Externalizing STs will measure Introverted on the MBTI because they are much more focused on things than people.

The modes in the MBTI and the HDM

The MBTI combines the S/N and the F/T dichotomies' preferred combinations of preferences in the same manner that the HDM combines S/N and F/T into modes:

MBTI	HDM
SFs (sensing plus feeling) are more interested in facts about people than things; make their decisions with personal warmth.	*SF* (Sensing Feeling) physical; gross-motor; grounded; uses emotional memory recall.
STs (sensing plus thinking) are objective people focused on collecting facts that can be found using the senses.	*ST* (Sensing Thinking) uses hands; fine motor; grounded; works procedurally to build tools.
NFs (intuition plus feeling) are not centered on the concrete situation and make their judgments based on feelings and with personal warmth.	*NF* (iNtuitive Feeling) concerned with people; verbal; uses emotional recall and the classic NF sensed-to-intuited metaphor.
NTs (intuition and thinking) are objective people who prefer impersonal analysis.	*NT* (iNtuitive Thinking) concerned with hierarchical arrangements; uses logic.

The MBTI preferences and the HDM modes line up more closely in N than they do in S. In particular, the MBTI ST preference does not place emphasis on the hand-eye coordination and procedural processing of the HDM ST mode.

Appendix C

THE OPERATOR IN ACTION

The CEST Operator cognitive processing profile is particularly adept at miming. For individuals with this profile, the physical acting out of a procedure is an important part of their communication. The following photos were taken from a videotape of an Operator describing a homemade underwater diving system with the hand pump on the boat deck and a helmet attached to his body. As he moves through the description, he mimes the bubbles going up from his shoulders, and not in the center where they would obscure his vision. Finally he describes fish swimming out in front of him and he is reaching out for them.

Notice too that the subject's eyes are focused on his hands. Operators think in body procedures expressed through manual dexterity, and communicating with the hands is more conscious than interacting with the listener.

GLOSSARY

NOTE: The glossary is organized alphabetically. Within each definition, words that are defined elsewhere in the glossary are *italicized*.

Abstraction: In humans, the *Left Procedural Cortex* can produce *practice sequences* of not only the *action directives* it uses to control the body and hands, but also the *action directives* it uses internally to process sensory information.

Applying *memetic processing* to the act of sensing is the key human cognitive ability. Repeated *episodes* of recognition of a perception are learned and stored as a *sequence*. This *sequence* is placed in the *Left Procedural Cortex's* part of the memory data store and becomes available as a possible annotation to all of the perceptual episodes that match it. These annotations are *abstractions*.

An *abstraction* can be made from any repeating perception—a visual image, a sound, a taste, the texture of an object, a smell, the emotion generated by a need, the feeling of the position of the muscles, pain, euphoria, or a *generalization* made from another *abstraction*. Anything that the brain can process can be turned into an *abstraction* and used to annotate perceptual bits of information.

Action directive: Each pairing of a *trigger* and a *response* along the path of the expression for an instinctual or memetic behavior forms an *action directive*. For example, *genes* code *action directives* that express as discrete cellular functions. When expressed genetically, they manifest as the performance of an *instinct*. When *action directives* are expressed memetically, they form the discrete body actions the brain manifests as *memes*.

Action plan: The *action directives* stored with a *now* in an *episode*. An action plan can be instinctual or memetic in humans.

Action sequence: A *sequence* of links stored in the *Left Procedural Cortex*. Each link refers to a unit of genetic action information that becomes part of a *sequence* delineating a larger and more complex behavior. *Action sequence*s are memetic and learned, and, unlike genetic-based instinctual actions linked to one perception, can be modified on the fly.

Action-taking: The areas at the front of the brain that facilitate *externalizing* processes.

Art: The representation and the transmission of *memes* packaged in *NF metaphors*. Art is truly intuitive—it uses tools to give *abstractions* physical form.

Associative linkages: The complex linking system used by higher mammals that is particularly well developed in primates. Associative linking connects multiple stored *episodes* based on a web of "similar enough" *features* within those *episodes*.

Example: The squirrel, another creature that, like primates, lives in the trees. A squirrel must balance and run in the constantly shifting environment of windblown branches. If the squirrel were only matching based on what it saw, it would quickly loses its balance and fall out of the tree. Instead, the squirrel takes into account vision, hearing, balance, wind speed, and movement of the branches and uses all of this information as a "landscape" of features within the current *now*. The squirrel can then match that landscape to many other different *episodes* in memory that are "similar enough" because they come very close to matching as many of the features present as possible. All of the possible matching *episodes* are part of the web of associative linkages. When enough features of an episode match, the same *instinctual action plan* can be activated.

Through associative linkages, the behavior of the past, though not memetic, is learned and carried forward. Higher mammals, including primates, have the most advanced brain structures to facilitate this kind of associative recall.

Attention: The focus that is placed on the *trigger* in the environment that affects the animal's needs the most. For example, a cat will focus all of its attention on a moving mouse because a mouse satisfies the need to eat, the need to hunt, and so on.

Australopithecus: A genus of bipedal ape that roamed the sub-Saharan plains of Africa approximately 4 million years ago. *Australopithecus afarensis* has long been considered our direct ancestor.

Awareness: The combination of *attention* to an actor in *consciousness* and the work applied to it in either the *sensing* or *intuitive models*.

Behavior: An *action sequence* or linked group of *action sequences* that can be repeated in response to similar circumstances.

Behavioral sequence: The *Left Procedural Cortex* maintains all of the processing architecture of the *Right Perceptual Cortex*, but instead of building the entirety of a *now* with the vast amount of sensory information included, it takes only the actions needed to respond to a situation and builds the entirety of a behavioral *sequence* instead. This behavior *sequence* is derived from a series of *nows*, from beginning to end. This behavior is a procedural "snapshot," which is stored as a *sequence*. A *sequence* can stand alone as a *meme* or be linked together with other *sequences* to form more complex *memes*.

Belief system: Everything tagged **true** is real; everything tagged **false** is fantasy. Across memetic organism boundaries, these tags aren't always equivalent, leading to fights, wars, and all-out attempts to smite unbelievers.

Closed belief systems have a very limited number of **true** abstractions allowing new matches into the believed section of the memory database. Basically, a new *meme* must come from an approved authority or it is **false**, and the approved authorities are severely restricted by the *memetic organism* to which the individual adheres.

Open belief systems have many **true** abstractions. An individual with an open belief system is constantly changing and accommodating new ideas.

Capacity: Each small triangle on the HDM maps a territory that is a static capacity of the human mind. There are sixteen capacities, with each capacity corresponding to a mechanism used to generate a certain type of *memetic processing*. The capacities reflect the brain's ability to evolve *memes* by using each of the four cognitive processing steps within each of the four modes.

Cognitive processing mode: One of four brain infrastructures humans use to organize and store knowledge. Depending on which mode a person uses, recalled memories will be sorted and processed in a particular manner. The brain processes the *memes* of each mode differently. The modes are *Sensing Feeling (SF), Sensing Thinking (ST), iNtuitive Feeling (NF), and iNtuitive Thinking (NT).*

Cognitive processing profile: The combination of the *cognitive processing mode* and *cognitive processing step* used by a human in *conscious* processing.

Cognitive processing steps: Humans use four *cognitive processing steps* during cognitive processing of a behavior that has not been previously mastered: *CI explore, CE try, DI evaluate,* and *DE implement.* Every person specializes their competence in one of these steps.

Competence transaction: The transaction within the HDM in which an individual operates in full *consciousness.* It is the main dynamic interaction of the individual's cognitive processing. In competence, an individual is aware of *effort, results,* and *process.*

Consciousness: A *meme* processor based on *language.*

Context: The environment. Context is everything that can be perceived either chemically for the cell, or with the senses for an organism.

Contextual Externalizing (CE): The "try" *cognitive processing step* used when an animal or a human tries an action in order to achieve a satisfactory state. In lower animals the actions and needs line up one-to-one, providing a strict adherence to predictable instinctive behaviors, for example, a lizard always grabbing for meat. In humans and other mammals, the animal has a choice of instincts from which to choose, which manifest as *learned behaviors.* Humans also have access to *memes.*

Contextual Internalizing (CI): The "explore" *cognitive processing step* used when an animal or a human uses its contextual *perception* to build an internal model of the external and internal environment.

Contextual Processing: The looping, perceptual processing that relies on trial and error: sense what is happening, try a response, sense, response, and repeat.

Cultural rules: Used to arbitrate between conflicting cultural *memes* in order to assure our behavioral alignment with the *memetic organisms* to which we are committed.

Deterministic Externalizing (DE): The "implement" *cognitive processing step* used to access and utilize a perfected action sequence in humans. Once a *sequence* has been perfected, the *action sequence* is linked to the episodic memory in the *Right Perceptual Cortex*. Once the behavior is *mastered*, the first three cognitive processing steps are skipped and the brain skips from recognizing a *trigger* to implementing it.

Deterministic Internalizing (DI): The "evaluate" *cognitive processing step*. In humans, the *Left Procedural Cortex is* differentiated from the *Right Perceptual Cortex* and now stores the *action sequences* associated with more complex behaviors, like throwing. The "perfect it" step is practice, and through practicing a complex *sequence*, humans perfect its implementation. This allows us to adjust our behaviors beyond instinct.

Deterministic processing: The type of processing where a *meme* is executed as an entire *sequence* of *action directives* that is triggered by the initial *now*. This kind of *sequential processing* relies on the brain's aggregation of sensory data just as instincts do, but, unlike a genetic instinctive response, a *sequence* can be quickly learned and perfected.

Deterministic replicator: The scripts that encode responses to environmental *triggers*. Replicators ride on a carrier, which functions within a medium. The carrier is *not* the replicator; the replicator is the script embedded in the carrier that codes for a specific set of actions. These actions are *expressed* when the organism is faced with the appropriate *trigger*.

There are two types of deterministic replicators: the *gene* and the *meme*.

Dichotomy: The steps and modes of the HDM form four dichotomies, which are divided into two groups. First are the *Contextual/Deterministic* and *Internalizing/Externalizing* dichotomies of the cognitive processing steps. Second are the *Sensing/iNtuitive* and *Feeling/Thinking* dichotomies of the cognitive processing modes.

DNA (deoxyribonucleic acid): The chemical carrying the genetic script within the nucleus of every cell of every living thing on earth. DNA allows the highly accurate transmission of species parameters from one generation to the next, including not only physical characteristics, but instincts, too.

Effort: In the area that is your competence transaction, you are aware of the *effort,* or energy, you put into processing consciously.

Emotional memory recall: People who process in either the *SF* or the *NF* modes recall one *episode* with one *sequence* of *action sequences.* This allows them to recall all of the episode, including the emotional context in which the originating perception took place.

When faced with a similar set of circumstances, the human brain meshes memory with new information to fit the current situation into that person's world model. People who process in the *SF* and *NF* modes recall and reprocess the emotional data associated with the circumstances along with other perceptual information.

Example: When we enter a familiar grocery store, we know our way around because we are meshing any new perceptions with recalled information about the store. People who use the *SF* and *NF* modes are also able to recall the emotions associated with the memories as well and will use that emotional information as part of their filter for new information. It allows them to determine if the situation gives them a "good" or "bad" feeling.

Emotional system: The system that checks if a *need state* will satisfactorily or unsatisfactorily be met by an *action.* Examples: Eating ensures survival, therefore eating carries positive emotional reinforcement. The emotional system resides in the limbic system of the brain.

Emotional tag: The emotional check on perception happens much faster than the cognitive process of checking for the correct *action plan.* The emotion is therefore part of the *episode* when the entire *now* is stored in memory. The recalled *episode* becomes emotional for the person—it was a good moment, or a bad moment, or a moment that satisfied the need for food, sex, or shelter.

Episode: When a snapshot is matched to an appropriate action, the whole *now* is stored as an *episode* in memory.

Episodic memory: The linked perceptual information and the instinctual actions expressed in a response that achieved an emotionally satisfactory state.

Evaluate: Please see **Deterministic Internalizing**.

Explore: Please see **Contextual Internalizing**.

Expression: A property of *deterministic replicators*. A replicator expresses when it plays out in response to an environmental *trigger*. Possible genetic actions include cellular functioning and instinctual behaviors. Possible memetic actions include the procedures needed to build a tangible item such as a screwdriver and the thinking involved in the creation of more *memes* that in turn can be used to produce more tangible items, like physics.

Externalize: The act of using the motor control areas in the front of the brain to *try* or *implement* in the current *now*.

Feature: Instead of matching to the whole *episode* built from the entirety of the *now*, an *ST* will use discrete features within the *episode* to mark a *trigger* for a *string meme*. For example, instead of matching to the perception of the entire scene, an *ST* will match to a type of tree.

Feeling: Cognition that uses single *episode* and *sequence* matching, thus making the *emotional tag* associated with the matched *episode* available for processing.

Gene: The *deterministic replicator* that is hard-coded in *deoxyribonucleic acid (DNA)* and provides scripts for operating cells. A *gene* rides on a specific segment of *DNA* and is known to control or regulate a process within an *organism,* may it be physiological or behavioral. The *gene* functions within the contextual framework of the biochemistry of the cell.

Generalization: *Abstractions, being sequences,* are not accessible to the right cortex, so the brain adds another step to make them available. When called upon, the *Left Procedural Cortex* will "play" the *abstraction* using the sensory cortices. This "playing" is perceived by the *Right Perceptual Cortex* as a perception, making it available for processing as part of an intuitive *episode.* Played *abstractions* are generalizations. Through generalizations, the brain overlays the *abstraction* onto its perception in a sensed episode. This effectively fills out a perception, extending the experience to include the *abstraction.*

Genome/genetic code: The *sequences* of *DNA* that carry the entire biological script of an *organism.*

Grammar: The socially agreed-upon rules of usage for combining symbols.

Hierarchical processing: The kind of cognition that uses *abstractions* and *generalizations* to extend access to memetic responses beyond linear connections. This type of processing allows complexity and innovation on a scale never before seen.

Hierarchy: The underlying cognitive processing that distinguishes humans from our hominid ancestors. Hierarchies are the method of organizing information into groupings under a category label.

Example: Language sorts and categorizes names under labels. Collie, German shepherd, and terrier are all symbols that are categorized under "dog."

In humans, category labels are generated by building a new *intuitive episode* from *features* abstracted from sensory episodes. For example, all of the similar "dog" features are extracted from all of the various breeds to form the **dog** abstraction.

Homo erectus: Unlike all previous ancestors whose remains have been found only in Africa, *H. erectus* was wide-ranging and has appeared in Africa, Asia, and Europe. There is evidence that *H. erectus* probably used fire, and they produced more sophisticated tools than did *H. habilis*. *H. erectus* lived between 1.8 million and 300,000 years ago. *H. erectus* probably developed the *ST cognitive processing mode.*

Homo habilis: The "handyman" was the first human ancestor to show evidence of tool use. *H. habilis* lived between 2.4 and 1.5 million years ago. It was during this period that our ancestors probably developed the *Left Procedural Cortex* and the *SF cognitive processing mode.*

Homo sapiens sapiens (Upper Paleolithic): Modern humans first appeared about 130,000 years ago, and at about 40,000 years ago, with the appearance of the Cro-Magnon culture, tool use became markedly more sophisticated than that of *H. erectus.* Over the next 20,000 years, fine artwork including decorated tools, beads, carvings, figurines, musical instruments, and spectacular cave paintings appeared. Perhaps the most important feature of this period of evolution was the development of spoken language. Paleolithic humans were the first to leave evidence of the *NF cognitive processing mode.*

Homo sapiens sapiens (modern): Approximately 8,000–5,000 years ago, humans developed overlapping *memetic organisms,* the *Self,* and *logic,* which is necessary to deal with the mingling groups. The Greeks and the Romans are examples of humans who used these memetic tools to develop the *NT cognitive processing mode.*

Hyperlinking: The process by which information is linked from within the content on a web page, that is, when a link on an underlined word takes the visitor to another page. Hyperlinking is one way to hierarchically connect information. The brain does a very similar organization of information by using *abstractions* as hyperlinks within an *episode.* The *abstraction* acts as the "word" to be "clicked" to allow a connection to be made to other episodes that also contain the *abstraction.*

Implement: Please see **Deterministic Externalizing**.

Instinct: The genetically determined behavior called upon when an animal's *now* indicates that an action is necessary for the animal to achieve a state supporting survival. Because instincts are genetically and therefore chemically based, they cannot be modified on the fly and respond only to mutations in the *genetic code*. They are the primitive driving forces behind everything we do to keep ourselves alive—eating, sleeping, mating, and avoiding pain.

Internalize: The *Contextual Internalizing step:* Building a model of the world by forming a snapshot in the perceptual processing areas of the brain. The *Deterministic Internalizing step:* Building a procedural *sequence-of-actions* snapshot in the procedural processing areas of the brain.

Intuitive episode: An *episode* built from *abstractions* and *generalizations*. The intuitive episode is based in concept and is the backbone of the *intuitive model*.

Intuitive model: The "symbolic reasoning" model of the world based on the construction and manipulation of *abstractions* and *hierarchies*. *Language, metaphor,* and *consciousness* are all part of the intuitive model, which runs in parallel to the *sensing model*.

Language: The combination of attaching *symbols* to *abstractions* and the rules of *grammar* for communicating those *symbols*. Also, language is a set of rules for forming hierarchical associations.

Learned Behavior: The associative matches that maximized benefit for the animal are called upon most often and form the basis of learned behavior.

Left Procedural Cortex: The area at the rear of the left cerebral cortex of the human brain where procedural linkages occur. Instead of remaining redundant with the right cortex as it has in other mammals, the left cortex differentiated in humans and now supports remembering *sequence*s of actions.

Linkage memory recall: People who process in either the *ST* or *NT* modes recall the links themselves between the perceptual and procedural, allowing a larger *sequence* to be recalled at one time. This allows for finer detailed work when, for example, making tools, programming computers, or developing complex mathematical theories. But, because the person is recalling linkages, he or she is divorced from the originating perception and does not have access to its emotions. Therefore, emotions are not used as part of that person's filter for new information.

Logic: The method of generating reasons that are considered valid and produce results considered to be true. This method was meticulously developed and perfected by the Greeks and has come to be called *logic*. *Logic* is fundamental to the operation of the *NT mode*. Like *language,* it is a set of rules for organizing the processes in the brain.

Mastered behavior: If an initial *now* occurs that can be matched to an episode that already contains a *procedural sequence*, the *CE try* and *DI evaluate* steps are not needed. This is a *mastered behavior*, and the brain jumps directly from *CI explore* to *DE implement* without using the CE and DI steps to create a new *meme*.

Medium: The local environment of the replicator. For the *gene,* it is the biochemical soup of the cell. For the *meme,* it is the *Left Procedural Cortex,* or the many external media humans use to communicate with each other. The medium in which a replicator exists is the only type of environment in which it can express and replicate.

Meme: The *deterministic r 'licator* that is created and stored in long-term memory in the *Left Procedural Cortex*. In its simplest form, the *meme* is a *sequence* of *action directive*s that are stored in the memory of the *Left Procedural Cortex*. This form of the *meme* is one *sequence* and is the basis of the *SF mode* cognitive processing infrastructure.

*Meme*s formed from stringing one *sequence* after another are *string memes,* and are the basis of the *ST mode* cognitive processing infrastructure.

*Meme*s formed by hierarchically ordering *sequences* of *action directives* are the basis of the *NF mode* cognitive processing infrastructure. The *NF* makes an *abstraction* that labels all of the associatively linked *action directives* involved with sensing a particular phenomenon. The *NF* then works with this virtual *abstraction*.

*Meme*s formed by logically ordering the output of the *NF mode* are the basis of the *NT mode* cognitive processing infrastructure.

The contextual framework of the *meme* is the *Left Procedural Cortex*.

Memes are processed only in the brain, but in the past few thousand years, modern humans have also stored *memes* externally in books, films, advertisements, design, and the like.

Memetic organisms: The memetically based entities that have emerged as modern human societies. In a memetic system, humans work together through memetic coherence. Each group speaks the same *language* and uses the same labels for the world. Each group tells its young the same *memes* in the same ways and creates the same images using the same tools. Examples: nations, religions, and corporations.

Metaphor: The linking of two ideas via the matching function of a cognitive processing mode. For example, *SFs* build *body-to-sensed* metaphors, *STs sensed-to-sensed*, *NFs sensed-to-intuited*, and *NTs intuited-to-intuited*.

Mimesis: The ability to use the hands to act out, or mime, intentional representations of a procedure.
Model: A "picture" built from all of the information about the world that an animal is capable of perceiving. Models are limited in scope and scale, and focus on the immediate environment and the *triggers* that most influence survival.

(NF) iNtuitive Feeling cognitive processing mode: The organizational mode using one *abstraction* coupled with one *sequence* of procedural information. Humans with competencies in this mode are communication-oriented. They structure perceptions in hypothetical, symbolic, what-if terms by building a hierarchy of perceptions based in *language*. Because they build a world model based in symbolic terms but still have access to *emotional memory recall*, NF people tend to find fulfillment in areas of verbal and emotional communication where they can fully use their symbolic representation of the world (words and aesthetics).

The NF mode of cognitive processing corresponds to Piaget's "concrete operational" stage of childhood development.

NF metaphor: Classic, literary metaphor structure comparing something concrete and known to something new and unknown.

Now: The sensory data that is processed into a snapshot of the current moment. This data is used to determine the correct reaction for that particular *now*. For animals, both the right and left cerebral cortices process *now* information.

The human left posterior parietal cerebral cortex does not process snapshots of *now*s but instead records and processes the *sequence*s of body actions resulting from a series of *now*s that are executed as *memes*.

(NT) iNtuitive Thinking cognitive processing mode: The organizational mode associating and recalling the links between *abstractions* and *sequences* of procedural information. Humans with competencies in this mode are logic-oriented and tend to structure complex hypothetical information as their "perceptions" and associate it with complex hierarchical procedural links. The NT mode is based on the existence of *logic,* which is used to structure the organization of NT *memes.* NT people tend to find fulfillment in areas of research and academics, and use the *linkage memory recall system.*

The NT mode of cognitive processing corresponds to Piaget's "formal operational" stage of childhood development.

Oldowan culture tools: The simple tools produced by *Homo habilis.*

Organism: A whole built from smaller units functioning *coherently.* For example, genetic organisms are built from cells, and memetic organisms are built from people.

Perception: The function of the brain that brings in and processes sensory information. This information is used to build a *now,* and trigger specific actions. The right posterior parietal cortex of the human brain remains perceptual and is the *Right Perceptual Cortex.*

Play transaction: The conscious transaction in which an individual is aware of *results,* but not *effort.*

Practice sequence: The "snapshot" of actions built by the *DI evaluate cognitive processing step.* See also **Procedural sequence.**

Procedural: The function of the left posterior parietal cortex of the human brain where *sequence*s of actions are created, stored, processed, and executed as *procedures* and *memes*. The left posterior parietal cortex of the human brain no longer processes perceptual information and now functions procedurally, and is the *Left Procedural Cortex*.

Procedural content: A property of *deterministic replicators*. *DNA* is not genetic unless it has a procedure to transmit. Letters are not *language* unless they form a word. A procedure must be present for a *gene* to express as a trait or for a *language* to be cognitively processed by a person and transformed into thought.

Procedural memory: The sequential and hierarchical organization of *action directive*s.

Procedural sequence: An entire *action sequence*—a whole throw, or the whole process of chipping a rock. Procedural *sequence*s fill memory storage units that had once been used to store individual perceptual episodes. Since procedural memory is stripped of all perceptual information, the new procedural *sequence* has room to hold information that transcends a single *now*.

Procedural snapshot: A *sequence* of *action directive*s derived over a series of *nows*. Please see **Procedural sequence**.

Procedure: A *sequence* of *action directives*, or the *meme* built from a combination of *sequence*s.

Process: The awareness of the procedures you use to do your work on the stage of perception, that is, the *cognitive processing step* you use to manipulate information within your mode.

Reasoning: The process of applying *logic* to generate new *reasons*.

Reasons: The purposes behind the cultural *rule-sets* that serve our *memetic organisms*. In building *reasons*, the early *NTs* abstracted the *why* of what we do and transformed these *whys* into another set of *abstractions*.

Response: What a living *organism* uses to counter an environmental *trigger* and to maximize the organism's benefit at that moment.

Result: The output generated by your cognitive work.

Right Perceptual Cortex: The area at the rear of the right cerebral cortex of the human brain where contextual perception occurs.

Rule: A behavior authorized by a memetic organism; a cultural taboo.

Rule-set: The *rules* organizing a component of cognition: For example, *grammar* is the rule-set of *language*, *logic* is the rule-set of *reasoning*, and the cultural rule-set is the rule-set that organizes social behavior within a *memetic organism*.

Scientific method: All reasons must be validated via experimentation and shown to operate in all possible situations as covered by the *hierarchy* in which they reside.

Secondary emotional system: In humans, the area in the right prefrontal cerebral cortex that houses an *emotional tagging* process associating emotional responses with *learned behaviors*. This allows emotional responses to be coupled to cultural contexts.

Self: The prioritizing system within consciousness that uses a hierarchy of allegiances to sort and order the control *memes* of multiple *memetic organisms*.

Sensing model: The model of the world built from perceptual information.

Sequence: The *sequence* of *action directives* derived from a series of *nows*. *Sequences* are put into place as *procedural snapshots* in the *Left Procedural Cortex*. When stored in memory, a *sequence* can stand alone as a *meme* or be linked together with other *sequences* to form more complex *memes*.

(SF) Sensing Feeling cognitive processing mode: The organizational mode based on *episodic memory*. Humans who use this mode are body-oriented. They structure incoming knowledge by associating one *episode* with one *sequence* of *procedural* links. The *episodic memory* represents an internal model of the tangible world, and in this mode, a one-to-one link is made to a corresponding *action sequence* in the *Left Procedural Cortex*. Because people with competencies in this mode have such close recall between the perception and the action, they tend to have a good consciousness of their bodies and the environment around them. They tend to find fulfillment in physical work such as athletics, and in body rhythms such as dancing. Because this mode links one-to-one, people who use this system to process information have access to *emotional memory recall*.

The SF mode of cognitive processing corresponds to Piaget's "sensorimotor" stage of childhood development.

Socialization: The transmission of the cultural *rule-set* of our *memetic organisms*.

Sociocognitive system: The integrated system of human cognition and our role as "selves" within *memetic organisms*.

(ST) Sensing Thinking cognitive processing mode: The organizational mode of associating and recalling the links between *episodes* and *procedural sequences*. Humans with competencies in this mode are hand-oriented and structure incoming knowledge as a list of links that allows them to remember and work with complex tasks in fine detail. Because their *episodic memory* represents a model of the tangible world, they tend to find fulfillment with physical, detailed work such as woodworking or surgery, or with developing schema as in mechanical engineering. People who operate in this mode use the *linkage memory recall system*.

The ST mode of cognitive processing corresponds to Piaget's "preoperational or symbolic" stage of childhood development.

String: To recreate an entire *meme*, the left cortex remembers *procedural sequences* one after another, forming a string that, when triggered, expresses as a single *meme* using multiple *sequences* of procedural information and executed over several *nows*.

Technology: Building tools to build tools to build even more highly refined tools.

Thinking: One-half of the Feeling/Thinking dichotomy. The thinking method of organization uses linkages as its method of associating *episodes* and *sequences*. *Memes* are therefore fragmented, and the holistic unit of behavior is not available for emotional checking.

Toil transaction: The conscious *transaction* in which an individual is aware of *effort* but not *results*.

Transaction: Human cognitive processing is not static and relies on the movement of information from one *capacity* to another. When using the capacities, the brain performs a dynamic interaction between two of them. These interactions are called transactions, and not all of them are conscious.

Trigger: The specific pattern of stimuli within the environment that triggers the expression of a replicator. A trigger is either stimulated by a chemical difference in the environment around a cell, or by a sensory perception in the case of more complex organisms.

Try: Please see **Contextual Externalizing**.

World-modeling: The areas at the back of the brain that facilitate *internalizing* processes.

REFERENCES AND SUGGESTED READINGS

Much of the HDM developed as a synthesis of the ideas and information from the following works. We've broken them down by subject and have listed major works first, followed by auxiliary works of interest.

Archaeology/Anthropology

"Hominidae: Species overview." *Archaeology Info* [cited November 2002]. Available at: http://www.archaeologyinfo.com/index.html. An excellent primer on the evolution of hominids.

Bahn, Paul, editor. *The Atlas of World Archaeology*. Checkmark Books, Facts on File, New York, 2000. An excellent primer on archaeology.

Bicchieri, M. G., editor *Hunters and Gatherers Today*. Holt, Rinehart, & Winston, New York, 1972. One of the definitive sources on how hunters and gatherers live today.

Bogucki, Peter. *The Origins of Human Society*. Blackwell Publishers, Oxford, 1999. An excellent look at archaeological evidence, climate, and the beginnings of human culture.

Kahler, Erich. *Man the Measure: A New Approach to History*. Pantheon Books, New York, 1943. A historical development of humanity and what makes us human.

Klein, Richard, with Blake Edgar. *The Dawn of Human Culture*. Nevraumont Publishing Group, Wiley and Sons, New York, 2002. Klein and Edgar examine the changes that occurred at the beginning of the intuitive model.

Rudgley, Richard. *The Lost Civilizations of the Stone Age*. Free Press, New York, 1999. A look at reinterpreting how advanced Stone Age cultures really were.

Scupin, Raymond, and Christopher DeCorse. *Anthropology: A Global Perspective*. Prentice Hall, New Jersey, 1992. An excellent global look at Ice Age humans.

Shostak, Marjorie. *Nisa: The Life and Words of a !Kung Woman*. Harvard University Press, Cambridge, 1981. Another definitive source on how hunters and gatherers live today.

White, Randall. *Prehistoric Art: The Symbolic Journey of Humankind*. Harry N. Abrams, New York, 2003. A brilliant and beautifully produced source investigating early human art.

"Cuneiform." *Encyclopedia Britannica,* 2003. Encyclopedia Britannica Premium Service, 14 Oct. 2003. http://www.britannica.com/eb/article?eu=119411. An overview of cuneiform writing.

Gluckman, Dan (producer), and Tim Lambert (director). *Ice World*. Wall to Wall Productions, for the Discovery Channel and Channel 4 TV, 2002 DVD. Available at: http://www.discovery.com. A wonderful teleplay reenacting the dawn of modern memetic organisms. Well made, and a very good place to start.

The Brain

Bear, Mark F., Barry W. Connors, and Michael A. Paradiso. *Neuroscience: Exploring the Brain*. 2nd ed. Lippincott Williams and Wilkins, Baltimore, 2001. One of the best introductory neuroscience texts available today.

Calvin, William. *The Throwing Madonna*. McGraw-Hill, New York, 1983. Calvin brings up a very important point in this work—why is it that humans can throw? He was first to realize that throwing may have been the first manifestation of what makes us human.

Curtis, W. John, and Danti Cicchetti. "Moving research on resilience into the twenty-first century: Theoretical and methodological considerations in examining the biological contributors to resilience." *Development and Psychopathology*. 15 (2003): 773–810.

Dunbar, Robin. "The social brain hypothesis." *Evolutionary Anthropology*. 6 (1998) issue 5: 178–90.

Gazzaniga, Michael S. "The Split Brain Revisited" *Scientific American*, pp. 50–55, July 1998.

Kent, Ernest W. *The Brain of Men and Machines*. BYTE/McGraw Hill, 1981. Kent examines the information-processing capabilities of the human brain in terms of its anatomy and physiology. Very few references take this approach and consider the brain as a system.

Klar, A. J. S. "A single locus, RIGHT, specifies preference for hand utilization in humans." *Cold Spring Harbor Symp. Quant. Biol.* 61: 59–65 (1996).

Llinas, Rodolfo R. *I of the Vortex: From Neurons To Self*. MIT Press, Cambridge, Mass., 2001. Llinas investigates the brain's capacity to predict by looking at sensory input and neurological oscillations.

Scientific American magazine, editors. *The Scientific American Book of the Brain.* The Lyons Press, New York, 1999. An excellent primer on what the brain does and how it does it.

Wilkins, W. K. and J. Wakefield. "Brain evolution and neurolinguistic precondi-tions." *Behavioral and Brain Sciences* 18 (1): 161–226 (1995).

Cognitive Processing Differences

Myers, Isabel Briggs, with Peter B. Myers. *Gifts Differing: Understanding Person-ality Type.* Davies-Black Publishing, Palo Alto, Calif., 1980. The definitive MBTI reference.

Other books of interest within this topic

Gardner, Howard. *Multiple Intelligences: The Theory in Practice, A Reader.* Basic Books, New York, 1993.

Gardner, Howard. *Intelligence Reframed: Multiple Intelligences for the twenty-first Century.* Basic Books, New York, 1999. Two books on Gardner's theory of intelligence differentiation.

McCaulley, M. H. *The Myers longitudinal medical study (Monograph II).* Center for Applications of Psychological Type, Gainesville, Fla., (1977).

McCaulley, M. H. *Application of the Myers-Briggs Type Indicator to medicine and other health professions (Monograph I).* Center for Applications of Psycho-logical Type, Gainesville, Fla., (1978).

Consciousness

Damasio, Antonio. *Descartes' Error.* Putnam, New York, 1994. Building upon the story of Phineas Gage and subsequent clinical research, Damasio describes a secondary emotional system situated in the right frontal lobe of the brain that provides the infrastructure for controlling social behaviors.

Damasio, Antonio. *The Feeling of What Happens.* Harcourt Brace, New York, 1999. Damasio continues his brilliant look at how emotions and conscious-ness interact in this follow-up to *Descartes' Error.*

Edelman, Gerald M. *The Remembered Present*, Basic Books, New York, 1989. Edelman discusses basic brain functions and reveals how the brain uses two methods simultaneously while processing information. This ensures accu-racy in the inherently inaccurate medium of brain biology.

Jaynes, Julian. *The Origin of Consciousness in the Breakdown of the Bicameral Mind.* Houghton Mifflin, 2nd printing, Boston, 1990. Jaynes' work, though missing the mark on when consciousness first appeared, is an excellent source describing what consciousness does. Jaynes also is the first to really look at how the Self functions.

Lowen, Walter. *Dichotomies of the Mind.* John Wiley and Sons, New York, 1982. Lowen's work is arguably the major source for the HDM and describes in a very detailed theory the workings of the cognitive processing profiles.

Neubauer, Peter, and Alexander Neubauer. *Nature's Thumbprint: The New Genetics of Personality.* Addison-Wesley, 1990. This is a review of three major studies of identical twins who were separated at birth and raised separately until adulthood. Results dramatically indicate the similarities in their development despite being raised in dissimilar environments.

Ornstein, Robert. *The Evolution of Consciousness.* Prentice Hall, New York, 1991. Ornstein shows the successive adaptations of our developing brains, which explains how we act today and points to how we develop a new conscious role to manage our increasingly technological society.

Other books of interest within this topic

Newberg, Andrew, Eugene D'Aquili, and Vince Rause. *Why God Won't Go Away.* Ballantine Books, New York, 2001. An interesting look at how the brain produces the religious experience.

Evolution

Calvin, William H. *A Brain for All Seasons: Human Evolution and the Abrupt Climate Change.* University of Chicago Press, Chicago and London, 2002. Calvin details how changes in environmental context lead to different aspects of human evolution.

Dawkins, Richard. *The Selfish Gene.* 2nd ed. Oxford University Press, Oxford, 1989. A classic look at the replicators that make humanity.

Dennett, Daniel C. *Darwin's Dangerous Idea: Evolution and the Meanings of Life.* A Touchstone Book published by Simon & Schuster, New York, 1995. Dennett takes an in-depth look at genetic and memetic evolution and details several of the replicator parallels between the two. Dennett also delves deeply into the memetic underpinnings of cultures.

Donald, Merlin. *Origins of the Modern Mind.* Harvard University Press, London, 1991. Donald's excellent book supplies the evolutionary map to Lowen's work as it details the four cognitive processing modes.

Morris, Richard. *The Evolutionists: The Struggle for Darwin's Soul.* W. H. Freeman, New York, 2001. A brilliant primer on the many debates within the study of evolution and who is doing the debating.

Plotkin, H. C., editor. *The Role of Behavior in Evolution.* MIT Press, 1988. This book contains several essays on the interaction of behavior and evolution, shining some light on the replicator-and-context exchange.

Spirov A. V., T. Bowler, and J. Reinitz. (2000) HOX-Pro: A Specialized Database for Clusters and Networks of Homeobox Genes, *Nucleic Acids Research,* 28: 337–40 [cited November 2003]. Available at: http://www.iephb.nw.ru/labs/lab38/spirov/hox_pro/shh.html.

History and Mythology

Thomas Cahill's "The Hinges of History" series:
  Cahill's beautiful narrative style brings to life several major turning points in the evolution of Western civilization.
  Cahill, Thomas. *How the Irish Saved Civilization.* Doubleday, New York, 1995.
  Cahill, Thomas. *The Gift of the Jews.* Doubleday, New York, 1998.
  Cahill, Thomas. *Desire of the Everlasting Hills: The World Before and After Jesus.* Doubleday, New York, 1999.

Campbell, Joseph. *Transformations of Myth through Time.* Harper & Row, New York, 1990. One of Campbell's definitive looks at mythology and its role in society.

Tingay, G. I. F and Badcock, J. *These Were the Romans.* 2nd ed. Dufour Editions, Chester Springs, Pa., 1989. An excellent primer on Roman life.

Other books of interest within this topic

Wells, Peters S. *The Barbarians Speak.* Princeton University Press, Princeton, N.J., 1999. An excellent investigation of the interactions between Rome and the peoples it conquered.

Languages and Their Architecture

Linguistics:

Chomsky, Noam. *Language and Mind.* Harcourt, Brace, & World, New York, 1968. One of the primary works by Chomsky.

Film Language

Bobker, Lee R. *Elements of Film.* 3d ed., Harcourt Brace Jovanovich, 2nd ed. San Diego, 1977.

Bordwell, David, and Kristin Thompson. *Film Art: An Introduction.* 2nd ed.

Alfred A. Knopf, New York, 1986.

Giannetti, Louis. *Understanding Movies.* 4th ed. Prentice-Hall, Englewood Cliffs, N.J., 1987.

Visual Languages

Canaday, John. *What Is Art? An Introduction To Painting, Sculpture, and Architecture.* Alfred A. Knopf, New York, 1983.

Zettl, Herbert. *Sight Sound Motion: Applied Media Aesthetics.* 2nd ed. Wadsworth Publishing, Belmont, Calif., 1990.

Other books of interest within this topic

Chomsky, Noam (edited by Nirmalangshu Mukherji; Bibudhendra Narayan Patnaik; and Rama Kant Agnihotri). *The Architecture of Language.* Oxford University Press, Oxford and New York, 2000. A discussion of linguistics given by Chomsky in New Delhi on January 1996.

Tufte, Edward R. *Visual Explanations: Images and Quantities, Evidence and Narrative.* Graphics Press, Cheshire, Conn. 1997. One of Tufte's books on presenting data visually.

Memetics

Aunger, Robert, editor. *Darwinizing Culture: The Status of Memetics as a Science.* Oxford University Press, Oxford and New York, 2000. An excellent source on the current state of memetics.

Aunger, Robert. *The Electric Meme: A New Theory of How We Think.* Free Press, a division of Simon & Schuster, New York, 2000. Aunger comes tantalizingly close to a true brain definition of the meme.

Blackmore, Susan. *The Meme Machine.* Oxford University Press, Oxford and New York, 1999. Blackmore's now classic look at meme and humanity is a good starting point, though misses the main engine of control meme processing, the Self.

Psychology

Cialdini, Robert B. *Influence: The Psychology of Persuasion.* 2nd printing. Quill/William Morrow, New York, 1993. Cialdini's book is an excellent description of how the creators of control memes work with the innate processes of the brain to grab attention and influence authorization.

Jung, C. G. (edited with an introduction by Violet Staub de Laszlo). *The Basic Writings of C. G. Jung.* Modern Library, New York, 1959. A collected work of Jung.

Detailed information concerning Jean Piaget's genetic epistemology: *Encyclopedia Britannica* "Human Behaviour" [accessed January 2, 2003] Available at: http://www.britannica.com/eb/article?eu=119312. A good primer for the work of Jean Piaget.

Other books of interest within this topic

Gladwell, Malcolm. *The Tipping Point.* Little, Brown, New York, 2000. Gladwell takes a fascinating and well-written look at how control memes move through society and how that movement is shaped by various cognitive processing profiles.

Social Systems

Balkin, J. M. *Cultural Software: A Theory of Ideology.* Yale University Press, New Haven & London, 1998. Balkin's work is an excellent look at how memes build cultures.

Citizen.org "NAFTA Chapter 11: Corporate Cases" [cited November 2003]. Available at: http://www.citizen.org/trade/nafta/CH__11/.

Kelly, Kevin. *Out of Control: The New Biology of Machines, Social Systems and the Economic World.* Perseus Books, Reading, Mass., 1994.

Korten, David C. *When Corporations Rule the World.* 2nd ed. Kumarian Press and Berrett-Koehler Publishers, Bloomfield, Conn., and San Francisco, 2001. The updated edition of Korten's look at multinational corporate memetic organisms.

Nisbett, Richard E. *The Geography of Thought.* Free Press, New York, 2003. A detailed look at the differences in Eastern and Western thought.

Putnam, Robert D. *Bowling Alone: The Collapse and Revival of American Community.* A Touchstone Book, published by Simon & Schuster, New York, 2000. Putnam's book details several of the changes that American society has undergone over the past half century.

Simon, Herbert A. *Reason in Human Affairs.* Stanford University Press, Stanford, Calif., 1983. Simon's brilliant work on reasoning and how it shapes modern culture.

Simmons, Rachel. *Odd Girl Out.* Harcourt, New York, 2002.

Wilson, David Sloan. *Darwin's Cathedral: Evolution, Religion, and the Nature of Society.* University of Chicago Press, Chicago and London, 2002. Wilson looks at the church as an organism, and delves into its memetic underpinnings.

Other books of interest within this topic

Kuhn, Thomas S. *The Structure of Scientific Revolutions.* 2nd ed., enlarged. University of Chicago Press, Chicago, 1970. Kuhn's book, though focused on science, speaks to the use of reason and how memetic organisms change in many circumstances.

INDEX

Symbols

A

B

Korten, David C. 323
Kuhn, Thomas 324

L

language xv, 12, 13, 17, 18, 21, 43, 57, 59, 61, 62, 63, 64, 67, 71, 72, 75, 76, 99, 100, 112, 115, 116, 124, 127, 180, 185, 193, 197, 216, 221, 226, 227, 228, 232, 236, 241, 287, 288, 289, 302, 307, 308, 309, 310, 312, 313
  body 63, 224, 245, 272
learned behavior 308, 313
Left Procedural Cortex 1, 5, 13, 15, 17, 18, 20, 23, 24, 28, 30, 31, 32, 33, 38, 39, 40, 41, 42, 43, 45, 49, 54, 57, 60, 64, 93, 94, 106, 110, 115, 119, 123, 299, 300, 301, 303, 306, 307, 308, 309, 312, 313, 314
Llinas, Rodolfo R. 318
logic 10, 12, 74, 75, 76, 77, 98, 116, 117, 118, 119, 131, 132, 200, 212, 215, 228, 241, 253, 263, 289, 290, 307, 309, 311, 312, 313
logic-oriented 6, 7, 8, 13, 62, 69, 74, 77, 100, 101, 116, 119, 120, 230, 295, 311
Lowen, Walter xvii, xviii, xxi, 10, 11, 51, 82, 102, 129, 293, 320

M

manners 288
marketing xviii, 250, 251, 252, 255, 257, 271, 273, 274, 275, 277, 280
mastered behavior 302, 303, 309
medium 309, 319
meme xxi, 1, 5, 6, 11, 12, 13, 14, 15, 17, 18, 20, 21, 24, 25, 28, 29, 30, 31, 32, 37, 38, 40, 43, 44, 49, 51, 53, 54, 55, 60, 61, 62, 63, 64, 67, 68, 72, 73, 75, 81, 82, 85, 93, 94, 97, 100, 101, 104, 106, 107, 111, 115, 116, 119, 127, 211, 219, 221, 222, 226, 227, 228, 229, 230, 231, 232, 233, 234, 235, 236, 237, 241, 245, 249, 253, 257, 263, 264, 273, 282, 290, 295, 299, 300, 301, 302, 303, 305, 309, 310, 311, 312, 313, 322, 323
  body meme 37, 39, 286
  control meme 322, 323
  gross motor 37, 38, 43, 44
  intuitive meme 64
  string meme 47, 49, 50, 51, 54, 60, 63, 72, 75, 76, 107, 109, 110, 116, 162, 185, 205, 245, 288, 305, 314
memetic organism 1, 6, 8, 14, 18, 44, 64, 66, 67, 72, 73, 74, 76, 221, 222, 228, 229, 232, 233, 234, 235, 237, 245, 263, 271, 274, 281, 282, 290, 301, 303, 307, 310, 311, 312, 313, 314, 323, 324
  civic 228
  corporation xv, 234, 271, 273, 310
  government 233
  religion 228, 232, 234, 310
memory 12, 18, 29, 30, 31, 50, 52, 65, 104, 109, 110, 128, 137, 151, 156, 166, 167, 170, 175, 189, 194, 205, 213, 217, 221, 233, 286, 295, 299, 300, 303, 304, 305, 309, 312, 313, 314